SPARK 2014 Reference Manual

Release 19.0w

AdaCore and Altran UK Ltd

Feb 13, 2018

CONTENTS

ONE

INTRODUCTION

SPARK 2014 is a programming language and a set of verification tools designed to meet the needs of high-assurance software development. SPARK 2014 is based on Ada 2012, both subsetting the language to remove features that defy verification and also extending the system of contracts by defining new Ada aspects to support modular, constructive, formal verification.

The new aspects support the analysis of incomplete programs, abstraction and refinement and facilitate deep static analysis to be performed including information-flow analysis and formal verification of an implementation against a specification.

Meaningful static analysis is possible on complete programs without the SPARK 2014 specific aspects and pragmas (for programs which are otherwise within the SPARK 2014 subset), in fact the formal verification of an implementation against a specification of a complete program is possible using only the Ada 2012 contracts. Without the SPARK 2014 specific aspects, however, analysis has to be performed on a completed program and cannot be applied constructively during its development.

SPARK 2014 is a much larger and more flexible language than its predecessor SPARK 2005. The language can be configured to suit a number of application domains and standards, from server-class high-assurance systems to embedded, hard real-time, critical systems.

A major feature of SPARK 2014 is the support for a mixture of proof and other verification methods such as testing, which facilitates the use of unit proof in place of unit testing; an approach now formalized in DO-178C and the DO-333 formal methods supplement. Certain units may be formally proven and other units validated through testing.

Ada 2012 introduced executable contracts such as Pre and Post conditions and new types of expression, in particular conditional expressions and quantifiers. SPARK 2014 uses these contracts and expressions and extends them with new aspects and pragmas.

The new aspects defined for SPARK 2014 all have equivalent pragmas which allows a SPARK 2014 program to be compiled by and executed by any Ada implementation; for instance an Ada 95 compiler provided that the use of Ada 2005 and Ada 2012 specific features is avoided. The SPARK 2014 attributes Update and Loop_Entry can be used only if the Ada implementation supports them.

The direct use of the new aspects requires an Ada 2012 compiler which supports them in a way consistent with the definition given here in the SPARK 2014 reference manual. The GNAT implementation is one such compiler.

As with the Ada 2012 contracts, the new SPARK 2014 aspects and pragmas have executable semantics and may be executed at run time. An expression in an Ada contract or SPARK 2014 aspect or pragma is called an *assertion expression* and it is the ability to execute such expressions which facilitates the mix of proof and testing.

The run-time checking of assertion expressions may be suppressed by using the Ada pragma Assertion_Policy but the static analysis and proof tools always use the assertion expressions whatever the assertion policy.

A special feature of SPARK 2014 is that numbers in assertion expressions may have extended or "infinite" arithmetic to make it simpler to write specifications as they can be written without having to consider the possibility of overflow within the specification. The numbers may therefore behave mathematically (see *Executable Contracts and Mathematical Numbers*).

1.1 Structure of Introduction

This introduction contains the following sections:

- Section *How to Read and Interpret this Manual* describes how to read and interpret this document.

- Section *Method of Description* describes the conventions used in presenting the definition of SPARK 2014.

- Section *Formal Analysis* gives a brief overview of the formal analysis to which SPARK 2014 programs are amenable.

- Section *Executable Contracts and Mathematical Numbers* gives a brief overview of the use of executable contracts.

- Section *Dynamic Semantics of SPARK 2014 Programs* gives details on the dynamic semantics of SPARK 2014.

- Section *SPARK 2014 Strategic Requirements* defines the overall goals to be met by the SPARK 2014 language and toolset.

- Section *Explaining the Strategic Requirements* provides expanded detail on the main strategic requirements.

1.2 How to Read and Interpret this Manual

This RM (reference manual) is *not* a tutorial guide to SPARK 2014. It is intended as a reference guide for users and implementors of the language. In this context, "implementors" includes those producing both compilers and verification tools.

This manual is written in the style and language of the Ada 2012 RM, so knowledge of Ada 2012 is assumed. Chapters 2 through 13 mirror the structure of the Ada 2012 RM. Chapters 14 onward cover all the annexes of the Ada 2012 RM. Moreover, this manual should be interpreted as an extension of the Ada 2012 RM (that is, SPARK 2014 is fully defined by this document taken together with the Ada 2012 RM).

The SPARK 2014 RM uses and introduces technical terms in its descriptions, those that are less well known or introduced are summarized in a *Glossary* following the sections covering the Ada annexes.

SPARK 2014 introduces a number of aspects. The language rules are written as if all the SPARK 2014 specific aspects are present but minimum requirements are placed on a tool which analyzes SPARK 2014 to be able to synthesize (from the source code) some of these aspects if they are not present. A tool may synthesize more aspects than the minimum required (see *Synthesis of SPARK 2014 Aspects*). An equivalent pragma is available for each of the new aspects but these are not covered explicitly in the language rules either. The pragmas used by SPARK 2014 are documented in *Language-Defined Pragmas (Annex L)*.

Readers interested in how SPARK 2005 constructs and idioms map into SPARK 2014 should consult the appendix *SPARK 2005 to SPARK 2014 Mapping Specification*.

1.3 Method of Description

In expressing the aspects, pragmas, attributes and rules of SPARK 2014, the following chapters of this document follow the notational conventions of the Ada 2012 RM (section 1.1.4).

The following sections are given for each new language feature introduced for SPARK 2014, following the Ada 2012 RM (other than *Verification Rules*, which is specific to SPARK 2014):

1. Syntax: this section gives the format of any SPARK 2014 specific syntax.

2. Legality Rules: these are rules that are enforced at compile time. A construct is legal if it obeys *all* of the Legality Rules.

3. Static Semantics: a definition of the compile-time effect of each construct.

4. Dynamic Semantics: a definition of the run-time effect of each construct.

5. Verification Rules: these rules define checks to be performed on the language feature that relate to static analysis rather than simple legality rules.

6. Name Resolution Rules: There are very few SPARK 2014 specific name resolution rules. Where they exist they are placed under this heading.

A section might not be present if there are no rules specific to SPARK 2014 associated with the language feature.

When presenting rules, additional text may be provided in square brackets [ ]. This text is redundant in terms of defining the rules themselves and simply provides explanatory detail.

In addition, examples of the use of the new features are given along with the language definition detail.

1.4 Formal Analysis

SPARK 2014 will be amenable to a range of formal analyses, including but not limited to the following static analysis techniques:

- Data-flow analysis, which considers the initialization of variables and the data dependencies of subprograms (which parameters and variables get read or written).

- Information-flow analysis, which also considers the coupling between the inputs and outputs of a subprogram (which input values of parameters and variables influence which output values). The term *flow analysis* is used to mean data-flow analysis and information-flow analysis taken together.

- Formal verification of robustness properties. In Ada terminology, this refers to the proof that certain predefined checks, such as the ones which could raise Constraint_Error, will never fail at run time and hence the corresponding exceptions will not be raised.

- Formal verification of functional properties, based on contracts expressed as preconditions, postconditions, type invariants and so on. The term *formal verification* is used to mean formal verification of robustness properties and formal verification of functional properties taken together.

Data and information-flow analysis is not valid and might not be possible if the legality rules of Ada 2012 and those presented in this document are not met. Similarly, a formal verification might not be possible if the legality rules are not met and may be unsound if data-flow errors are present.

1.4.1 Further Details on Formal Verification

Many Ada constructs have dynamic semantics which include a requirement that some error condition must or may[1] be checked, and some exception must or may[1] be raised, if the error is detected (see Ada 2012 RM 1.1.5(5-8)). For example, evaluating the name of an array component includes a check that each index value belongs to the corresponding index range of the array (see Ada 2012 RM 4.1.1(7)).

For every such run-time check a corresponding obligation to prove that the error condition cannot be true is introduced. In particular, this rule applies to the run-time checks associated with any assertion (see Ada 2012 RM (11.4.2)); the one exception to this rule is pragma `Assume` (see *Proof Pragmas*).

In addition, the generation of verification conditions is unaffected by the suppression of checks (e.g., via pragma `Suppress`) or the disabling of assertions (e.g., via pragma `Assertion_Policy`). In other words, suppressing or disabling a check does not prevent generation of its associated verification conditions. Similarly, the verification

---

[1] In the case of some bounded errors, performing a check (and raising an exception if the check fails) is permitted but not required.

conditions generated to ensure the absence of numeric overflow for operations of a floating point type T are unaffected by the value of T'Machine_Overflows.

All such generated verification conditions must be discharged before the formal program verification phase may be considered to be complete.

A SPARK 2014 implementation has the option of treating any construct which would otherwise generate an unsatisfiable verification condition as illegal, even if the construct will never be executed. For example, a SPARK 2014 implementation might reject the declaration

```
X : Positive := 0;
```

in almost any context. [Roughly speaking, if it can be determined statically that a runtime check associated with some construct will inevitably fail whenever the construct is elaborated, then the implementation is allowed (but not required) to reject the construct just as if the construct violated a legality rule.] For purposes of this rule, the Ada rule that Program_Error is raised if a function "completes normally without executing a return statement" is treated as a check associated with the end of the function body's sequence_of_statements. [This treatment gives SPARK 2014 implementations the option of imposing simpler (but more conservative) rules to ensure that the end of a function is not reachable. Strictly speaking, this rule gives SPARK 2014 implementations the option of rejecting many things that should not be rejected (e.g., "pragma Assert (False);" in an unreachable arm of a case statement); reasonable implementations will not misuse this freedom.]

Formal verification of a program may depend on properties of either the machine on which it is to be executed or on properties of the tools used to compile and build it. For example, a program might depend on the bounds of the type Standard.Long_Integer or on the implementation-dependent bounds chosen for the unconstrained base subtype associated with a declaration like "type T is range 1 .. 10;". In such cases it must be possible to provide the needed information as explicit inputs to the formal verification process. The means by which this is accomplished is not specified as part of the SPARK 2014 language definition.

1.5 Executable Contracts and Mathematical Numbers

Contracts, in the form of assertion expressions, are executable in Ada and SPARK 2014 and have the same semantics in both. The new aspects and pragmas introduced by SPARK 2014 where they are assertion expressions are also executable. Executable contracts have a number of advantages but also a few drawbacks that SPARK 2014 to a large extent mitigates.

The Ada pragma Assertion_Policy controls whether contracts and assertion expressions in general are executed and checked at run-time. Assertion expressions are always significant in static analysis and proof and, indeed, form the basis of the specification against which the implementation is verified.

In summary, Ada 2012 in itself enables contract-based, dynamic verification of complex properties of a program. SPARK 2014 enables contract-based static deductive verification of a large subset of Ada 2012.

1.5.1 The Advantages of Executable Contracts

The possibility of making assertions and contracts executable benefits the programmer in a number of ways:

- it gives the programmer a gentle introduction to the use of contracts, and encourages the development of assertions and code in parallel. This is natural when both are expressed in the same programming language;

- executable assertions can be enabled and checked at run time, and this gives valuable information to the user. When an assertion fails, it means that the code failed to obey desired properties (i.e., the code is erroneous), or that the intent of the code has been incorrectly expressed (i.e., the assertion is erroneous) and experience shows that both situations arise equally often. In any case, the understanding of the code and properties of the programmer are improved. This also means that users get immediate benefits from writing additional assertions and contracts, which greatly encourages the adoption of contract-based programming;

- contracts can be written and dynamically verified even when the contracts or the program are too complex for automatic proof. This includes programs that explicitly manipulate pointers, for example.

Executable contracts can be less expressive than pure mathematical ones, or more difficult to write in some situations but SPARK 2014 has features to largely mitigate these issues as described in the following subsections.

1.5.2 Mathematical Numbers and Arithmetic

In Ada numeric overflow may occur when evaluating an assertion expression this adds to the complexity of writing contracts and specifications using them, for instance, the expression

```
Post => X = (Y + Z) / 100
```

might raise a run-time exception if Y is an integer and Y + Z > Integer'Last even if the entire expression is less then Integer'Last.

SPARK 2014 mandates that there is an operational mode where such expressions (at least for Integer types) are treated as mathematical and the above expression shall not overflow and will not raise an exception. In this mode the assertion expressions may still be executable and use extended or infinite precision numbers. This mode might be acceptable if assertion expressions are not to be executed in the delivered code or if the overhead of executing contracts is not an issue.

If the mode is not chosen, then SPARK 2014 requires checks that have to be proven to demonstrate that an overflow cannot occur. In the above example the checks would not be provable and the postcondition would have to be rewritten something like:

```
Post => X = Integer ((Long_Integer (Y) + Long_Integer (Z)) / 100)
```

The way in which this operational mode is selected is tool dependent and shall be described in the user manual accompanying the tool.

1.5.3 Libraries for Specification and Proof

It is intended that SPARK 2014 will have available libraries (as packages) of common paradigms such as sets that might be difficult to express in executable contracts but the underlying model of the library packages will have a more expressive specification along with axioms that will make automatic proof of (executable) contracts using these libraries practical.

1.6 Dynamic Semantics of SPARK 2014 Programs

Every valid SPARK 2014 program is also a valid Ada 2012 program, although for a general Ada 2012 compiler, SPARK 2014 specific aspects may have to be replaced by their equivalent pragmas. The SPARK 2014 dynamic semantics are the same as Ada 2012 with the exception of some new aspects, pragmas and attributes which have dynamic semantics and the mathematical arithmetic in assertion expressions. Additionally, the new dynamic semantics only affect assertion expressions so if assertion expressions are ignored then the dynamic semantics of an Ada 2012 program are the same as a SPARK 2014 program.

SPARK 2014 programs that have failed their static analysis checks can still be valid Ada 2012 programs. An incorrect SPARK 2014 program with, say, flow analysis anomalies or undischarged verification conditions can still be executed as long as the Ada compiler in question finds nothing objectionable. What one gives up in this case is the formal analysis of the program, such as proof of absence of run-time errors or the static checks performed by flow analysis such as the proof that all variables are initialized before use.

SPARK 2014 may make use of certain aspects, attributes and pragmas which are not defined in the Ada 2012 reference manual. Ada 2012 explicitly permits implementations to provide implementation-defined aspects, attributes and pragmas. If a SPARK 2014 program uses one of these aspects (e.g., Global), or attributes (e.g., Update) then it can only be compiled and executed by an implementation which supports the construct in a way consistent with the definition given here in the SPARK 2014 reference manual.

If the equivalent pragmas are used instead of the implementation-defined aspects and if the use of implementation-defined attributes is avoided, then a SPARK 2014 program may be compiled and executed by any Ada implementation (whether or not it recognizes the SPARK 2014 pragmas). Ada specifies that unrecognized pragmas are ignored: an Ada compiler that ignores the pragma is correctly implementing the dynamic semantics of SPARK 2014 and the SPARK 2014 tools will still be able to undertake all their static checks and proofs. If an Ada compiler defines a pragma with the same name as a SPARK 2014 specific pragma but has different semantics, then the compilation or execution of the program may fail.

1.7 Main Program

There is no aspect or pragma in SPARK 2014 indicating that a subprogram is a main program. Instead it is expected that any implementation of SPARK 2014 will have its own mechanism to allow the tools to identify the main program (albeit not within the language itself).

1.8 SPARK 2014 Strategic Requirements

The following requirements give the principal goals to be met by SPARK 2014. Some are expanded in subsequent sections within this chapter.

- The SPARK 2014 language subset shall embody the largest subset of Ada 2012 to which it is currently practical to apply automatic formal verification, in line with the goals below. However, future advances in verification research and computing power may allow for expansion of the language and the forms of verification available. See section *Principal Language Restrictions* for further details.

- The use of Ada 2012 preconditions, postconditions and other assertions dictates that SPARK 2014 shall have executable semantics for assertion expressions. Such expressions may be executed, proven or both. To avoid having to consider potential numeric overflows when defining an assertion expression SPARK 2014 mandates a mode whereby extended or infinite integer arithmetic is supported for assertion expressions. The way in which this mode is selected is tool dependent and shall be described in the user guide for the tool. If this mode is not active, verification conditions to demonstrate the absence of overflow in assertion expressions will be present.

- SPARK 2014 shall provide for mixing of verification evidence generated by formal analysis [for code written in the SPARK 2014 subset] and evidence generated by testing or other traditional means [for code written outside of the core SPARK 2014 language, including legacy Ada code, or code written in the SPARK 2014 subset for which verification evidence could not be generated]. See section *Combining Formal Verification and Testing* for further details. Note, however, that a core goal of is to provide a language expressive enough for the whole of a program to be written in SPARK 2014, making it potentially entirely provable largely using automatic proof tools.

- SPARK 2014 shall support *constructive*, modular development which allows contracts to be specified on the declaration of program units and allows analysis and verification to be performed based on these contracts as early as possible in the development lifecycle, even before the units are implemented. As units are implemented the implementation is verified against its specification given in its contract. The contracts are specified using SPARK 2014 specific aspects.

- A SPARK 2014 analysis tool is required to synthesize at least some of the SPARK 2014 specific aspects, used to specify the contract of a program unit, if a contract is not explicitly specified, for instance the *Global Aspects* and the *Depends Aspects* from the implementation of the unit if it exists. The minimum requirements are given in *Synthesis of SPARK 2014 Aspects* but a particular tool may provide more precise synthesis and the synthesis of more aspects. The synthesized aspect is used in the analysis of the unit if the aspect is not explicitly specified. The synthesis of SPARK 2014 specific aspects facilitates different development strategies and the analysis of pre-existing code (see section *Synthesis of SPARK 2014 Aspects*).

- Although a goal of SPARK 2014 is to provide a language that supports as many Ada 2012 features as practical, there is another goal which is to support good programming practice guidelines and coding standards applicable to certain domains or standards. This goal is met either by standard Ada Restrictions and Profile pragmas, or via existing tools (e.g., pragma Restriction_Warnings in GNAT, or the coding standard checker gnatcheck).

- SPARK 2014 shall allow the mixing of code written in the SPARK 2014 subset with code written in full Ada 2012. See section *In and Out of SPARK 2014* for further details.

- Many systems are not written in a single programming language. SPARK 2014 shall support the development, analysis and verification of programs which are only partly in SPARK 2014, with other parts in another language, for instance, C. SPARK 2014 specific aspects manually specified at unit level will form the boundary interface between the SPARK 2014 and other parts of the program.

- SPARK 2014 shall support entities which do not affect the functionality of a program but may be used in the test and verification of a program. See section *Adding Code for Specification and Verification*.

- SPARK 2014 shall provide counterparts of all language features and analysis modes provided in SPARK 83/95/2005, unless it has been identified that customers do not find them useful.

- Enhanced support for specifying and verifying properties of secure systems shall be provided (over what is available in SPARK 2005). [The features to provide this enhanced support are not yet fully defined and will not be implemented until after release 1 of the SPARK 2014 tools.]

- SPARK 2014 shall support the analysis of external communication channels, which are typically implemented using volatile variables. See section *External State* for further details.

- The language shall offer an unambiguous semantics. In Ada terminology, this means that all erroneous and unspecified behaviour shall be eliminated either by direct exclusion or by adding rules which indirectly guarantee that some implementation-dependent choice, other than the fundamental data types and constants, cannot effect the externally-visible behaviour of the program. For example, Ada does not specify the order in which actual parameters are evaluated as part of a subprogram call. As a result of the SPARK rules which prevent the evaluation of an expression from having side effects, two implementations might choose different parameter evaluation orders for a given call but this difference won't have any observable effect. [This means undefined, implementation-defined and partially-specified features may be outside of SPARK 2014 by definition, though their use could be allowed and a warning or error generated for the user. See section *In and Out of SPARK 2014* for further details.] Where the possibility of ambiguity still exists it is noted, namely the reading of an invalid value from an external source and the use of Unchecked_Conversion, otherwise There are no known ambiguities in the language presented in this document.

- SPARK 2014 shall support provision of "formal analysis" as defined by DO-333, which states "an analysis method can only be regarded as formal analysis if its determination of a property is sound. Sound analysis means that the method never asserts a property to be true when it is not true." A language with unambiguous semantics is required to achieve this and additionally any other language feature that for which sound analysis is difficult or impractical will be eliminated or its use constrained to meet this goal. See section *Principal Language Restrictions* for further details.

1.9 Explaining the Strategic Requirements

The following sections provide expanded detail on the main strategic requirements.

1.9.1 Principal Language Restrictions

To facilitate formal analyses and verification, SPARK 2014 enforces a number of global restrictions to Ada 2012. While these are covered in more detail in the remaining chapters of this document, the most notable restrictions are:

- The use of access types and allocators is not permitted.

- All expressions (including function calls) are free of side-effects.

- Aliasing of names is not permitted in general but the renaming of entities is permitted as there is a static relationship between the two names. In analysis all names introduced by a renaming declaration are replaced by the name of the renamed entity. This replacement is applied recursively when there are multiple renames of an entity.

- The goto statement is not permitted.

- The use of controlled types is not currently permitted.

- Tasks and protected objects are permitted only if the Ravenscar profile (or the Extended Ravenscar profile) is specified.

- Raising and handling of exceptions is not currently permitted (exceptions can be included in a program but proof must be used to show that they cannot be raised).

1.9.2 Combining Formal Verification and Testing

There are common reasons for combining formal verification on some part of a codebase and testing on the rest of the codebase:

1. Formal verification is only applicable to a part of the codebase. For example, it might not be possible to apply the necessary formal verification to Ada code that is not in SPARK 2014.

2. Formal verification only gives strong enough results on a part of the codebase. This might be because the desired properties cannot be expressed formally, or because proof of these desired properties cannot be sufficiently automated.

3. Formal verification might be only cost-effective on a part of the codebase. (And it may be more cost-effective than testing on this part of the codebase.)

Since the combination of formal verification and testing cannot guarantee the same level of assurance as when formal verification alone is used, the goal when combining formal verification and testing is to reach a level of confidence at least as good as the level reached by testing alone.

Mixing of formal verification and testing requires consideration of at least the following three issues.

Demarcating the Boundary between Formally Verified and Tested Code

Contracts on subprograms provide a natural boundary for this combination. If a subprogram is proved to respect its contract, it should be possible to call it from a tested subprogram. Conversely, formal verification of a subprogram (including absence of run-time errors and contract checking) depends on called subprograms respecting their own contracts, whether these are verified by formal verification or testing.

In cases where the code to be tested is not SPARK 2014, then additional information may be provided in the code – possibly at the boundary – to indicate this (see section *In and Out of SPARK 2014* for further details).

Checks to be Performed at the Boundary

When a tested subprogram T calls a proved subprogram P, then the precondition of P must hold. Assurance that this is true is generated by executing the assertion that P's precondition holds during the testing of T.

Similarly, when a proved subprogram P calls a tested subprogram T, formal verification will have shown that the precondition of T holds. Hence, testing of T must show that the postcondition of T holds by executing the corresponding assertion. This is a necessary but not necessarily sufficient condition. Dynamically, there is no check that the subprogram has not updated entities not included in the postcondition.

In general, formal verification works by imposing requirements on the callers of proved code, and these requirements should be shown to hold even when formal verification and testing are combined. Any tool set that proposes a combination of formal verification and testing for SPARK 2014 should provide a detailed process for doing so, including any necessary additional testing of proof assumptions.

Conditions that Apply to the Tested Code

The unit of test and formal verification is a subprogram (the sequence of statements of a package body is regarded as a subprogram). There are several sources of conditions that apply to a tested subprogram:

- The need to validate a partial proof of a subprogram that calls a subprogram that is not itself proven but is only tested.

- The need to validate the assumptions on which a proof of a subprogram is based when a tested subprogram calls it.

- A tested subprogram may be flow analyzed if it is in SPARK 2014 even if it is not formally proven.

- A tested subprogram may have properties that are formally proven.

Flow analysis of a non-proven subprogram

If a subprogram is in SPARK 2014 but is too complex or difficult to prove formally then it still may be flow analyzed which is a fast and efficient process. Flow analysis in the absence proof of has a number of significant benefits as the subprogram implementation is

- checked that it is in SPARK 2014;

- checked that there are no uses of initialized variables;

- checked that there are no ineffective statements; and

- checked against its specified Global and Depends aspects if they exist or alternatively facilitating their synthesis. This is important because this automatically checks one of the conditions on tested subprograms which are called from proven code (see *Conditions on a tested subprogram which is called from a partially proven subprogram*).

Proving properties of a tested subprogram

A tested subprogram which is in SPARK may have properties, such as the absence of run-time exceptions proven even though the full functionality of the subprogram is tested rather than proven. The extent to which proof is performed is controlled using pragma Assume (see *Proof Pragmas*).

To perform proof of absence of run-time exceptions but not the postcondition of a subprogram a pragma Assume stating the postcondition is placed immediately prior to each exit point from the subprogram (each return statement or the end of the body). Parts of the postcondition may be proved using a similar scheme.

If the proof of absence of one or more run-time exceptions is not proven automatically or takes too long to prove then pragma Assume may be used to suppress the proof of a particular check.

Pragma Assume informs the proof system that the assumed expression is always True and so the prover does not attempt to prove it. In general pragma Assume should be used with caution but it acts as a pragma Assert when the subprogram code is run. Therefore, in a subprogram that is tested it acts as an extra test.

Conditions on a tested subprogram which is called from a partially proven subprogram

When a subprogram which is to be partially proven calls a tested (but not proven subprogram) then the following conditions must be met by the called subprogram:

- if it is in SPARK 2014 then it should be flow analyzed to demonstrate that the implementation satisfies the Global aspect and Depends aspects pf the subprogram if they are given, otherwise conservative approximations will be synthesized from the implementation of the subprogram;

- if it is not in SPARK 2014 then at least a Global aspect shall be specified for the subprogram. The Global aspect must truthfully represent the global variables and state abstractions known to the SPARK 2014 program (not just the calling subprogram) and specify whether each of the global items are an Input, an Output or is In_Out. The onus is on the user to show that the Global (and Depends) aspect is correct as the SPARK 2014 tools do not check this because the subprogram is not in SPARK 2014;

- it shall not update any variable or state abstraction known to the SPARK 2014 program, directly or indirectly, apart from through an actual parameter of the subprogram or a global item listed in its Global aspect. Updating a variable or state abstraction through an object of an access type or through a subprogram call is an indirect update. Here again, if the subprogram is not in SPARK 2014 and cannot be flow analyzed, the onus is on the user to show this condition is met; and

- if it has a postcondition sufficient testing to demonstrate to a high-level of confidence that the postcondition is always True must be performed.

A tool set may provide further tools to demonstrate that the Global aspects are satisfied by a non-SPARK 2014 subprogram and possibly partially check the post condition.

Conditions on a tested subprogram which is calls a proven subprogram

A tested (but not proven) subprogram which calls a proven subprogram must satisfy the following conditions:

- if it is in SPARK 2014 then flow analysis of the tested subprogram should be performed. This demonstrates that all variables and state abstractions which are inputs to the called subprogram are initialized and that the outputs of the called subprogram are used;

- if it is not in SPARK 2014 the user must ensure that all variables and state abstractions that are inputs to the called subprogram are initialized prior to calling the subprogram. This is the responsibility of the user as the SPARK 2014 tools cannot check this as the subprogram is not in SPARK 2014; and

- if it is in SPARK 2014 it may be possible to prove that the precondition of the called subprogram is always satisfied even if no other proof is undertaken, otherwise sufficient testing must be performed by the user to demonstrate to a high-level of confidence that the precondition of the subprogram will always be True when the subprogram is called. The proof of the called subprogram relies on its precondition evaluating to True.

1.9.3 Adding Code for Specification and Verification

Often extra entities, such as types, variables and functions may be required only for test and verification purposes. Such entities are termed *ghost* entities and their use is restricted so that they do not affect the functionality of the program. Complete removal of *ghost* entities has no functional impact on the program.

SPARK 2014 supports ghost subprograms, types, objects, and packages. Ghost subprograms may be executable or non-executable. Non-executable ghost subprograms have no implementation and can be used for the purposes of formal verification only. Such functions may have their specification defined within an external proof tool to facilitate formal verification. This specification is outside of the SPARK 2014 language and toolset and therefore cannot be checked by the tools. An incorrect definition of function may lead to an unsound proof which is of no use. Ideally any definition will be checked for soundness by the external proof tools.

If the postcondition of a function, F, can be specified in SPARK 2014 as F'Result = E, then the postcondition may be recast as the expression of an `expression_function_declaration` as shown below:

```
function F (V : T) return T1 is (E);
```

The default postcondition of an expression function is F'Result = E making E both the implementation and the expression defining the postcondition of the function. This is useful, particularly for ghost functions, as the expression which acts as the postcondition might not give the most efficient implementation but if the function is a ghost function this might not matter.

1.9.4 Synthesis of SPARK 2014 Aspects

SPARK 2014 supports a *constructive* analysis style where all program units require contracts specified by SPARK 2014 specific aspects to be provided on their declarations. Under this constructive analysis style, these contracts have to be designed and added at an early stage to assist modular analysis and verification, and then maintained by the user as a program evolves. When the body of a unit is implemented (or modified) it is checked that it conforms to its contract. However, it is mandated that a SPARK 2014 analysis tool shall be able to synthesize a conservative approximation of at least a minimum of SPARK 2014 specific aspects from the source code of a unit.

Synthesis of SPARK 2014 aspects is fundamental to the analysis of pre-existing code where no SPARK 2014 specific aspects are provided.

A SPARK 2014 analysis tool is required to be capable of synthesizing at least a basic, conservative *Global Aspects*, *Depends Aspects* , *Refined_Global Aspects*, *Refined_Depends Aspects*, *Abstract_State Aspects*, *Refined_State Aspects*, *Initializes Aspects* and *Default_Initial_Condition Aspects* from either the implementation code or from other SPARK 2014 aspects as follows:

- if subprogram has no Depends aspect but has a Global aspect, an approximation of the Depends aspect is obtained by constructing a `dependency_relation` by assuming that each output is dependent on every input, where outputs are all of the parameters of mode out and in-out, plus all the `global_items` that have a `mode_selector` of Output or In_Out, and inputs are all the parameters of mode in and in-out, plus all the `global_items` that have a `mode_selector` of Input or In_Out. This is a conservative approximation;

- if a subprogram has a Depends aspect but no Global aspect then the Global aspect is determined by taking each `input` of the `dependency_relation` which is not also an `output` and adding this to the Global aspect with a `mode_selector` of Input. Each `output` of the `dependency_relation` which is not also an `input` is added to the Global aspect with a `mode_selector` of Output. Finally, any other `input` and `output` of the `dependency_relation` which has not been added to the Global aspect is added with a `mode_selector` of In_Out;

- if neither a Global or Depends aspect is present, then first the globals of a subprogram are determined from an analysis of the entire program code. This is achieved in some tool dependent way. The globals of each subprogram determined from this analysis is used to synthesize the Global aspects and then from these the Depends aspects are synthesized as described above;

- if an Abstract_State is specified on a package and a Refined_State aspect is specified in its body, then Refined_Global and Refined_Depends aspects shall be synthesized in the same way as described above. From the Refined_Global, Refined_Depends and Refined_State aspects the abstract Global and Depends shall be synthesized if they are not present.

- if no abstract state aspect is specified on a package but it contains hidden state, then each variable that makes up the hidden state has a Abstract_State synthesized to represent it. At least a crude approximation of a single state abstraction for every variable shall be provided. A Refined_State aspect shall be synthesized which shows the constituents of each state.

- if no Default_Initial_Condition is specified for a private type declaration, then the synthesized value of this aspect of the type is determined by whether the full view of the private type defines full default initialization (see SPARK RM 3.1). If it does, then the synthesized aspect value is a static *Boolean*_expression having the value True; if it does not, then the synthesized aspect value is a null literal.

The syntheses described above do not include all of the SPARK 2014 aspects and nor do the syntheses cover all facets of the aspects. In complex programs where extra or more precise aspects are required they might have to be specified manually.

An analysis tool may provide the synthesis of more aspects and more precise synthesis of the mandatory ones.

Some use cases where the synthesis of aspects is likely to be required are:

- Code has been developed as SPARK 2014 but not all the aspects are included on all subprograms by the developer. This is regarded as *generative analysis*, where the code was written with the intention that it would be analyzed.

- Code is in maintenance phase, it might or might not have all of the SPARK 2014 specific aspects. If there are aspects missing they are automatically for analysis purposes when possible. This is also regarded as generative analysis.

- Legacy code is analyzed which has no or incomplete SPARK 2014 specific aspects This is regarded as *retrospective analysis*, where code is being analyzed that was not originally written with analysis in mind. Legacy code will typically have a mix of SPARK 2014 and non-SPARK 2014 code (and so there is an interaction with the detail presented in section *In and Out of SPARK 2014*). This leads to two additional process steps that might be necessary:

  - An automatic identification of what code is in SPARK 2014 and what is not.

  - Manual definition of the boundary between the SPARK 2014 and non-SPARK 2014 code by explicitly specifying accurate and truthful contracts using SPARK 2014 specific aspects on the declarations of non-SPARK 2014 program units.

1.9.5 In and Out of SPARK 2014

There are various reasons why it may be necessary to combine SPARK 2014 and non-SPARK 2014 in the same program, such as (though not limited to):

- Use of language features that are not amenable to formal verification (and hence where formal verification will be mixed with testing).

- Use of libraries that are not written in SPARK 2014.

- Need to analyze legacy code that was not developed as SPARK 2014.

Hence, it must be possible within the language to indicate what parts are (intended to be) in and what parts are (intended to be) out, of SPARK 2014.

The default is to assume none of the program text is in SPARK 2014, although this can be overridden. A new aspect *SPARK_Mode* is provided, which may be applied to a unit declaration or a unit body, to indicate when a unit declaration or just its body is in SPARK and should be analyzed. If just the body is not in SPARK 2014 a SPARK 2014 compatible contract may be supplied on the declaration which facilitates the analysis of units which use the declaration. The tools cannot check that the the given contract is met by the body as it is not analyzed. The burden falls on the user to ensure that the contract represents the behavior of the body as seen by the SPARK 2014 parts of the program and – if this is not the case – the assumptions on which the analysis of the SPARK 2014 code relies may be invalidated.

In general a definition may be in SPARK 2014 but its completion need not be.

A finer grain of mixing SPARK 2014 and Ada code is also possible by justifying certain warnings and errors. Warnings may be justified at a project, library unit, unit, and individual warning level. Errors may be justifiable at the individual error level or be unsuppressible errors.

Examples of this are:

- A declaration occurring immediately within a unit might not be in, or might depend on features not in, the SPARK 2014 subset. The declaration might generate a warning or an error which may be justifiable. This does not necessarily render the whole of the program unit not in SPARK 2014. If the declaration generates a warning, or if the error is justified, then the unit is considered to be in SPARK 2014 except for the errant declaration.

- It is the use of the entity declared by the errant declaration, for instance a call of a subprogram or the denoting of an object in an expression (generally within the statements of a body) that will result in an unsuppressible error. The body of a unit causing the unsuppressible message (or declaration if this is the cause) will need to be marked as not in SPARK 2014 to prevent its future analysis.

Hence, SPARK 2014 and non-SPARK 2014 code may mix at a fine level of granularity. The following combinations may be typical:

- Package (or generic package) specification in SPARK 2014. Package body entirely not in SPARK 2014.

- Visible part of package (or generic package) specification in SPARK 2014. Private part and body not in SPARK 2014.

- Package specification in SPARK 2014. Package body almost entirely in SPARK 2014, with a small number of subprogram bodies not in SPARK 2014.

- Package specification in SPARK 2014, with all bodies imported from another language.

- Package specification contains a mixture of declarations which are in SPARK 2014 and not in SPARK 2014. A client of the package may be in SPARK 2014 if it only references SPARK 2014 declarations; the presence of non-SPARK 2014 constructs in a referenced package specification does not by itself mean that a client is not in SPARK 2014.

Such patterns are intended to allow for mixed-language programming, mixed-verification using different analysis tools, and mixed-verification between formal verification and more traditional testing. A condition for safely combining the results of formal verification with other verification results is that formal verification tools explicitly list the assumptions that were made to produce their results. The proof of a property may depend on the assumption of other user-specified properties (for example, preconditions and postconditions) or implicit assumptions associated with the foundation and hypothesis on which the formal verification relies (for example, initialization of inputs and outputs, or non-aliasing between parameters). When a complete program is formally verified, these assumptions are discharged by the proof tools, based on the global guarantees provided by the strict adherence to a given language subset. No such guarantees are available when only part of a program is formally verified. Thus, combining these results with other verification results depends on the verification of global and local assumptions made during formal verification.

Full details on the SPARK_Mode aspect are given in the SPARK Toolset User's Guide (*Identifying SPARK Code*).

1.9.6 External State

A variable or a state abstraction may be specified as external state to indicate that it represents an external communication channel, for instance, to a device or another subsystem. An external variable may be specified as volatile. A volatile state need not have the same value between two reads without an intervening update. Similarly an update of a volatile variable might not have any effect on the internal operation of a program, its only effects are external to the program. These properties require special treatment of volatile variables during flow analysis and formal verification.

SPARK 2014 follows the Ada convention that a read of a volatile variable may have an external effect as well as reading the value of the variable. SPARK 2014 extends this notion to cover updates of a volatile variable such that an update of a volatile variable may also have some other observable effect. SPARK 2014 further extends these principles to apply to state abstractions. (see section *External State*).

LEXICAL ELEMENTS

SPARK 2014 supports the full Ada 2012 language with respect to lexical elements. Users may choose to apply restrictions to simplify the use of wide character sets and strings.

2.1 Character Set

No extensions or restrictions.

2.2 Lexical Elements, Separators, and Delimiters

No extensions or restrictions.

2.3 Identifiers

No extensions or restrictions.

2.4 Numeric Literals

No extensions or restrictions.

2.5 Character Literals

No extensions or restrictions.

2.6 String Literals

No extensions or restrictions.

2.7 Comments

No extensions or restrictions.

2.8 Pragmas

SPARK 2014 introduces a number of new pragmas that facilitate program verification. These are described in the relevant sections of this document.

2.9 Reserved Words

No extensions or restrictions.

CHAPTER
THREE

DECLARATIONS AND TYPES

No extensions or restrictions.

3.1 Declarations

The view of an entity is in SPARK 2014 if and only if the corresponding declaration is in SPARK 2014. When clear from the context, we say *entity* instead of using the more formal term *view of an entity*. If the initial declaration of an entity (e.g., a subprogram, a private type, or a deferred constant) requires a completion, it is possible that the initial declaration might be in SPARK 2014 (and therefore can be referenced in SPARK 2014 code) even if the completion is not in SPARK 2014. [This distinction between views is much less important in "pure" SPARK 2014 than in the case where SPARK_Mode is used (as described in the SPARK Toolset User's Guide) to allow mixing of SPARK 2014 and non-SPARK 2014 code.]

A type is said to *define full default initialization* if it is

- a scalar type with a specified Default_Value; or

- an array-of-scalar type with a specified Default_Component_Value; or

- an array type whose element type defines default initialization; or

- a record type, type extension, or protected type each of whose `component_declarations` either includes a `default_expression` or has a type which defines full default initialization and, in the case of a type extension, is an extension of a type which defines full default initialization; or

- a task type; or

- a private type whose Default_Initial_Condition aspect is specified to be a *Boolean*_expression.

[The discriminants of a discriminated type play no role in determining whether the type defines full default initialization.]

3.2 Types and Subtypes

No extensions or restrictions.

3.2.1 Type Declarations

Legality Rules

1. Named access-to-constant types are permitted in SPARK 2014. All other access type declarations are not permitted in SPARK 2014, as well as all forms of anonymous access types.

3.2.2 Subtype Declarations

A `constraint` in SPARK 2014 cannot be defined using variable expressions except when it is the `range` of a `loop_parameter_specification`. Dynamic subtypes are permitted but they must be defined using constants whose values may be derived from expressions containing variables. Note that a formal parameter of a subprogram of mode **in** is a constant and may be used in defining a constraint. This restriction gives an explicit constant which can be referenced in analysis and proof.

An expression with a *variable input* reads a variable or calls a function which (directly or indirectly) reads a variable.

Legality Rules

1. [A `constraint`, excluding the `range` of a `loop_parameter_specification`, shall not be defined using an expression with a variable input; see *Expressions* for the statement of this rule.]

3.2.3 Classification of Operations

No restrictions or extensions.

3.2.4 Subtype Predicates

Static predicates are in SPARK 2014. Dynamic predicates are also in SPARK 2014, but are subject to some restrictions.

Legality Rules

1. [A Dynamic_Predicate expression shall not have a variable input; see *Expressions* for the statement of this rule.]

2. If a Dynamic_Predicate applies to the subtype of a composite object, then a verification condition is generated to ensure that the object satisfies its predicate immediately after any subcomponent or slice of the given object is either

    - the target of an assignment statement or;
    - an actual parameter of mode **out** or **in out** in a call.

    [These verification conditions do not correspond to any run-time check. Roughly speaking, if object X is of subtype S, then verification conditions are generated as if an implicitly generated

    > pragma Assert (X in S);

    were present immediately after any assignment statement or call which updates a subcomponent (or slice) of X.]

    [No such proof obligations are generated for assignments to subcomponents of the result object of an aggregate, an extension aggregate, or an update expression (see section *Update Expressions*). These are assignment operations but not assignment statements.]

3.3 Objects and Named Numbers

3.3.1 Object Declarations

The Boolean aspect Constant_After_Elaboration may be specified as part of the declaration of a library-level variable. If the aspect is directly specified, the aspect_definition, if any, shall be a static [Boolean] expression. [As with most Boolean-valued aspects,] the aspect defaults to False if unspecified and to True if it is specified without an aspect_definition.

A variable whose Constant_After_Elaboration aspect is True, or any part thereof, is said to be *constant after elaboration*. [The Constant_After_Elaboration aspect indicates that the variable will not be modified after execution of the main subprogram begins (see section *Tasks and Synchronization*).]

A stand-alone constant is a *constant with variable inputs* if its initialization expression depends on:

- A variable or parameter; or

- Another *constant with variable inputs*

Otherwise, a stand-alone constant is a *constant without variable inputs*.

Verification Rules

1. Constants without variable inputs shall not be denoted in Global, Depends, Initializes or Refined_State aspect specifications. [Two elaborations of such a constant declaration will always yield equal initialization expression values.]

Examples

```
A : constant Integer := 12;
--  No variable inputs

B : constant Integer := F (12, A);
--  No variable inputs if F is a function without global inputs (although
--  it could have global proof inputs)

C : constant Integer := Param + Var;
--  Constant with variable inputs
```

3.3.2 Number Declarations

No extensions or restrictions.

3.4 Derived Types and Classes

The following rules apply to derived types in SPARK 2014.

Legality Rules

1. A private type that is not visibly tagged but whose full view is tagged cannot be derived.

[The rationale for this rule is that, otherwise, given that visible operations on this type cannot have class-wide preconditions and postconditions, it is impossible to check the verification rules associated to overridding operations on the derived type.]

3.5 Scalar Types

The Ada RM states that, in the case of a fixed point type declaration, "The base range of the type does not necessarily include the specified bounds themselves". A fixed point type for which this inclusion does not hold is not in SPARK 2014.

For example, given

```
type T is delta 1.0 range -(2.0 ** 31) .. (2.0 ** 31);
```

it might be the case that (2.0 ** 31) is greater than T'Base'Last. If this is the case, then the type T is not in SPARK 2014.

[This rule applies even in the case where the bounds specified in the `real_range_specification` of an `ordinary_fixed_point_definition` define a null range.]

3.6 Array Types

No extensions or restrictions.

3.7 Discriminants

The following rules apply to discriminants in SPARK 2014.

Legality Rules

1. The type of a `discriminant_specification` shall be discrete.

2. A `discriminant_specification` shall not occur as part of a derived type declaration.

3. [The `default_expression` of a `discriminant_specification` shall not have a variable input; see *Expressions* for the statement of this rule.]

3.8 Record Types

Default initialization expressions must not have variable inputs in SPARK 2014.

Legality Rules

1. If at least one nondiscriminant component (either explicitly declared or inherited) of a record type or type extension either is of a type which defines full default initialization or is declared by a `component_declaration` which includes a `default_expression`, and if that component's type has at least one elementary nondiscriminant part, then the record type or type extension shall define full default initialization.

   [The enforcement of this rule may require looking at the `full_type_declaration` of a `private_type` declaration if the private type's Default_Initial_Condition aspect is not specified.]

   [In the unusual case of a nondiscriminant component which has no nondiscriminant scalar parts (e.g., an array of null records), the preceding "at least one elementary" wording means that the component is ignored for purposes of this rule.]

2. [The `default_expression` of a `component_declaration` shall not have any variable inputs, nor shall it contain a name denoting the current instance of the enclosing type; see *Expressions* for the statement of this rule.]

[The rules in this section apply to any `component_declaration`; this includes the case of a `component_declaration` which is a `protected_element_declaration`. In other words, these rules also apply to components of a protected type.]

3.9 Tagged Types and Type Extensions

Legality Rules

1. No construct shall introduce a semantic dependence on the Ada language defined package Ada.Tags. [See Ada RM 10.1.1 for the definition of semantic dependence. This rule implies, among other things, that any use of the Tag attribute is not in SPARK 2014.]

2. The identifier External_Tag shall not be used as an `attribute_designator`.

3.9.1 Type Extensions

Legality Rules

1. A type extension shall not be declared within a subprogram body, block statement, or generic body which does not also enclose the declaration of each of its ancestor types.

3.9.2 Dispatching Operations of Tagged Types

No extensions or restrictions.

3.9.3 Abstract Types and Subprograms

No extensions or restrictions.

3.9.4 Interface Types

No extensions or restrictions.

3.10 Access Types

Access types allow the creation of aliased data structures and objects, which notably complicate the specification and verification of a program's behavior. Therefore, the following rules are applied in SPARK 2014.

Legality Rules

1. All forms of access type and parameter declarations are prohibited. [This follows from the rule forbidding use of the Ada reserved word **access**.]

2. The attribute 'Access shall not be denoted.

3.11 Declarative Parts

No extensions or restrictions.

NAMES AND EXPRESSIONS

The term *assertion expression* denotes an expression that appears inside an assertion, which can be a pragma Assert, a precondition or postcondition, a type invariant or (subtype) predicate, or other assertions introduced in SPARK 2014.

4.1 Names

Legality Rules

1. Neither `explicit_dereference` nor `implicit_dereference` are in SPARK 2014.

4.1.1 Indexed Components

No extensions or restrictions.

4.1.2 Slices

No extensions or restrictions.

4.1.3 Selected Components

Some constructs which would unconditionally raise an exception at run time in Ada are rejected as illegal in SPARK 2014 if this property can be determined prior to formal program verification.

Legality Rules

1. If the prefix of a record component selection is known statically to be constrained so that the selected component is not present, then the component selection (which, in Ada, would raise Constraint_Error if it were to be evaluated) is illegal.

4.1.4 Attributes

Many of the Ada language defined attributes are in SPARK 2014 but there are exclusions. For a full list of attributes supported by SPARK 2014 see *Language-Defined Attributes*.

A SPARK 2014 implementation is permitted to support other attributes which are not Ada or SPARK 2014 language defined attributes and these should be documented in the User Guide for the tool.

Legality Rules

1. The prefix of a '*Access* `attribute_reference` shall be a constant without variable input. [This ensures that information flows through such access values only depend on assignments to the access objects, not assignments to the accessed objects. See *Object Declarations*.]

4.1.5 User-Defined References

Legality Rules

1. User-defined references are not allowed.

2. The aspect Implicit_Dereference is not permitted.

4.1.6 User-Defined Indexing

Legality Rules

1. User-defined indexing is not allowed.

2. The aspects Constant_Indexing and Variable_Indexing are not permitted.

4.2 Literals

Legality Rules

1. The literal **null** representing an access value is not allowed.

4.3 Aggregates

Legality Rules

1. The box symbol, <>, shall not be used in an aggregate unless the type(s) of the corresponding component(s) define full default initialization.

2. If the `ancestor_part` of an `extension_aggregate` is a `subtype_mark`, then the type of the denoted subtype shall define full default initialization.

[The box symbol cannot be used in an aggregate to produce an uninitialized scalar value or a composite value having an uninitialized scalar value as a subcomponent. Similarly for an ancestor subtype in an extension aggregate.]

4.4 Expressions

An expression is said to be *side-effect free* if the evaluation of the expression does not update any object. The evaluation of an expression free from side-effects only retrieves or computes a value.

Legality Rules

1. An expression shall be side-effect free. [Strictly speaking, this "rule" is a consequence of other rules, most notably the rule that a function cannot have outputs other than its result.]

2. An expression (or range) in SPARK 2014 occurring in certain contexts (listed below) shall not have a variable input. This means that such an expression shall not read a variable, nor shall it call a function which (directly or indirectly) reads a variable. These contexts include:

- a constraint other than the range of a loop parameter specification (see *Subtype Declarations*);
- the default_expression of a component declaration (see *Record Types*);
- the default_expression of a discriminant_specification (see *Discriminants*);
- a Dynamic_Predicate aspect specification (see *Subtype Predicates*);
- a Type_Invariant aspect specification (see *Type Invariants*);
- an indexing expression of an indexed_component or the discrete_range of a slice in an object renaming declaration which renames part of that index or slice (see *Object Renaming Declarations*);
- a generic actual parameter corresponding to a generic formal object having mode **in** (see *Generic Instantiation*);
- the declaration and body of a user-defined equality operation on a record type (see *Overloading of Operators*).

    [This avoids the case where such a record type is a component of another composite type, whose predefined equality operation now depends on variables through the primitive equality operation on its component.]

[An expression in one of these contexts may read a constant which is initialized with the value of a variable.]

[These rules simplify analysis by eliminating the need to deal with implicitly created anonymous constants. An expression which does not have a variable input will always yield the same result if it is (conceptually, for purposes of static analysis) reevaluated later. This is not true of an expression that has a variable input because the value of the variable might have changed.]

[For purposes of these rules, the current instance of a type or subtype is not considered to be a variable input in the case of a Dynamic_Predicate or Type_Invariant condition, but is considered to be a variable input in the case of the default_expression of a component declaration.]

4.4.1 Update Expressions

The Update attribute provides a way of overwriting specified components of a copy of a given composite value.

For a prefix X that denotes an object of a nonlimited record type or record extension T, the attribute

```
X'Update ( record_component_association_list )
```

is defined and yields a value of type T and is a *record update expression*.

For a prefix X that denotes an object of a nonlimited one dimensional array type T, the attribute

```
X'Update ( array_component_association {, array_component_association} )
```

is defined and yields a value of type T and is an *array update expression*.

For a prefix X that denotes an object of a nonlimited multidimensional array type T, the attribute

```
X'Update ( multidimensional_array_component_association
       {, multidimensional_array_component_association} )
```

is defined and yields a value of type T and is a *multi-dimensional array update*. Where multidimensional_array_component_association has the following syntax:

Syntax

```
multidimensional_array_component_association ::=
  index_expression_list_list => expression
index_expression_list_list ::=
  index_expression_list { | index_expression_list }
index_expression_list ::=
  ( expression {, expression} )
```

Legality Rules

1. The box symbol, <>, may not appear in any expression appearing in an *update expression*.

Dynamic Semantics

2. In all cases (i.e., whether T is a record type, a record extension type, or an array type - see below), evaluation of X'Update begins with the creation of an anonymous object of type T which is initialized to the value of X in the same way as for an occurrence of X'Old (except that the object is constrained by its initial value but not constant).

3. Next, components of this object are updated as described in the following subsections. The attribute reference then denotes a constant view of this updated object. The master and accessibility level of this object are defined as for the anonymous object of an aggregate.

4. The assignments to components of the result object described in the following subsections are assignment operations and include performance of any checks associated with evaluation of the target component name or with implicit conversion of the source value to the component subtype.

Record Update Expressions

For a record update expression of type T the following are required.

Legality Rules

5. The record_component_association_list shall have one or more record_component_associations, each of which shall have a non-**others** component_choice_list and an expression.

6. Each selector_name of each record_component_name shall denote a distinct non discriminant component of T.

7. Each record_component_association's associated components shall all be of the same type. The expected type and applicable index constraint of the expression is defined as for a record_component_association occurring within a record aggregate.

8. Each selector of all component_choice_lists of a record update expression shall denote a distinct component.

Dynamic Semantics

9. For each component for which an expression is provided, the expression value is assigned to the corresponding component of the result object. The order in which the components are updated is unspecified.

[Components in a record update expression must be distinct. The following is illegal

```
Some_Record'Update
  (Field_1 => ... ,
   Field_2 => ... ,
   Field_1 => ... ); -- illegal; components not distinct
```

because the order of component updates is unspecified.]

Array Update Expressions

For an array update expression of type `T` the following are required.

Legality Rules

10. Each `array_component_association` of the attribute reference shall have one or more `array_component_associations`, each of which shall have an expression.

11. The expected type and applicable index constraint of the expression is defined as for an `array_component_association` occurring within an array aggregate of type `T`. The expected type for each `discrete_choice` is the index type of `T`.

12. The reserved word **others** shall not occur as a `discrete_choice` of an `array_component_association` of the `attribute_reference`.

Dynamic Semantics

13. The discrete choices and array component expressions are evaluated. Each array component expression is evaluated once for each associated component, as for an array aggregate. For each such associated component of the result object, the expression value is assigned to the component.

14. Evaluations and updates are performed in the order in which the `array_component_associations` are given; within a single `array_component_association`, in the order of the `discrete_choice_list`; and within the range of a single `discrete_choice`, in ascending order.

[Note: the `Update` attribute for an array object allows multiple assignments to the same component, as in either

```
Some_Array'Update (1 .. 10 => True, 5 => False)
```

or

```
Some_Array'Update (Param_1'Range => True, Param_2'Range => False)
-- ok even if the two ranges overlap]
```

Multi-dimensional Array Update Expressions

For a multi-dimensional array update expression of type `T` the following are required.

Legality Rules

15. The expected type and applicable index constraint of the expression of a `multidimensional_array_component_association` are defined as for the expression of an `array_component_association` occurring within an array aggregate of type `T`.

16. The length of each `index_expression_list` shall equal the dimensionality of `T`. The expected type for each expression in an `index_expression_list` is the corresponding index type of `T`.

Dynamic Semantics

17. For each `multidimensional_array_component` association (in the order in which they are given) and for each `index_expression_list` (in the order in which they are given), the index values of the `index_expression_list` and the expression are evaluated (in unspecified order) and the expression value is assigned to the component of the result object indexed by the given index values. Each array component expression is evaluated once for each associated `index_expression_list`.

Examples

```
1   package Update_Examples
2     with SPARK_Mode
3   is
4      type Rec is record
5         X, Y : Integer;
6      end record;
7
8      type Arr is array (1 .. 3) of Integer;
9
10     type Arr_2D is array (1 .. 3, 1 .. 3) of Integer;
11
12     type Nested_Rec is record
13        A : Integer;
14        B : Rec;
15        C : Arr;
16        D : Arr_2D;
17     end record;
18
19     type Nested_Arr is array (1 .. 3) of Nested_Rec;
20
21     -- Simple record update
22     procedure P1 (R : in out Rec)
23       with Post => R = R'Old'Update (X => 1);
24     -- this is equivalent to:
25     --    R = (X => 1,
26     --         Y => R'Old.Y)
27
28     -- Simple 1D array update
29     procedure P2 (A : in out Arr)
30       with Post => A = A'Old'Update (1 => 2);
31     -- this is equivalent to:
32     --    A = (1 => 2,
33     --         2 => A'Old (2),
34     --         3 => A'Old (3));
35
36     -- 2D array update
37     procedure P3 (A2D : in out Arr_2D)
38       with Post => A2D = A2D'Old'Update ((1, 1) => 1,
39                                           (2, 2) => 2,
40                                           (3, 3) => 3);
41     -- this is equivalent to:
42     --    A2D = (1 => (1 => 1,
43     --                 2 => A2D'Old (1, 2),
44     --                 3 => A2D'Old (1, 3)),
45     --           2 => (2 => 2,
46     --                 1 => A2D'Old (2, 1),
47     --                 3 => A2D'Old (2, 3)),
48     --           3 => (3 => 3,
49     --                 1 => A2D'Old (3, 1),
50     --                 2 => A2D'Old (3, 2)));
51
52     -- Nested record update
53     procedure P4 (NR : in out Nested_Rec)
54       with Post => NR = NR'Old'Update (A => 1,
55                                         B => NR'Old.B'Update (X => 1),
56                                         C => NR'Old.C'Update (1 => 5));
57     -- this is equivalent to:
58     --    NR = (A => 1,
```

```
59    --            B.X => 1,
60    --            B.Y => NR'Old.B.Y,
61    --            C (1) => 5,
62    --            C (2) => NR'Old.C (2),
63    --            C (3) => NR'Old.C (3),
64    --            D => NR'Old.D)
65
66    -- Nested array update
67    procedure P5 (NA : in out Nested_Arr)
68      with Post =>
69        NA = NA'Old'Update (1 => NA'Old (1)'Update
70                                   (A => 1,
71                                    D => NA'Old (1).D'Update ((2, 2) => 0)),
72                            2 => NA'Old (2)'Update
73                                   (B => NA'Old (2).B'Update (X => 2)),
74                            3 => NA'Old (3)'Update
75                                   (C => NA'Old (3).C'Update (1 => 5)));
76    -- this is equivalent to:
77    --    NA = (1 => (A => 1,
78    --                B => NA'Old (1).B,
79    --                C => NA'Old (1).C,
80    --                D => NA'Old (1).D),
81    --          2 => (B.X => 2,
82    --                B.Y => NA'Old (2).B.Y,
83    --                A => NA'Old (2).A,
84    --                C => NA'Old (2).C,
85    --                D => NA'Old (2).D),
86    --          3 => (C => (1 => 5,
87    --                      2 => NA'Old (3).C (2),
88    --                      3 => NA'Old (3).C (3)),
89    --                A => NA'Old (3).A,
90    --                B => NA'Old (3).B,
91    --                D => NA'Old (3).D));
92
93    end Update_Examples;
```

4.5 Operators and Expression Evaluation

Ada grants implementations the freedom to reassociate a sequence of predefined operators of the same precedence level even if this changes the behavior of the program with respect to intermediate overflow (see Ada 2012 RM 4.5). SPARK 2014 assumes that an implementation does not take advantage of this permission; in particular, a proof of the absence of intermediate overflow in this situation may depend on this assumption.

A SPARK 2014 tool is permitted to provide a warning where operators may be re-associated by a compiler.

[The GNAT Ada 2012 compiler does not take advantage of this permission. The GNAT compiler also provides an option for rejecting constructs to which this permission would apply. Explicit parenthesization can always be used to force a particular association in this situation.]

4.6 Type Conversions

No extensions or restrictions.

4.7 Qualified Expressions

No extensions or restrictions.

4.8 Allocators

Legality Rules

1. The use of allocators is not permitted.

4.9 Static Expressions and Static Subtypes

No extensions or restrictions.

CHAPTER

FIVE

STATEMENTS

SPARK 2014 restricts the use of some statements, and adds a number of pragmas which are used for verification, particularly involving loop statements.

5.1 Simple and Compound Statements - Sequences of Statements

SPARK 2014 excludes certain kinds of statements that complicate verification.

Legality Rules

1. A `simple_statement` shall not be a `goto_statement`, a `requeue_statement`, an `abort_statement`, or a `code_statement`.

2. A `compound_statement` shall not be an `accept_statement` or a `select_statement`.

3. A statement is only in SPARK 2014 if all the constructs used in the statement are in SPARK 2014.

5.2 Assignment Statements

No extensions or restrictions.

5.3 If Statements

No extensions or restrictions.

5.4 Case Statements

No extensions or restrictions.

5.5 Loop Statements

5.5.1 User-Defined Iterator Types

Legality Rules

1. The generic package Ada.Iterator_Interfaces shall not be referenced. [In particular, Ada.Iterator_Interfaces shall not be instantiated. An alternative mechanism for defining iterator types is described in the next section.]

5.5.2 Generalized Loop Iteration

Static Semantics

1. Ada's generalized loop iteration is supported in SPARK 2014, but only in a modified form. Ada's existing generalized loop iteration is defined in terms of other constructs which are not in SPARK 2014 (e.g., access discriminants).

2. Instead, SPARK 2014 provides a new mechanism for defining an iterable container type (see Ada RM 5.5.1). Iteration over the elements of an object of such a type is then allowed as for any iterable container type (see Ada RM 5.5.2), although with dynamic semantics as described below. Similarly, SPARK 2014 provides a new mechanism for defining an iterator type (see Ada RM 5.5.1), which then allows generalized iterators as for any iterator type (see Ada RM 5.5.2). Other forms of generalized loop iteration are not in SPARK 2014.

3. The type-related operational representation aspect Iterable may be specified for any non-array type. The `aspect_definition` for an Iterable aspect specification for a subtype of a type T shall follow the following grammar for `iterable_specification`:

```
iterable_specification ::=
  (First       => name,
   Next        => name,
   Has_Element => name[,
   Element     => name])
```

4. If the aspect Iterable is visibly specified for a type, the (view of the) type is defined to be an iterator type (view). If the aspect Iterable is visibly specified for a type and the specification includes an Element argument then the (view of the) type is defined to be an iterable container type (view). [The visibility of an aspect specification is defined in Ada RM 8.8]. [Because other iterator types and iterable container types as defined in Ada RM 5.5.1 are necessarily not in SPARK 2014, this effectively replaces, rather than extends, those definitions].

Legality Rules

5. Each of the four (or three, if the optional argument is omitted) names shall denote an explicitly declared primitive function of the type, referred to respectively as the First, Next, Has_Element, and Element functions of the type. All parameters of all four subprograms shall be of mode In.

6. The First function of the type shall take a single parameter, which shall be of type T. The "iteration cursor subtype" of T is defined to be result subtype of the First function. The First function's name shall be resolvable from these rules alone. [This means the iteration cursor subtype of T can be determined without examining the other subprogram names]. The iteration cursor subtype of T shall be definite and shall not be limited.

7. The Next function of the type shall have two parameters, the first of type T and the second of the cursor subtype of T; the result subtype of the function shall be the cursor subtype of T.

8. The Has_Element function of the type shall have two parameters, the first of type T and the second of the cursor subtype of T; the result subtype of the function shall be Boolean.

9. The Element function of the type, if one is specified, shall have two parameters, the first of type T and the second of the cursor subtype of T; the default element subtype of T is then defined to be the result subtype of the Element function.

10. Reverse container element iterators are not in SPARK 2014. The loop parameter of a container element iterator is a constant object.

11. A container element iterator shall only occur as the loop_parameter_specification of a quantified_expression[, and not as the iteration_scheme of a loop statement].

12. Iteration associated with a generalized iterator or a container element iterator procedes as follows. An object of the iteration cursor subtype of T (hereafter called "the cursor") is created and is initialized to the result of calling First, passing in the given container object. Each iteration begins by calling Has_Element, passing in the container and the cursor. If False is returned, execution of the associated loop is completed. If True is returned then iteration continues and the loop parameter for the next iteration of the loop is either (in the case of a generalized iterator) the cursor or (in the case of a container element iterator) the result of calling the Element function, passing in the container and the cursor. At the end of the iteration, Next is called (passing in the container and the cursor) and the result is assigned to the cursor.

5.5.3 Loop Invariants, Variants and Entry Values

Two loop-related pragmas, Loop_Invariant and Loop_Variant, and a loop-related attribute, Loop_Entry are defined. The pragma Loop_Invariant is used to specify the essential non-varying properties of a loop. Pragma Loop_Variant is intended for use in ensuring termination. The Loop_Entry attribute is used to refer to the value that an expression had upon entry to a given loop in much the same way that the `Old` attribute in a subprogram postcondition can be used to refer to the value an expression had upon entry to the subprogram.

Syntax

```
loop_variant_parameters ::= loop_variant_item {, loop_variant_item}
loop_variant_item       ::= change_direction => discrete_expression
change_direction        ::= Increases | Decreases
```

where `discrete_expression` is an `expression` of a discrete type.

Static Semantics

1. Pragma Loop_Invariant is like a pragma Assert except it also acts as a *cut point* in formal verification. A cut point means that a prover is free to forget all information about modified variables that has been established within the loop. Only the given Boolean expression is carried forward.

2. Pragma Loop_Variant is used to demonstrate that a loop will terminate by specifying expressions that will increase or decrease as the loop is executed.

Legality Rules

3. Loop_Invariant is an assertion just like pragma Assert with respect to syntax of its Boolean actual parameter, name resolution, legality rules and dynamic semantics, except for extra legality rules given below.

4. Loop_Variant is an assertion and has an expected actual parameter which is a specialization of an Ada expression. Otherwise, it has the same name resolution and legality rules as pragma Assert, except for extra legality rules given below.

5. The following constructs are said to be *restricted to loops*:

    - A Loop_Invariant pragma;

    - A Loop_Variant pragma;

    - A `block_statement` whose `sequence_of_statements` or `declarative_part` immediately includes a construct which is restricted to loops.

6. A construct which is restricted to loops shall occur immediately within either:

    - the `sequence_of_statements` of a `loop_statement`; or

    - the `sequence_of_statements` or `declarative_part` of a `block_statement`.

The construct is said to apply to the innermost enclosing loop.

[Roughly speaking, a Loop_Invariant or Loop_Variant pragma shall only occur immediately within a loop statement except that intervening block statements are ignored for purposes of this rule.]

7. The expression of a `loop_variant_item` shall be of any discrete type.

8. Two Loop_Invariant or Loop_Variant pragmas which apply to the same loop shall occur in the same `sequence_of_statements`, separated only by [zero or more] other Loop_Invariant or Loop_Variant pragmas.

Dynamic Semantics

9. Other than the above legality rules, pragma Loop_Invariant is equivalent to pragma `Assert`. Pragma Loop_Invariant is an assertion (as defined in Ada RM 11.4.2(1.1/3)) and is governed by the Loop_Invariant assertion aspect [and may be used in an Assertion_Policy pragma].

10. The elaboration of a Checked Loop_Variant pragma begins by evaluating the `discrete_expressions` in textual order. For the first elaboration of the pragma within a given execution of the enclosing loop statement, no further action is taken. For subsequent elaborations of the pragma, one or more of these expression results are each compared to their corresponding result from the previous iteration as follows: comparisons are performed in textual order either until unequal values are found or until values for all expressions have been compared. In either case, the last pair of values to be compared is then checked as follows: if the `change_direction` for the associated `loop_variant_item` is Increases (respectively, Decreases) then a check is performed that the expression value obtained during the current iteration is greater (respectively, less) than the value obtained during the preceding iteration. The exception Assertions.Assertion_Error is raised if this check fails. All comparisons and checks are performed using predefined operations. Pragma Loop_Variant is an assertion (as defined in Ada RM 11.4.2(1.1/3)) and is governed by the Loop_Variant assertion aspect [and may be used in an Assertion_Policy pragma].

Examples

The following example illustrates some pragmas of this section

```
1  procedure Loop_Var_Loop_Invar is
2     type Total is range 1 .. 100;
3     subtype T is Total range 1 .. 10;
4     I : T := 1;
5     R : Total := 100;
6  begin
7     while I < 10 loop
8        pragma Loop_Invariant (R >= 100 - 10 * I);
9        pragma Loop_Variant (Increases => I,
10                             Decreases => R);
11       R := R - I;
12       I := I + 1;
13    end loop;
14 end Loop_Var_Loop_Invar;
```

Note that in this example, the loop variant is unnecessarily complex, stating that I increases is enough to prove termination of this simple loop.

Attribute Loop_Entry

Static Semantics

1. For a prefix *X* that denotes an object of a nonlimited type, the following attribute is defined:

```
X'Loop_Entry [(loop_name)]
```

2. X'Loop_Entry [(loop_name)] denotes a constant object of the type of X. [The value of this constant is the value of X on entry to the loop that is denoted by `loop_name` or, if no `loop_name` is provided, on entry to the closest enclosing loop.]

Legality Rules

3. A Loop_Entry `attribute_reference` *applies to* a `loop_statement` in the same way that an `exit_statement` does (see Ada RM 5.7). For every rule about `exit_statements` in the Name Resolution Rules and Legality Rules sections of Ada RM 5.7, a corresponding rule applies to Loop_Entry `attribute_references`.

4. In many cases, the language rules pertaining to the Loop_Entry attribute match those pertaining to the Old attribute (see Ada LRM 6.1.1), except with "Loop_Entry" substituted for "Old". These include:

   • prefix name resolution rules (including expected type definition)

   • nominal subtype definition

   • accessibility level definition

   • run-time tag-value determination (in the case where *X* is tagged)

   • interactions with abstract types

   • interactions with anonymous access types

   • forbidden attribute uses in the prefix of the `attribute_reference`.

   The following rules are not included in the above list; corresponding rules are instead stated explicitly below:

   • the requirement that an Old `attribute_reference` shall only occur in a postcondition expression;

   • the rule disallowing a use of an entity declared within the postcondition expression;

   • the rule that a potentially unevaluated Old `attribute_reference` shall statically denote an entity;

   • the prefix of the `attribute_reference` shall not contain a Loop_Entry `attribute_reference`.

5. A Loop_Entry `attribute_reference` shall occur within a Loop_Variant or Loop_Invariant pragma, or an Assert, Assume or Assert_And_Cut pragma appearing in a position where a Loop_Invariant pragma would be allowed.

   [Roughly speaking, a Loop_Entry `attribute_reference` can occur in an Assert, Assume or Assert_And_Cut pragma immediately within a loop statement except that intervening block statements are ignored for purposes of this rule.]

6. The prefix of a Loop_Entry `attribute_reference` shall not contain a use of an entity declared within the `loop_statement` but not within the prefix itself.

   [This rule is to allow the use of I in the following example:

```
loop
   pragma Assert
      ((Var > Some_Function (Param => (for all I in T => F (I))))'Loop_Entry);
```

   In this example the value of the inequality ">" that would have been evaluated on entry to the loop is obtained even if the value of Var has since changed].

7. The prefix of a Loop_Entry `attribute_reference` shall statically denote an entity, or shall denote an `object_renaming_declaration`, if

- the `attribute_reference` is potentially unevaluated; or

- the `attribute_reference` does not apply to the innermost enclosing `loop_statement`.

[This rule follows the corresponding Ada RM rule for 'Old. The prefix of an Old attribute_reference that is potentially unevaluated shall statically denote an entity and have the same rationale. If the following was allowed:

```
procedure P (X : in out String; Idx : Positive) is
begin
   Outer :
      loop
         if Idx in X'Range then
            loop
               pragma Loop_Invariant (X(Idx) > X(Idx)'Loop_Entry(Outer));
```

this would introduce an exception in the case where Idx is not in X'Range.]

Dynamic Semantics

8. For each X'Loop_Entry other than one occurring within an Ignored assertion expression, a constant is implicitly declared at the beginning of the associated loop statement. The constant is of the type of X and is initialized to the result of evaluating X (as an expression) at the point of the constant declaration. The value of X'Loop_Entry is the value of this constant; the type of X'Loop_Entry is the type of X. These implicit constant declarations occur in an arbitrary order.

9. The previous paragraph notwithstanding, the implicit constant declaration is not elaborated if the `loop_statement` has an `iteration_scheme` whose evaluation yields the result that the `sequence_of_statements` of the `loop_statement` will not be executed (loosely speaking, if the loop completes after zero iterations).

[Note: This means that the constant is not elaborated unless the loop body will execute (or at least begin execution) at least once. For example, a while loop

```
while <condition> do
   sequence_of_statements; -- contains Loop_Entry uses
end loop;
```

may be thought of as being transformed into

```
if <condition> then
   declare
   ... implicitly declared Loop_Entry constants
   begin
      loop
         sequence_of_statements;
         exit when not <condition>;
      end loop;
   end;
end if;
```

The rule also prevents the following example from raising Constraint_Error:

```
declare
   procedure P (X : in out String) is
   begin
      for I in X'Range loop
         pragma Loop_Invariant (X(X'First)'Loop_Entry >= X(I));
         X := F(X); -- modify X
      end loop;
```

```
      end P;
      Length_Is_Zero : String := "";
 begin
      P (Length_Is_Zero);
end; -- ...]
```

Examples

```
1    type Array_Of_Int is array (1 .. 10) of Integer;
2
3    procedure Reverse_Order (A : in out Array_Of_Int)
4      with Post => (for all J in A'Range => A (J) = A'Old (A'Last - J + 1) and
5                    A (A'Last - J + 1) = A'Old (J))
6    is
7       Temp : Integer;
8    begin
9       for Index in A'First .. (A'Last + 1) / 2 loop
10         Temp := A (Index);
11         A (Index) := A (A'Last - Index + 1);
12         A (A'Last - Index + 1) := Temp;
13         pragma Loop_Invariant
14            (-- Elements that have been visited so far are swapped
15            (for all J in A'First .. Index =>
16               A (J) = A'Loop_Entry (A'Last - J + 1) and
17               A (A'Last - J + 1) = A'Loop_Entry (J))
18            and then
19            -- Elements not yet visited are unchanged
20            (for all J in Index + 1 .. A'Last - Index =>
21               A (J) = A'Loop_Entry (J)));
22
23      end loop;
24   end Reverse_Order;
```

5.6 Block Statements

No extensions or restrictions.

5.7 Exit Statements

No extensions or restrictions.

5.8 Goto Statements

Legality Rules

1. The goto statement is not permitted.

5.9 Proof Pragmas

This section discusses the pragmas Assert_And_Cut and Assume.

Two SPARK 2014 pragmas are defined, Assert_And_Cut and Assume. Each is an assertion and has a single Boolean parameter (an assertion expression) and may be used wherever pragma Assert is allowed.

Assert_And_Cut may be used within a subprogram when the given expression sums up all the work done so far in the subprogram, so that the rest of the subprogram can be verified (informally or formally) using only the entry preconditions, and the expression in this pragma. This allows dividing up a subprogram into sections for the purposes of testing or formal verification. The pragma also serves as useful documentation.

A Boolean expression which is an actual parameter of pragma Assume can be assumed to be True for the remainder of the subprogram. If the Assertion_Policy is Check for pragma Assume and the Boolean expression does not evaluate to True, the exception Assertions.Assertion_Error will be raised. However, in proof, no verification of the expression is performed and in general it cannot. It has to be used with caution and is used to state axioms.

Static Semantics

1. Pragma Assert_And_Cut is an assertion the same as a pragma Assert except it also acts as a cut point in formal verification. The cut point means that a prover is free to forget all information about modified variables that has been established from the statement list before the cut point. Only the given Boolean expression is carried forward.

2. Pragma Assume is an assertion the same as a pragma Assert except that there is no verification condition to prove the truth of the Boolean expression that is its actual parameter. [Pragma Assume indicates to proof tools that the expression can be assumed to be True.]

Legality Rules

3. Pragmas Assert_And_Cut and Assume have the same syntax for their Boolean actual parameter, name resolution rules and dynamic semantics as pragma Assert.

Verification Rules

4. The verification rules for pragma Assume are significantly different to those of pragma Assert. [It would be difficult to overstate the importance of the difference.] Even though the dynamic semantics of pragma Assume and pragma Assert are identical, pragma Assume does not introduce a corresponding verification condition. Instead the prover is given permission to assume the truth of the assertion, even though this has not been proven. [A single incorrect Assume pragma can invalidate an arbitrarily large number of proofs - the responsibility for ensuring correctness rests entirely upon the user.]

Examples

```
1   function F (S : String) return Integer
2     with SPARK_Mode,
3           Post => F'Result in 0 .. 999
4   is
5       subtype Control_Chars is Character range '0' .. '3';
6       Control_Char : Control_Chars ;
7       Valid : Boolean;
8   begin
9       if S'Length >= 6 then
10          Valid := S (S'First .. S'First + 3) = "ABCD";
11          if Valid and then S (S'First + 4) in Control_Chars then
12              Valid := True;
13              Control_Char := S (S'First + 4);
14          else
15              Valid := False;
16          end if;
17      else
18          Valid := False;
19      end if;
20
21      pragma Assert_And_Cut (if Valid then Control_Char in Control_Chars);
```

```ada
22
23    -- A conditional flow error will be reported when it used in the following
24    -- case as statement flow analysis techniques cannot determine that
25    -- Control_Char is initialized when Valid is True.
26    -- The Assert_And_Cut verifies that Control_Char is initialized if Valid
27    -- is True and the conditional flow which raised the error cannot occur.
28    -- The complicated decision process and the details of the string S are
29    -- not required to prove the postcondition and so the Assert_And_Cut
30    -- cuts out all of the unnecessary complex information gathered from this
31    -- process from the proof tool and the eye of the human viewer.
32
33    if Valid then
34       case Control_Char is
35          when '0' => return 0;
36          when '1' => return 7;
37          when '2' => return 42;
38          when '3' => return 99;
39       end case;
40    else
41       return 999;
42    end if;
43 end F;
```

```ada
1  -- The up-time timer is updated once a second
2  package Up_Timer
3     with SPARK_Mode
4  is
5     type Time_Register is limited private;
6     type Times is range 0 .. 2**63 - 1;
7
8     procedure Inc (Up_Time : in out Time_Register);
9
10    function Get (Up_Time : Time_Register) return Times;
11
12 private
13    type Time_Register is record
14       Time : Times := 0;
15    end record;
16 end Up_Timer;
```

```ada
1  package body Up_Timer
2     with SPARK_Mode
3  is
4     procedure Inc (Up_Time : in out Time_Register) is
5     begin
6        -- The up timer is incremented every second.
7        -- The system procedures require that the system is rebooted
8        -- at least once every three years - as the Timer_Reg is a 64 bit
9        -- integer it cannot reach Times'Last before a system reboot.
10       pragma Assume (if Times'Last = 2**63 - 1 then Up_Time.Time < Times'Last);
11
12       -- Without the previous assume statement it would not be possible
13       -- to prove that the following addition would not overflow.
14       Up_Time.Time := Up_Time.Time + 1;
15    end Inc;
16
17    function Get (Up_Time : Time_Register) return Times is (Up_Time.Time);
```

```
18  end Up_Timer;
```

SUBPROGRAMS

6.1 Subprogram Declarations

We distinguish the *declaration view* introduced by a `subprogram_declaration` from the *implementation view* introduced by a `subprogram_body` or an `expression_function_declaration`. For subprograms that are not declared by a `subprogram_declaration`, the `subprogram_body` or `expression_function_declaration` also introduces a declaration view which may be in SPARK 2014 even if the implementation view is not.

Rules are imposed in SPARK 2014 to ensure that the execution of a function call does not modify any variables declared outside of the function. It follows as a consequence of these rules that the evaluation of any SPARK 2014 expression is side-effect free.

We also introduce the notion of a *global item*, which is a name that denotes a global object or a state abstraction (see *Abstraction of State*). Global items are presented in Global aspects (see *Global Aspects*).

An *entire object* is an object which is not a subcomponent of a larger containing object. More specifically, an *entire object* is an object declared by an `object_declaration` (as opposed to, for example, a slice or the result object of a function call) or a formal parameter of a subprogram. In particular, a component of a protected unit is not an *entire object*.

Static Semantics

1. The *exit* value of a global item or parameter of a subprogram is its value immediately following the successful call of the subprogram.

2. The *entry* value of a global item or parameter of a subprogram is its value at the call of the subprogram.

3. An *output* of a subprogram is a global item or parameter whose final value may be updated by a successful call to the subprogram. The result of a function is also an output. A global item or parameter which is an external state with the property Async_Readers => True, and for which intermediate values are written during an execution leading to a successful call, is also an output even if the final state is the same as the initial state. (see *External State*). [On the contrary, a global item or parameter is not an output of the subprogram if it is updated only on paths that lead to an explicit `raise_statement` or to a `pragma Assert (statically_False)` or to a call to a subprogram marked `No_Return`.]

4. An *input* of a subprogram is a global item or parameter whose initial value may be used in determining the exit value of an output of the subprogram. For a global item or parameter which is an external state with Async_Writers => True, each successive value read from the external state is also an input of the subprogram (see *External State*). As a special case, a global item or parameter is also an input if it is mentioned in a `null_dependency_clause` in the Depends aspect of the subprogram (see *Depends Aspects*).

5. An output of a subprogram is said to be *fully initialized* by a call if all parts of the output are initialized as a result of any successful execution of a call of the subprogram. In the case of a parameter X of a class-wide type T'Class, this set of "all parts" is not limited to the (statically known) parts of T. For example, if the underlying dynamic tag of X is T2'Tag, where T2 is an extension of T that declares a component C, then C would be

included in the set. In this case, this set of "all parts" is not known statically. [In order to fully initialize such a parameter, it is necessary to use some form of dispatching assignment. This can be done by either a direct (class-wide) assignment to X, passing X as an actual out-mode parameter in a call where the formal parameter is of a class-wide type, or passing X as a controlling out-mode parameter in a dispatching call.] The meaning of "all parts" in the case of a parameter of a specific tagged type is determined by the applicable Extensions_Visible aspect (see *Extensions_Visible Aspects*). [A state abstraction cannot be fully initialized by initializing individual constituents unless its refinement is visible.]

Legality Rules

5. A function declaration shall not have a `parameter_specification` with a mode of **out** or **in out**. This rule also applies to a `subprogram_body` for a function for which no explicit declaration is given.

6.1.1 Preconditions and Postconditions

Legality Rules

1. The corresponding expression for an inherited Pre'Class or Post'Class of an inherited subprogram S of a tagged type T shall not call a non-inherited primitive function of type T.

[The notion of corresponding expression is defined in Ada RM 6.1.1(18/4) as follows: If a Pre'Class or Post'Class aspect is specified for a primitive subprogram S of a tagged type T, or such an aspect defaults to True, then a corresponding expression also applies to the corresponding primitive subprogram S of each descendant of T.]

[The rationale for this rule is that, otherwise, if the contract applicable to an inherited subprogram changes due to called subprograms in its contract being overridden, then the inherited subprogram would have to be re-verified for the derived type. This rule forbids the cases that require re-verification.]

2. The Pre aspect shall not be specified for a primitive operation of a type T at a point where T is tagged. [Pre'Class should be used instead to express preconditions.]

[The rationale for this rule is that, otherwise, the combination of dynamic semantics and verification rules below would force an identical Pre'Class each time Pre is used on a dispatching operation.]

3. A subprogram_renaming_declaration shall not declare a primitive operation of a tagged type.

[Consider

```
package Outer is
   type T is tagged null record;
   package Nested is
      procedure Op (X : T) with Pre => ..., Post => ... ;
      -- not a primitive, so Pre/Post specs are ok
   end Nested;
   procedure Renamed_Op (X : T) renames Nested.Op; -- illegal
end Outer;
```

Allowing this example in SPARK would introduce a case of a dispatching operation which is subject to a Pre (and Post) aspect specification. This rule is also intended to avoid problematic interactions between the Pre/Pre'Class/Post/Post'Class aspects of the renamed subprogram and the Pre'Class/Post'Class inheritance associated with the declaration of a primitive operation of a tagged type.

Note that a dispatching subprogram can be renamed as long as the renaming does not itself declare a dispatching operation. Note also that this rule would never apply to a renaming-as-body.]

Verification Rules

For a call on a nondispatching operation, a verification condition is introduced (as for any run-time check) to ensure that the specific precondition check associated with the statically denoted callee will succeed. Upon entry to such a subprogram, the specific preconditions of the subprogram may then be assumed.

For a call (dispatching or not) on a dispatching operation, a verification condition is introduced (as for any run-time check) to ensure that the class-wide precondition check associated with the statically denoted callee will succeed.

The verification condition associated with the specific precondition of a dispatching subprogram is imposed on the callee, as opposed to on callers of the subprogram. Upon entry to a subprogram, the class-wide preconditions of the subprogram may be assumed. Given this, the specific preconditions of the subprogram must be proven.

The callee is responsible for discharging the verification conditions associated with any postcondition checks, class-wide or specific. The success of these checks may then be assumed by the caller.

In the case of an overriding dispatching operation whose Pre'Class attribute is explicitly specified, a verification condition is introduced to ensure that the specified Pre'Class condition is implied by the Pre'Class condition of the overridden inherited subprogram(s). Similarly, in the case of an overriding dispatching operation whose Post'Class attribute is explicitly specified, a verification condition is introduced to ensure that the specified Post'Class condition implies the Post'Class condition of the overridden inherited subprogram(s). [These verification conditions do not correspond to any run-time check. They are intended to, in effect, require users to make explicit the implicit disjunction/conjunction of class-wide preconditions/postconditions that is described in Ada RM 6.1.1.]

6.1.2 Subprogram Contracts

In order to extend Ada's support for specification of subprogram contracts (e.g., the Pre and Post) by providing more precise and/or concise contracts, the SPARK 2014 aspects, Global, Depends, and Contract_Cases are defined.

Legality Rules

1. The Global, Depends and Contract_Cases aspects may be specified for a subprogram with an `aspect_specification`. More specifically, such aspect specifications are allowed in the same contexts as Pre or Post aspect specifications. [In particular, these aspects may be specified for a generic subprogram but not for an instance of a generic subprogram.]

See section *Contract Cases* for further detail on Contract_Case aspects, section *Global Aspects* for further detail on Global aspects and section *Depends Aspects* for further detail on Depends aspects.

6.1.3 Contract Cases

The Contract_Cases aspect provides a structured way of defining a subprogram contract using mutually exclusive subcontract cases. The final case in the Contract_Case aspect may be the keyword **others** which means that, in a specific call to the subprogram, if all the `conditions` are False this `contract_case` is taken. If an **others** `contract_case` is not specified, then in a specific call of the subprogram exactly one of the guarding `conditions` should be True.

A Contract_Cases aspect may be used in conjunction with the language-defined aspects Pre and Post in which case the precondition specified by the Pre aspect is augmented with a check that exactly one of the `conditions` of the `contract_case_list` is satisfied and the postcondition specified by the Post aspect is conjoined with conditional expressions representing each of the `contract_cases`. For example:

```
procedure P (...)
   with Pre  => General_Precondition,
        Post => General_Postcondition,
        Contract_Cases => (A1 => B1,
                           A2 => B2,
                           ...
                           An => Bn);
```

is short hand for

```
procedure P (...)
  with Pre  => General_Precondition
                  and then Exactly_One_Of (A1, A2, ..., An),
       Post => General_Postcondition
                  and then (if A1'Old then B1)
                  and then (if A2'Old then B2)
                  and then ...
                  and then (if An'Old then Bn);
```

where

> A1 .. An are Boolean expressions involving the entry values of formal parameters and global objects and
>
> B1 .. Bn are Boolean expressions that may also use the exit values of formal parameters, global objects and results.
>
> `Exactly_One_Of(A1,A2...An)` evaluates to True if exactly one of its inputs evaluates to True and all other of its inputs evaluate to False.

The Contract_Cases aspect is specified with an `aspect_specification` where the `aspect_mark` is Contract_Cases and the `aspect_definition` must follow the grammar of `contract_case_list` given below.

Syntax

```
contract_case_list   ::= (contract_case {, contract_case})
contract_case        ::= condition => consequence
                       | others => consequence
```

where

> `consequence` ::= *Boolean*_expression

Legality Rules

1. A Contract_Cases aspect may have at most one **others** `contract_case` and if it exists it shall be the last one in the `contract_case_list`.

2. A `consequence` expression is considered to be a postcondition expression for purposes of determining the legality of Old or Result `attribute_references`.

Static Semantics

3. A Contract_Cases aspect is an assertion (as defined in RM 11.4.2(1.1/3)); its assertion expressions are as described below. Contract_Cases may be specified as an `assertion_aspect_mark` in an Assertion_Policy pragma.

Dynamic Semantics

4. Upon a call of a subprogram which is subject to an enabled Contract_Cases aspect, Contract_Cases checks are performed as follows:

   - Immediately after the specific precondition expression is evaluated and checked (or, if that check is disabled, at the point where the check would have been performed if it were enabled), all of the `conditions` of the `contract_case_list` are evaluated in textual order. A check is performed that exactly one (if no **others** `contract_case` is provided) or at most one (if an **others** `contract_case` is provided) of these `conditions` evaluates to True; Assertions.Assertion_Error is raised if this check fails.

   - Immediately after the specific postcondition expression is evaluated and checked (or, if that check is disabled, at the point where the check would have been performed if it were enabled), exactly one of the `consequences` is evaluated. The `consequence` to be evaluated is the one corresponding to the one `condition` whose evaluation yielded True (if such a `condition` exists), or to the **others** `contract_case` (if every `condition`'s evaluation yielded False). A check is performed that the evaluation of the selected `consequence` evaluates to True; Assertions.Assertion_Error is raised if this check fails.

5. If an Old `attribute_reference` occurs within a `consequence` other than the `consequence` selected for (later) evaluation as described above, then the associated implicit constant declaration (see Ada RM 6.1.1) is not elaborated. [In particular, the prefix of the Old `attribute_reference` is not evaluated].

Verification Rules

The verification conditions associated with the Contract_Cases runtime checks performed at the beginning of a call are assigned in the same way as those associated with a specific precondition check. More specifically, the verification condition is imposed on the caller or on the callee depending on whether the subprogram in question is a dispatching operation.

Examples

```
-- This subprogram is specified using a Contract_Cases aspect.
-- The prover will check that the cases are disjoint and
-- cover the domain of X.
procedure Incr_Threshold (X : in out Integer; Threshold : in Integer)
   with Contract_Cases => (X < Threshold  => X = X'Old + 1,
                           X >= Threshold => X = X'Old);

-- This is the equivalent specification not using Contract_Cases.
-- It is noticeably more complex and the prover is not able to check
-- for disjoint cases or that he domain of X is covered.
procedure Incr_Threshold_1 (X : in out Integer; Threshold : in Integer)
   with Pre  => (X < Threshold and not (X = Threshold))
                     or else (not (X < Threshold) and X = Threshold),
        Post => (if X'Old < Threshold then X = X'Old + 1
                 elsif X'Old = Threshold then X = X'Old);

-- Contract_Cases can be used in conjunction with  pre and postconditions.
procedure Incr_Threshold_2 (X : in out Integer; Threshold : in Integer)
   with Pre  => X in 0 .. Threshold,
        Post => X >= X'Old,
        Contract_Cases => (X < Threshold => X = X'Old + 1,
                           X = Threshold => X = X'Old);
```

6.1.4 Global Aspects

A Global aspect of a subprogram lists the global items whose values are used or affected by a call of the subprogram.

The Global aspect shall only be specified for the initial declaration of a subprogram (which may be a declaration, a body or a body stub), of a protected entry, or of a task unit. The implementation of a subprogram body shall be consistent with the subprogram's Global aspect. Similarly, the implementation of an entry or task body shall be consistent with the entry or task's Global aspect.

Note that a Refined_Global aspect may be applied to a subprogram body when using state abstraction; see section *Refined_Global Aspects* for further details.

The Global aspect is introduced by an `aspect_specification` where the `aspect_mark` is Global and the `aspect_definition` must follow the grammar of `global_specification`

For purposes of the rules concerning the Global, Depends, Refined_Global, and Refined_Depends aspects, when any of these aspects are specified for a task unit the task unit's body is considered to be the body of a nonreturning procedure and the current instance of the task unit is considered to be a formal parameter (of that notional procedure) of mode **in out**. [For example, rules which refer to the "subprogram body" refer, in the case of a task unit, to the task body.] [Because a task (even a discriminated task) is effectively a constant, one might think that a mode of **in** would make more sense. However, the current instance of a task unit is, strictly speaking, a variable; for example, it may be passed as an actual **out** or **in out** mode parameter in a call.] The Depends and Refined_Depends aspect of a task unit T need not mention this implicit parameter; an implicit specification of "T => T" is assumed, although this may be confirmed explicitly.

Similarly, for purposes of the rules concerning the Global, Refined_Global, Depends, and Refined_Depends aspects as they apply to protected operations, the current instance of the enclosing protected unit is considered to be a formal parameter (of mode **in** for a protected function, of mode **in out** otherwise) and a protected entry is considered to be a protected procedure. [For example, rules which refer to the "subprogram body" refer, in the case of a protected entry, to the entry body. As another example, the Global aspect of a subprogram nested within a protected operation might name the current instance of the protected unit as a global in the same way that it might name any other parameter of the protected operation.]

[Note that AI12-0169 modifies the Ada RM syntax for an `entry_body` to allow an optional `aspect_specification` immediately before the `entry_barrier`. This is relevant for aspects such as Refined_Global and Refined_Depends.]

Syntax

```
global_specification        ::= (moded_global_list {, moded_global_list})
                              | global_list
                              | null_global_specification
moded_global_list           ::= mode_selector => global_list
global_list                 ::= global_item
                              | (global_item {, global_item})
mode_selector               ::= Input | Output | In_Out | Proof_In
global_item                 ::= name
null_global_specification   ::= null
```

Static Semantics

1. A `global_specification` that is a `global_list` is shorthand for a `moded_global_list` with the `mode_selector` Input.

2. A `global_item` is *referenced* by a subprogram if:

   * It denotes an input or an output of the subprogram, or;

   * Its entry value is used to determine the value of an assertion expression within the subprogram, or;

   * Its entry value is used to determine the value of an assertion expression within another subprogram that is called either directly or indirectly by this subprogram.

3. A `null_global_specification` indicates that the subprogram does not reference any `global_item` directly or indirectly.

4. If a subprogram's Global aspect is not otherwise specified and either

   * the subprogram is a library-level subprogram declared in a library unit that is declared pure (i.e., a subprogram to which the implementation permissions of Ada RM 10.2.1 apply); or

   * a Pure_Function pragma applies to the subprogram

   then a Global aspect of *null* is implicitly specified for the subprogram.

Name Resolution Rules

5. A `global_item` shall denote an entire object or a state abstraction. [This is a name resolution rule because a `global_item` can unambiguously denote a state abstraction even if a function having the same fully qualified name is also present].

Legality Rules

6. The Global aspect may only be specified for the initial declaration of a subprogram (which may be a declaration, a body or a body stub), of a protected entry, or of a task unit.

7. A `global_item` occurring in a Global aspect specification of a subprogram shall not denote a formal parameter of the subprogram.

8. A `global_item` shall not denote a state abstraction whose refinement is visible. [A state abstraction cannot be named within its enclosing package's body other than in its refinement. Its constituents shall be used rather than the state abstraction.]

9. Each `mode_selector` shall occur at most once in a single Global aspect.

10. A function subprogram shall not have a `mode_selector` of Output or In_Out in its Global aspect.

11. The `global_items` in a single Global aspect specification shall denote distinct entities.

12. If a subprogram is nested within another and if the `global_specification` of the outer subprogram has an entity denoted by a `global_item` with a `mode_specification` of Input or the entity is a formal parameter with a mode of **in**, then a `global_item` of the `global_specification` of the inner subprogram shall not denote the same entity with a `mode_selector` of In_Out or Output.

Dynamic Semantics

There are no dynamic semantics associated with a Global aspect as it is used purely for static analysis purposes and is not executed.

Verification Rules

13. For a subprogram that has a `global_specification`, an object (except a constant without variable inputs) or state abstraction that is declared outside the scope of the subprogram, shall only be referenced within its implementation if it is a `global_item` in the `global_specification`.

14. A `global_item` shall occur in a Global aspect of a subprogram if and only if it denotes an entity (except for a constant without variable inputs) that is referenced by the subprogram.

15. Where the refinement of a state abstraction is not visible (see *State Refinement*) and a subprogram references one or more of its constituents the constituents may be represented by a `global_item` that denotes the state abstraction in the `global_specification` of the subprogram. [The state abstraction encapsulating a constituent is known from the Part_Of indicator on the declaration of the constituent.]

16. Each entity denoted by a `global_item` in a `global_specification` of a subprogram that is an input or output of the subprogram shall satisfy the following mode specification rules [which are checked during analysis of the subprogram body]:

    • a `global_item` that denotes an input but not an output has a `mode_selector` of Input;

    • a `global_item` has a `mode_selector` of Output if:

        – it denotes an output but not an input, other than the use of a discriminant or an attribute related to a property, not its value, of the `global_item` [examples of attributes that may be used are A'Last, A'First and A'Length; examples of attributes that are dependent on the value of the object and shall not be used are X'Old and X'Update] and

        – is always fully initialized by a call of the subprogram;

    • otherwise the `global_item` denotes both an input and an output, and has a `mode_selector` of In_Out.

[For purposes of determining whether an output of a subprogram shall have a `mode_selector` of Output or In_Out, reads of array bounds, discriminants, or tags of any part of the output are ignored. Similarly, for purposes of determining whether an entity is fully initialized as a result of any successful execution of the call, only nondiscriminant parts are considered. This implies that given an output of a discriminated type that is not known to be constrained ("known to be constrained" is defined in Ada RM 3.3), the discriminants of the output might or might not be updated by the call.]

17. An entity that is denoted by a `global_item` which is referenced by a subprogram but is neither an input nor an output but is only referenced directly, or indirectly in assertion expressions has a `mode_selector` of Proof_In.

18. A `global_item` shall not denote a constant object other than a formal parameter [of an enclosing subprogram] of mode **in**, a generic formal object of mode **in**, or a *constant with variable inputs*.

   If a `global_item` denotes a generic formal object of mode **in**, then the corresponding `global_item` in an instance of the generic unit may denote a constant which has no variable inputs. [This can occur if the corresponding actual parameter is an expression which has no variable inputs]. Outside of the instance, such a `global_item` is ignored. For example,

```
generic
   Xxx : Integer;
package Ggg is
   procedure Ppp (Yyy : in out Integer) with Global => Xxx,
                                             Depends => (Yyy =>+ Xxx);
end Ggg;

package body Ggg is
   procedure Ppp (Yyy : in out Integer) is
   begin
      Yyy := Integer'Max (Xxx, Yyy);
   end Ppp;
end Ggg;

package Iii is new Ggg
  (Xxx => 123); -- actual parameter lacks variable inputs

procedure Qqq (Zzz : in out Integer) with Global => null,
                                          Depends => (Zzz =>+ null);
procedure Qqq (Zzz : in out Integer) is
begin
   Iii.Ppp (Yyy => Zzz);
end Qqq;

-- Qqq's Global and Depends aspects don't mention Iii.Xxx even though
-- Qqq calls Iii.Ppp which does reference Iii.Xxx as a global.
-- As seen from outside of Iii, Iii.Ppp's references to Iii.Xxx in its
-- Global and Depends aspect specifications are ignored.
```

19. The `mode_selector` of a `global_item` denoting a *constant with variable inputs* shall be Input or Proof_In.

20. The `mode_selector` of a `global_item` denoting a variable marked as a *constant after elaboration* shall be Input or Proof_In [, to ensure that such variables are only updated directly by package elaboration code]. A subprogram or entry having such a `global_item` shall not be called during library unit elaboration[, to ensure only the final ("constant") value of the object is referenced].

Examples

```
with Global => null; -- Indicates that the subprogram does not reference
                     -- any global items.
with Global => V;    -- Indicates that V is an input of the subprogram.
with Global => (X, Y, Z); -- X, Y and Z are inputs of the subprogram.
with Global => (Input    => V); -- Indicates that V is an input of the subprogram.
```

```
with Global => (Input    => (X, Y, Z));  -- X, Y and Z are inputs of the subprogram.
with Global => (Output   => (A, B, C));  -- A, B and C are outputs of
                                         -- the subprogram.
with Global => (In_Out   => (D, E, F));  -- D, E and F are both inputs and
                                         -- outputs of the subprogram
with Global => (Proof_In => (G, H));     -- G and H are only used in
                                         -- assertion expressions within
                                         -- the subprogram

with Global => (Input    => (X, Y, Z),
                Output   => (A, B, C),
                In_Out   => (P, Q, R),
                Proof_In => (T, U));
                -- A global aspect with all types of global specification
```

6.1.5 Depends Aspects

A Depends aspect defines a *dependency relation* for a subprogram which may be given in the `aspect_specification` of the subprogram. A dependency relation is a sort of formal specification which specifies a simple relationship between inputs and outputs of the subprogram. It may be used with or without a postcondition.

The Depends aspect shall only be specified for the initial declaration of a subprogram (which may be a declaration, a body or a body stub), of a protected entry, or of a task unit.

Unlike a postcondition, the Depends aspect must be complete in the sense that every input and output of the subprogram must appear in it. A postcondition need only specify properties of particular interest.

Like a postcondition, the dependency relation may be omitted from a subprogram declaration when it defaults to the conservative relation that each output depends on every input of the subprogram. A particular SPARK 2014 tool may synthesize a more accurate approximation from the subprogram implementation if it is present (see *Synthesis of SPARK 2014 Aspects*).

For accurate information flow analysis the Depends aspect should be present on every subprogram.

A Depends aspect for a subprogram specifies for each output every input on which it depends. The meaning of *X depends on Y* in this context is that the input value(s) of *Y* may affect:

- the exit value of *X*; and

- the intermediate values of *X* if it is an external state (see section *External State*), or if the subprogram is a nonreturning procedure [, possibly the notional nonreturning procedure corresponding to a task body].

This is written *X* => *Y*. As in UML, the entity at the tail of the arrow depends on the entity at the head of the arrow.

If an output does not depend on any input this is indicated using a **null**, e.g., *X* => **null**. An output may be self-dependent but not dependent on any other input. The shorthand notation denoting self-dependence is useful here, X =>+ **null**.

Note that a Refined_Depends aspect may be applied to a subprogram body when using state abstraction; see section *Refined_Depends Aspects* for further details.

See section *Global Aspects* regarding how the rules given in this section apply to protected operations and to task bodies.

The Depends aspect is introduced by an `aspect_specification` where the `aspect_mark` is Depends and the `aspect_definition` must follow the grammar of `dependency_relation` given below.

Syntax

```
dependency_relation    ::= null
                          | (dependency_clause {, dependency_clause})
dependency_clause       ::= output_list =>[+] input_list
                          | null_dependency_clause
null_dependency_clause  ::= null => input_list
output_list             ::= output
                          | (output {, output})
input_list              ::= input
                          | (input {, input})
                          | null
input                   ::= name
output                  ::= name | function_result
```

where

> `function_result` is a function Result `attribute_reference`.

Name Resolution Rules

1. An `input` or `output` of a `dependency_relation` shall denote only an entire object or a state abstraction. [This is a name resolution rule because an `input` or `output` can unambiguously denote a state abstraction even if a function having the same fully qualified name is also present.]

Legality Rules

2. The Depends aspect shall only be specified for the initial declaration of a subprogram (which may be a declaration, a body or a body stub), of a protected entry, or of a task unit.

3. An `input` or `output` of a `dependency_relation` shall not denote a state abstraction whose refinement is visible [a state abstraction cannot be named within its enclosing package's body other than in its refinement].

4. The *explicit input set* of a subprogram is the set of formal parameters of the subprogram of mode **in** and **in out** along with the entities denoted by `global_items` of the Global aspect of the subprogram with a `mode_selector` of Input and In_Out.

5. The *input set* of a subprogram is the explicit input set of the subprogram augmented with those formal parameters of mode **out** and those `global_items` with a `mode_selector` of Output having discriminants, array bounds, or a tag which can be read and whose values are not implied by the subtype of the parameter. More specifically, it includes formal parameters of mode **out** and `global_items` with a `mode_selector` of Output which are of an unconstrained array subtype, an unconstrained discriminated subtype, a tagged type (with one exception), or a type having a subcomponent of an unconstrained discriminated subtype. The exception mentioned in the previous sentence is in the case where the formal parameter is of a specific tagged type and the applicable Extensions_Visible aspect is False. In that case, the tag of the parameter cannot be read and so the fact that the parameter is tagged does not cause it to included in the subprogram's *input_set*, although it may be included for some other reason (e.g., if the parameter is of an unconstrained discriminated subtype).

6. The *output set* of a subprogram is the set of formal parameters of the subprogram of mode **in out** and **out** along with the entities denoted by `global_items` of the Global aspect of the subprogram with a `mode_selector` of In_Out and Output and (for a function) the `function_result`.

7. The entity denoted by each `input` of a `dependency_relation` of a subprogram shall be a member of the input set of the subprogram.

8. Every member of the explicit input set of a subprogram shall be denoted by at least one `input` of the `dependency_relation` of the subprogram.

9. The entity denoted by each `output` of a `dependency_relation` of a subprogram shall be a member of the output set of the subprogram.

10. Every member of the output set of a subprogram shall be denoted by exactly one `output` in the `dependency_relation` of the subprogram.

11. For the purposes of determining the legality of a Result `attribute_reference`, a `dependency_relation` is considered to be a postcondition of the function to which the enclosing `aspect_specification` applies.

12. In a `dependency_relation` there can be at most one `dependency_clause` which is a `null_dependency_clause` and if it exists it shall be the last `dependency_clause` in the `dependency_relation`.

13. An entity denoted by an `input` which is in an `input_list` of a `null_dependency_clause` shall not be denoted by an `input` in another `input_list` of the same `dependency_relation`.

14. The `input`s in a single `input_list` shall denote distinct entities.

15. A `null_dependency_clause` shall not have an `input_list` of **null**.

Static Semantics

16. A `dependency_clause` with a "+" symbol in the syntax `output_list =>+ input_list` means that each `output` in the `output_list` has a *self-dependency*, that is, it is dependent on itself. [The text (A, B, C) =>+ Z is shorthand for (A => (A, Z), B => (B, Z), C => (C, Z)).]

17. A `dependency_clause` of the form A =>+ A has the same meaning as A => A. [The reason for this rule is to allow the short hand: ((A, B) =>+ (A, C)) which is equivalent to (A => (A, C), B => (A, B, C)).]

18. A `dependency_clause` with a **null** `input_list` means that the final value of the entity denoted by each `output` in the `output_list` does not depend on any member of the input set of the subprogram (other than itself, if the `output_list =>+` **null** self-dependency syntax is used).

19. The `input`s in the `input_list` of a `null_dependency_clause` may be read by the subprogram but play no role in determining the values of any outputs of the subprogram.

20. A Depends aspect of a subprogram with a **null** `dependency_relation` indicates that the subprogram has no `input`s or `output`s. [From an information flow analysis viewpoint it is a null operation (a no-op).]

21. A function without an explicit Depends aspect specification has the default `dependency_relation` that its result is dependent on all of its inputs. [Generally an explicit Depends aspect is not required for a function declaration.]

22. A procedure without an explicit Depends aspect specification has a default `dependency_relation` that each member of its output set is dependent on every member of its input set. [This conservative approximation may be improved by analyzing the body of the subprogram if it is present.]

Dynamic Semantics

There are no dynamic semantics associated with a Depends aspect as it is used purely for static analysis purposes and is not executed.

Verification Rules

23. Each entity denoted by an `output` given in the Depends aspect of a subprogram shall be an output in the implementation of the subprogram body and the output shall depend on all, but only, the entities denoted by the `input`s given in the `input_list` associated with the `output`.

24. Each output of the implementation of the subprogram body is denoted by an `output` in the Depends aspect of the subprogram.

25. Each input of the implementation of a subprogram body is denoted by an `input` of the Depends aspect of the subprogram.

26. If not all parts of an output are updated, then the updated entity is dependent on itself as the parts that are not updated have their current value preserved.

    [In the case of a parameter of a tagged type (specific or class-wide), see the definition of "fully initialized" for a clarification of what the phrase "all parts" means in the preceding sentence.]

```
procedure P (X, Y, Z in : Integer; Result : out Boolean)
  with Depends => (Result => (X, Y, Z));
-- The exit value of Result depends on the entry values of X, Y and Z

procedure Q (X, Y, Z in : Integer; A, B, C, D, E : out Integer)
  with Depends => ((A, B) => (X, Y),
                   C       => (X, Z),
                   D       => Y,
                   E       => null);
-- The exit values of A and B depend on the entry values of X and Y.
-- The exit value of C depends on the entry values of X and Z.
-- The exit value of D depends on the entry value of Y.
-- The exit value of E does not depend on any input value.

procedure R (X, Y, Z : in Integer; A, B, C, D : in out Integer)
  with Depends => ((A, B) =>+ (A, X, Y),
                   C       =>+ Z,
                   D       =>+ null);
-- The "+" sign attached to the arrow indicates self-dependency, that is
-- the exit value of A depends on the entry value of A as well as the
-- entry values of X and Y.
-- Similarly, the exit value of B depends on the entry value of B
-- as well as the entry values of A, X and Y.
-- The exit value of C depends on the entry value of C and Z.
-- The exit value of D depends only on the entry value of D.

procedure S
  with Global  => (Input  => (X, Y, Z),
                   In_Out => (A, B, C, D)),
       Depends => ((A, B) =>+ (A, X, Y, Z),
                   C       =>+ Y,
                   D       =>+ null);
-- Here globals are used rather than parameters and global items may appear
-- in the Depends aspect as well as formal parameters.

function F (X, Y : Integer) return Integer
  with Global  => G,
       Depends => (F'Result => (G, X),
                   null     => Y);
-- Depends aspects are only needed for special cases like here where the
-- parameter Y has no discernible effect on the result of the function.
```

6.1.6 Class-Wide Global and Depends Aspects

The Global'Class and Depends'Class aspects may be specified for a dispatching subprogram just as the Global and Depends aspects may be specified for any subprogram (dispatching or not). [The syntax, static semantics, and legality rules are all the same, except that the Depends'Class aspect of a subprogram is checked for consistency with the Global'Class aspect of the subprogram rather than with the Global aspect.]

Verification Rules

When analyzing a dispatching call, the Global and Depends aspects of the statically denoted callee play no role; the corresponding class-wide aspects are used instead.

[No relationship between the Global'Class/Depends'Class aspects of a subprogram and the subprogram's implementation is explicitly verified. This is instead accomplished implicitly by checking the consistency of the subprogram's implementation with its Global/Depends aspects (as described in preceding sections) and then checking (as described in this section) the consistency of the Global/Depends aspects with the Global'Class/Depends'Class aspects.]

Static Semantics

A Global or Global'Class aspect specification G2 is said to be a *valid overriding* of another such specification, G1, if the following conditions are met:

- each Input-mode item of G2 is an Input-mode or an In_Out-mode item of G1 or a direct or indirect constituent thereof; and

- each In_Out-mode item of G2 is an In_Out-mode item of G1 or a direct or indirect constituent thereof; and

- each Output-mode item of G2 is an Output-mode or In_Out-mode item of G1 or a direct or indirect constituent therof; and

- each Output-mode item of G1 which is not a state abstraction whose refinement is visible at the point of G2 is an Output-mode item of G2; and

- for each Output-mode item of G1 which is a state abstraction whose refinement is visible at the point of G2, each direct or indirect constituent thereof is an Output-mode item of G2.

A Depends or Depends'Class aspect specification D2 is said to be a *valid overriding* of another such specification, D1, if the set of dependencies of D2 is a subset of the dependencies of D1 or, in the case where D1 mentions a state abstraction whose refinement is visible at the point of D2, if D2 is derivable from such a subset as described in *Refined_Depends Aspects*.

Legality Rules

The Global aspect of a subprogram shall be a valid overriding of the Global'Class aspect of the subprogram. The Global'Class aspect of an an overriding subprogram shall be a valid overriding of the Global'Class aspect(s) of the overridden inherited subprogram(s).

The Depends aspect of a subprogram shall be a valid overriding of the Depends'Class aspect of the subprogram. The Depends'Class aspect of an an overriding subprogram shall be a valid overriding of the Depends'Class aspect(s) of the overridden inherited subprogram(s).

6.1.7 Extensions_Visible Aspects

1. The Extensions_Visible aspect provides a mechanism for ensuring that "hidden" components of a formal parameter of a specific tagged type are unreferenced. For example, if a formal parameter of a specific tagged type T is converted to a class-wide type and then used as a controlling operand in a dispatching call, then the (dynamic) callee might reference components of the parameter which are declared in some extension of T. Such a use of the formal parameter could be forbidden via an Extensions_Visible aspect specification as described below. The aspect also plays a corresponding role in the analysis of callers of the subprogram.

Static Semantics

2. Extensions_Visible is a Boolean-valued aspect which may be specified for a noninstance subprogram or a generic subprogram. If directly specified, the aspect_definition shall be a static [Boolean] expression. The aspect is inherited by an inherited primitive subprogram. If the aspect is neither inherited nor directly specified for a subprogram, then the aspect is False, except in the case of the predefined equality operator of a type extension. In that case, the aspect value is that of the primitive [(possibly user-defined)] equality operator for the parent type.

Legality Rules

3. If the Extensions_Visible aspect is False for a subprogram, then certain restrictions are imposed on the use of any parameter of the subprogram which is of a specific tagged type (or of a private type whose full view is a specific tagged type). Such a parameter shall not be converted (implicitly or explicitly) to a class-wide

type. Such a parameter shall not be passed as an actual parameter in a call to a subprogram whose Extensions_Visible aspect is True. These restrictions also apply to any parenthesized expression, qualified expression, or type conversion whose operand is subject to these restrictions, to any Old, Update, or Loop_Entry `attribute_reference` whose prefix is subject to these restrictions, and to any conditional expression having at least one dependent_expression which is subject to these restrictions. [A subcomponent of a parameter is not itself a parameter and is therefore not subject to these restrictions. A parameter whose type is class-wide is not subject to these restrictions. An Old, Update, or Loop_Entry `attribute_reference` does not itself violate these restrictions (despite the fact that (in the tagged case) each of these attributes yields a result having the same underlying dynamic tag as their prefix).]

4. A subprogram whose Extensions_Visible aspect is True shall not override an inherited primitive operation of a tagged type whose Extensions_Visible aspect is False. [The reverse is allowed.]

5. If a nonnull type extension inherits a procedure having both a False Extensions_Visible aspect and one or more controlling out-mode parameters, then the inherited procedure requires overriding. [This is because the inherited procedure would not initialize the noninherited component(s).]

6. The Extensions_Visible aspect shall not be specified for a subprogram which has no parameters of either a specific tagged type or a private type unless the subprogram is declared in an instance of a generic unit and the corresponding subprogram in the generic unit satisfies this rule. [Such an aspect specification, if allowed, would be ineffective.]

7. [These rules ensure that the value of the underlying tag (at run time) of the actual parameter of a call to a subprogram whose Extensions_Visible aspect is False will have no effect on the behavior of that call. In particular, if the actual parameter has any additional components which are not components of the type of the formal parameter, then these components are unreferenced by the execution of the call.]

Verification Rules

8. SPARK 2014 requires that an actual parameter corresponding to an in mode or in out mode formal parameter in a call shall be fully initialized before the call; similarly, the callee is responsible for fully initializing any out-mode parameters before returning.

9. In the case of a formal parameter of a specific tagged type T (or of a private type whose full view is a specific tagged type), the set of components which shall be initialized in order to meet these requirements depends on the Extensions_Visible aspect of the callee. If the aspect is False, then that set of components is the [statically known] set of nondiscriminant components of T. If the aspect is True, then this set is the set of nondiscriminant components of the specific type associated with the tag of the corresponding actual parameter. [In general, this is not statically known. This set will always include the nondiscriminant components of T, but it may also include additional components.]

10. [To put it another way, if the applicable Extensions_Visible aspect is True, then the initialization requirements (for both the caller and the callee) for a parameter of a specific tagged type T are the same as if the formal parameter's type were T'Class. If the aspect is False, then components declared in proper descendants of T need not be initialized. In the case of an out mode parameter, such initialization by the callee is not only not required, it is effectively forbidden because such an out-mode parameter could not be fully initialized without some form of dispatching (e.g., a class-wide assignment or a dispatching call in which an out-mode parameter is a controlling operand). Such a dispatching assignment will always fully initialize its controlling out-mode parameters, regardless of the Extensions_Visible aspect of the callee. An assignment statement whose target is of a class-wide type T'Class is treated, for purposes of formal verification, like a call to a procedure with two parameters of type T'Class, one of mode out and one of mode in.]

11. [In the case of an actual parameter of a call to a subprogram whose Extensions_Visible aspect is False where the corresponding formal parameter is of a specific tagged type T, these rules imply that formal verification can safely assume that any components of the actual parameter which are not components of T will be neither read nor written by the call.]

6.2 Formal Parameter Modes

In flow analysis, particularly information flow analysis, the update of a component of composite object is treated as updating the whole of the composite object with the component set to its new value and the remaining components of the composite object with their value preserved.

This means that if a formal parameter of a subprogram is a composite type and only individual components, but not all, are updated, then the mode of the formal parameter should be **in out**.

In general, it is not possible to statically determine whether all elements of an array have been updated by a subprogram if individual array elements are updated. The mode of a formal parameter of an array with such updates should be **in out**.

A formal parameter with a mode of **out** is treated as not having an entry value (apart from any discriminant or attributes of properties of the formal parameter). Hence, a subprogram cannot read a value of a formal parameter of mode **out** until the subprogram has updated it.

Verification Rules

1. A subprogram formal parameter of a composite type which is updated but not fully initialized by the subprogram shall have a mode of **in out**.

2. A subprogram formal parameter of mode **out** shall not be read by the subprogram until it has been updated by the subprogram. The use of a discriminant or an attribute related to a property, not its value, of the formal parameter is not considered to be a read of the formal parameter. [Examples of attributes that may be used are A'First, A'Last and A'Length; examples of attributes that are dependent on the value of the formal parameter and shall not be used are X'Old and X'Update.]

Examples

```
1   -- The following example is acceptable in Ada
2   -- but will raise a flow anomaly in SPARK stating that
3   -- X may not be initialized because an out parameter indicates
4   -- that the entire String is initialized.
5   procedure Param_1_Illegal (X : out String)
6   is
7   begin
8      if X'Length > 0 and X'First = 1 then
9         X (1) := '?';
10     end if;
11  end Param_1_Illegal;
```

```
1   -- In SPARK the parameter mode should be in out meaning that the
2   -- entire array is initialized before the call to the subprogram.
3   procedure Param_1_Legal (X : in out String)
4   is
5   begin
6      if X'Length > 0 and X'First = 1 then
7         X (1) := '?';
8      end if;
9   end Param_1_Legal;
```

6.3 Subprogram Bodies

6.3.1 Conformance Rules

No extensions or restrictions.

6.3.2 Inline Expansion of Subprograms

No extensions or restrictions.

6.4 Subprogram Calls

No extensions or restrictions.

6.4.1 Parameter Associations

No extensions or restrictions.

6.4.2 Anti-Aliasing

An alias is a name which refers to the same object as another name. The presence of aliasing is inconsistent with the underlying flow analysis and proof models used by the tools which assume that different names represent different entities. In general, it is not possible or is difficult to deduce that two names refer to the same object and problems arise when one of the names is used to update the object (although object renaming declarations are not problematic in SPARK 2014).

A common place for aliasing to be introduced is through the actual parameters and between actual parameters and global variables in a procedure call. Extra verification rules are given that avoid the possibility of aliasing through actual parameters and global variables. A function is not allowed to have side-effects and cannot update an actual parameter or global variable. Therefore, function calls cannot introduce aliasing and are excluded from the anti-aliasing rules given below for procedure calls.

Static Semantics

1. Two names that denote parts of the same unsynchronized (see section *Tasks and Synchronization*) stand-alone object whose Constant_After_Elaboration aspect is False, or which denote parts of the same unsynchronized parameter, are said to *potentially introduce aliasing*. [This definition has the effect of exempting most synchronized objects from the anti-aliasing rules given below; aliasing of most synchronized objects via parameter passing is allowed.]

Verification Rules

2. A procedure call shall not pass two actual parameters which potentially introduce aliasing unless either

   - both of the corresponding formal parameters are of mode **in**; or

   - at least one of the corresponding formal parameters is of mode **in** and is of a by-copy type.

3. If an actual parameter in a procedure call and a `global_item` referenced by the called procedure potentially introduce aliasing, then

   - the mode of the corresponding formal parameter shall be **in**; and

- if the `global_item`'s mode is Output or In_Out, then the parameter's corresponding formal parameter shall be of a by-copy type.

4. Where one of these rules prohibits the occurrence of an object V or any of its subcomponents as an actual parameter, the following constructs are also prohibited in this context:

   - A type conversion whose operand is a prohibited construct;

   - A call to an instance of Unchecked_Conversion whose operand is a prohibited construct;

   - A qualified expression whose operand is a prohibited construct;

   - A prohibited construct enclosed in parentheses.

Examples

```ada
 1  procedure Anti_Aliasing is
 2     type Rec is record
 3        X : Integer;
 4        Y : Integer;
 5     end record;
 6
 7     type Arr is array (1 .. 10) of Integer;
 8
 9     type Arr_With_Rec is array (1 .. 10) of Rec;
10
11     Local_1, Local_2 : Integer := 0;
12
13     Rec_1 : Rec := (0, 0);
14
15     Arr_1 : arr := (others => 0);
16
17     Arr_Rec : Arr_With_Rec := (others => (0, 0));
18
19     procedure One_In_One_Out (X : in Integer; Y : in out Integer)
20     is
21     begin
22        Y := X + Y;
23     end One_In_One_Out;
24
25     procedure Two_In_Out (X, Y : in out Integer) with Global => null
26     is
27        Temp : Integer;
28     begin
29        Temp := Y;
30        Y := X + Y;
31        X := Temp;
32     end Two_In_Out;
33
34     procedure With_In_Global (I : in out Integer)
35       with Global => Local_1
36     is
37     begin
38        I := I + Local_1;
39     end With_In_Global;
40
41     procedure With_In_Out_Global (I : in Integer)
42       with Global => (In_Out => Local_1)
43     is
44     begin
45        Local_1 := I + Local_1;
```

```
46    end With_In_Out_Global;

47
48    procedure With_Composite_In_Out_Global (I : in Integer)
49      with Global => (In_Out => Rec_1)
50    is
51    begin
52       Rec_1.X := I + Rec_1.X;
53    end With_Composite_In_Out_Global;

54
55 begin
56    -- This is ok because parameters are by copy and there
57    -- is only one out parameter
58    One_In_One_Out (Local_1, Local_1);

59
60    -- This is erroneous both parameters are in out and
61    -- the actual parameters overlap
62    Two_In_Out (Local_1, Local_1);

63
64    -- This is ok the variables do not overlap even though
65    -- they are part of the same record.
66    Two_In_Out (Rec_1.X, Rec_1.Y);

67
68    -- This is ok the variables do not overlap they
69    -- can statically determined to be distinct elements
70    Two_In_Out (Arr_1 (1), Arr_1 (2));

71
72    -- This is erroneous because it cannot be determined statically
73    -- whether the elements overlap
74    Two_In_Out (Arr_1 (Local_1), Arr_1 (Local_2));

75
76    -- This is ok the variables do not overlap they
77    -- can statically determined to be distinct components
78    Two_In_Out (Arr_Rec (Local_1).X , Arr_Rec (Local_2).Y);

79
80    -- This erroneous Global and formal in out parameter overlap.
81    With_In_Global (Local_1);

82
83    -- This erroneous Global In_Out and formal parameter overlap.
84    With_In_Out_Global (Local_1);

85
86    -- This erroneous Global In_Out and formal parameter overlap.
87    With_Composite_In_Out_Global (Rec_1.Y);

88
89 end Anti_Aliasing;
```

6.5 Return Statements

No extensions or restrictions.

6.5.1 Nonreturning Procedures

Verification Rules

1. A call to a nonreturning procedure introduces an obligation to prove that the statement will not be executed, much like the verification condition associated with

```
pragma Assert (False);
```

[In other words, the verification conditions introduced for a call to a nonreturning procedure are the same as those introduced for a runtime check which fails unconditionally. See also section *Exceptions*, where a similar verification rule is imposed on `raise_statements`.]

6.6 Overloading of Operators

Legality Rules

1. **[The declaration and body of a user-defined equality operation on a record** type shall not have any variable inputs; see *Expressions* for the statement of this rule.]

6.7 Null Procedures

No extensions or restrictions.

6.8 Expression Functions

Legality Rules

1. Contract_Cases, Global and Depends aspects may be applied to an expression function as for any other function declaration if it does not have a separate declaration. If it has a separate declaration then the aspects are applied to that. It may have refined aspects applied (see *State Refinement*).

Examples

```
function Expr_Func_1 (X : Natural; Y : Natural) return Natural is (X + Y)
  with Pre => X <= Natural'Last - Y;
```

6.9 Ghost Entities

Ghost entities are intended for use in discharging verification conditions and in making it easier to express assertions about a program. The essential property of ghost entities is that they have no effect on the dynamic behavior of a valid SPARK program. More specifically, if one were to take a valid SPARK program and remove all ghost entity declarations from it and all "innermost" statements, declarations, and pragmas which refer to those declarations (replacing removed statements with null statements when syntactically required), then the resulting program might no longer be a valid SPARK program (e.g., it might no longer be possible to discharge all of the program's verification conditions) but its dynamic semantics (when viewed as an Ada program) should be unaffected by this transformation. [This transformation might affect the performance characteristics of the program (e.g., due to no longer evaluating provably true assertions), but that is not what we are talking about here. In rare cases, it might be necessary to make a small additional change after the removals (e.g., adding an Elaborate_Body pragma) in order to avoid producing a library package that no longer needs a body (see Ada RM 7.2(4))].

Static Semantics

1. SPARK 2014 defines the Boolean-valued representation aspect Ghost. Ghost is an aspect of all entities (e.g., subprograms, types, objects). An entity whose Ghost aspect is True is said to be a ghost entity; terms such as "ghost function" or "ghost variable" are defined analogously (e.g., a function whose Ghost aspect is True is said to be a ghost function). In addition, a subcomponent of a ghost object is a ghost object.

Ghost is an assertion aspect. [This means that Ghost can be named in an Assertion_Policy pragma.]

2. The Ghost aspect of an entity declared inside of a ghost entity (e.g., within the body of a ghost subprogram) is defined to be True. The Ghost aspect of an entity implicitly declared as part of the explicit declaration of a ghost entity (e.g., an implicitly declared subprogram associated with the declaration of a ghost type) is defined to be True. The Ghost aspect of a child of a ghost library unit is defined to be True.

3. A statement or pragma is said to be a "ghost statement" if

   - it occurs within a ghost subprogram or package; or

   - it is a call to a ghost procedure; or

   - it is an assignment statement whose target is a ghost variable; or

   - it is a pragma which encloses a name denoting a ghost entity or which specifies an aspect of a ghost entity.

4. If the Ghost assertion policy in effect at the point of a ghost statement or the declaration of a ghost entity is Ignore, then the elaboration of that construct (at run time) has no effect, other Ada or SPARK 2014 rules notwithstanding. Similarly, the elaboration of the completion of a ghost entity has no effect if the Ghost assertion policy in effect at the point of the entity's initial declaration is Ignore. [A Ghost assertion policy of Ignore can be used to ensure that a compiler generates no code for ghost constructs.] Such a declaration is said to be a *disabled ghost declaration*; terms such as "disabled ghost type" and "disabled ghost subprogram" are defined analogously.

Legality Rules

5. The Ghost aspect may only be specified [explicitly] for the declaration of a subprogram, a generic subprogram, a type (including a partial view thereof), an object (or list of objects, in the case of an `aspect_specification` for an `object_declaration` having more than one `defining_identifier`), a package, or a generic package. The Ghost aspect may be specified via either an `aspect_specification` or via a pragma. The representation pragma Ghost takes a single argument, a name denoting one or more entities whose Ghost aspect is then specified to be True. [In particular, SPARK 2014 does not currently include any form of ghost components of non-ghost record types, or ghost parameters of non-ghost subprograms. SPARK 2014 does define ghost state abstractions, but these are described elsewhere.]

6. A Ghost aspect value of False shall not be explicitly specified except in a confirming aspect specification. [For example, a non-ghost declaration cannot occur within a ghost subprogram.]

   The value specified for the Ghost assertion policy in an Assertion_Policy pragma shall be either Check or Ignore. [In other words, implementation-defined assertion policy values are not permitted.] The Ghost assertion policy in effect at any point of a SPARK program shall be either Check or Ignore.

7. A ghost type or object shall not be effectively volatile. A ghost object shall not be imported or exported. [In other words, no ghost objects for which reading or writing would constitute an external effect (see Ada RM 1.1.3).]

8. A ghost primitive subprogram of a non-ghost type extension shall not override an inherited non-ghost primitive subprogram. A non-ghost primitive subprogram of a type extension shall not override an inherited ghost primitive subprogram. [A ghost subprogram may be a primitive subprogram of a non-ghost tagged type. A ghost type extension may have a non-ghost parent type or progenitor; primitive subprograms of such a type may override inherited (ghost or non-ghost) subprograms.]

9. A Ghost pragma which applies to a declaration occuring in the visible part of a package shall not occur in the private part of that package. [This rule is to ensure that the ghostliness of a visible entity can be determined without having to look into the private part of the enclosing package.]

10. A ghost entity shall only be referenced:

    - from within an assertion expression; or

- from within an aspect specification [(i.e., either an `aspect_specification` or an aspect-specifying pragma)]; or

- within the declaration or completion of a ghost entity (e.g., from within the body of a ghost subprogram); or

- within a ghost statement; or

- within a `with_clause` or `use_clause`; or

- within a renaming_declaration which either renames a ghost entity or occurs within a ghost subprogram or package.

11. A ghost entity shall not be referenced within an aspect specification [(including an aspect-specifying pragma)] which specifies an aspect of a non-ghost entity except in the following cases:

    - the reference occurs within an assertion expression which is not a predicate expression; or

    - the specified aspect is either Global, Depends, Refined_Global, Refined_Depends, Initializes, or Refined_State. [For example, the Global aspect of a non-ghost subprogram might refer to a ghost variable.]

    [Predicate expressions are excluded because predicates participate in membership tests; no Assertion_Policy pragma has any effect on this participation. In the case of a Static_Predicate expression, there are also other reasons (e.g., case statements).]

12. An **out** or **in out** mode actual parameter in a call to a ghost subprogram shall be a ghost variable.

13. If the Ghost assertion policy in effect at the point of the declaration of a ghost entity is Ignore, then the Ghost assertion policy in effect at the point of any reference to that entity shall be Ignore. If the Ghost assertion policy in effect at the point of the declaration of a ghost variable is Check, then the Ghost assertion policy in effect at the point of any assignment to a part of that variable shall be Check. [This includes both assignment statements and passing a ghost variable as an **out** or **in out** mode actual parameter.]

14. An Assertion_Policy pragma specifying a Ghost assertion policy shall not occur within a ghost subprogram or package. If a ghost entity has a completion then the Ghost assertion policies in effect at the declaration and at the completion of the entity shall be the same. [This rule applies to subprograms, packages, types, and deferred constants.]

    The Ghost assertion policies in effect at the point of the declaration of an entity and at the point of an aspect specification which applies to that entity shall be the same.

15. The Ghost assertion policies in effect at the declaration of a state abstraction and at the declaration of each constituent of that abstraction shall be the same.

16. The Ghost assertion policies in effect at the declaration of a primitive subprogram of a ghost tagged type and at the declaration of the ghost tagged type shall be the same.

17. If a tagged type is not a disabled ghost type, and if a primitive operation of the tagged type overrides an inherited operation, then the corresponding operation of the ancestor type shall be a disabled ghost subprogram if and only if the overriding subprogram is a disabled ghost subprogram.

18. If the Ghost assertion policy in effect at the point of an a reference to a Ghost entity which occurs within an assertion expression is Ignore, then the assertion policy which governs the assertion expression (e.g., Pre for a precondition expression, Assert for the argument of an Assert pragma) shall [also] be Ignore.

19. A ghost type shall not have a task or protected part. A ghost object shall not be of a type which yields synchronized objects (see section *Tasks and Synchronization*). A ghost object shall not have a volatile part. A synchronized state abstraction shall not be a ghost state abstraction (see *Abstract_State Aspects*).

Verification Rules

20. A ghost procedure shall not have a non-ghost [global] output.

21. An output of a non-ghost subprogram other than a state abstraction or a ghost global shall not depend on a ghost input. [It is intended that this follows as a consequence of other rules. Although a non-ghost state abstraction output which depends on a ghost input may have a non-ghost constituent, other rules prevent such a non-ghost constituent from depending on the ghost input.]

22. A ghost procedure shall not have an effectively volatile global input with the properties Async_Writers or Effective_Reads set to True. [This rule says, in effect, that ghost procedures are subject to the same restrictions as non-ghost nonvolatile functions with respect to reading volatile objects.] A name occurring within a ghost statement shall not denote an effectively volatile object with the properties Async_Writers or Effective_Reads set to True. [In other words, a ghost statement is subject to effectively the same restrictions as a ghost procedure.]

23. If the Ghost assertion policy in effect at the point of the declaration of a ghost variable or ghost state abstraction is Check, then the Ghost assertion policy in effect at the point of any call to a procedure for which that variable or state abstraction is a global output shall be Check.

Examples

```
function A_Ghost_Expr_Function (Lo, Hi : Natural) return Natural is
  (if Lo > Integer'Last - Hi then Lo else ((Lo + Hi) / 2))
  with Pre         => Lo <= Hi,
       Post        => A_Ghost_Expr_Function'Result in Lo .. Hi,
       Ghost;

function A_Ghost_Function (Lo, Hi : Natural) return Natural
  with Pre         => Lo <= Hi,
       Post        => A_Ghost_Function'Result in Lo .. Hi,
       Ghost;
-- The body of the function is declared elsewhere.

function A_Nonexecutable_Ghost_Function (Lo, Hi : Natural) return Natural
  with Pre         => Lo <= Hi,
       Post        => A_Nonexecutable_Ghost_Function'Result in Lo .. Hi,
       Ghost,
       Import;
-- The body of the function is not declared elsewhere.
```

PACKAGES

Verification Rules

1. In SPARK 2014 the elaboration of a package shall only update, directly or indirectly, variables declared immediately within the package.

7.1 Package Specifications and Declarations

7.1.1 Abstraction of State

The variables declared within a package but not within a subprogram body or block which does not also enclose the given package constitute the *persistent state* of the package. A package's persistent state is divided into *visible state* and *hidden state*. If a declaration that is part of a package's persistent state is visible outside of the package, then it is a constituent of the package's visible state; otherwise it is a constituent of the package's hidden state.

Though the variables may be hidden they still form part (or all) of the persistent state of the package and the hidden state cannot be ignored. *State abstraction* is the means by which this hidden state is represented and managed. A state abstraction represents one or more declarations which are part of the hidden state of a package.

SPARK 2014 extends the concept of state abstraction to provide hierarchical data abstraction whereby the state abstraction declared in a package may contain the persistent state of other packages given certain restrictions described in *Abstract_State, Package Hierarchy and Part_Of*. This provides data refinement similar to the refinement available to types whereby a record may contain fields which are themselves records.

Static Semantics

1. The visible state of a package P consists of:

   - any variables, or *constants with variable inputs*, declared immediately within the visible part of package P; and

   - the state abstractions declared by the Abstract_State aspect specification (if any) of package P; and

   - the visible state of any packages declared immediately within the visible part of package P.

2. The hidden state of a package P consists of:

   - any variables, or *constants with variable inputs*, declared immediately in the private part or body of P; and

   - the visible state of any packages declared immediately within the private part or body of P.

3. The preceding two rules notwithstanding, an object or state abstraction whose Part_Of aspect refers to a task or protected unit is not (directly) part of the visible state or hidden state of any package (see section *Tasks and Synchronization*).

7.1.2 External State

External state is a state abstraction or variable representing something external to a program. For instance, an input or output device, or a communication channel to another subsystem such as another SPARK 2014 program.

Updating external state might have some external effect. It could be writing a value to be read by some external device or subsystem which then has a potential effect on that device or subsystem. Similarly the value read from an external state might depend on a value provided by some external device or subsystem.

Ada uses the terms external readers and writers to describe entities external to a program which interact with the program through reading and writing data. Of particular concern to SPARK 2014 are external readers and writers which are not strictly under control of the program. It is not known precisely when a value will be written or read by an external reader or writer. These are called *asynchronous readers* and *asynchronous writers* in SPARK 2014.

Each read or update of an external state might be significant, for instance reading or writing a stream of characters to a file, or individual reads or writes might not be significant, for instance reading a temperature from a device or writing the same value to a lamp driver or display. SPARK 2014 provides a mechanism to indicate whether a read or write is always significant.

A type is said to be *effectively volatile* if it is either a volatile type, an array type whose Volatile_Component aspect is True, or an array type whose component type is effectively volatile, a protected type, or a descendant of the type Ada.Synchronous_Task_Control.Suspension_Object. An *effectively volatile object* is a volatile object or an object of an effectively volatile type.

External state is an effectively volatile object or a state abstraction which represents one or more effectively volatile objects (or it could be a null state abstraction; see *Abstract_State Aspects*). [The term "external" does not necessarily mean that this state is accessed outside of the SPARK portion of the program (although it might be); it refers to the state being potentially visible to multiple tasks (as well as to the outside world), so that it is externally visible from the perspective of any one task.]

Four Boolean valued *properties* of external states that may be specified are defined:

- Async_Readers - a component of the system external to the program might read/consume a value written to an external state.

- Async_Writers - a component of the system external to the program might update the value of an external state.

- Effective_Writes - every update of the external state is significant.

- Effective_Reads - every read of the external state is significant.

These properties may be specified for an effectively volatile object as Boolean aspects or as external properties of an external state abstraction.

The Boolean aspect Volatile_Function may be specified as part of the (explicit) initial declaration of a function. A function whose Volatile_Function aspect is True is said to be a *volatile function*. A protected function is also defined to be a *volatile function*, as is an instance of Unchecked_Conversion where one or both of the actual Source and Target types are effectively volatile types. [Unlike nonvolatile functions, two calls to a volatile function with all inputs equal need not return the same result. However note that the rule that a function must not have any output still applies; in effect this bans a volatile function from reading an object with Effective_Reads => True.]

A protected function whose Volatile_Function aspect is False is said to be "nonvolatile for internal calls".

Legality Rules

1. If an external state is declared without any of the external properties specified then all of the properties default to a value of True.

2. If just the name of the property is given then its value defaults to True [for instance Async_Readers defaults to Async_Readers => True].

3. A property may be explicitly given the value False [for instance Async_Readers => False].

4. If any one property is explicitly defined, all undefined properties default to a value of False.

5. The expression defining the Boolean valued property shall be static.

6. Only the following combinations of properties are valid:

Async_Readers	Async_Writers	Effective_Writes	Effective_Reads
True	–	True	–
–	True	–	True
True	–	–	–
–	True	–	–
True	True	True	–
True	True	–	True
True	True	–	–
True	True	True	True

[Another way of expressing this rule is that Effective_Reads can only be True if Async_Writers is True and Effective_Writes can only be True if Async_Readers is True.]

Static Semantics

7. Every update of an external state is considered to be read by some external reader if Async_Readers => True.

8. Each successive read of an external state might have a different value [written by some external writer] if Async_Writers => True.

9. If Effective_Writes => True, then every value written to the external state is significant. [For instance writing a sequence of values to a port.]

10. If Effective_Reads => True, then every value read from the external state is significant. [For example a value read from a port might be used in determining how the next value is processed.]

11. Each update of an external state has no external effect if both Async_Readers => False and Effective_Writes => False.

12. Each successive read of an external state will result in the last value explicitly written [by the program] if Async_Writers => False.

13. Every explicit update of an external state might affect the next value read from the external state even if Async_Writers => True.

14. An external state which has the property Async_Writers => True need not be initialized before being read although explicit initialization is permitted. [The external state might be initialized by an external writer.]

15. A subprogram whose Volatile_Function aspect is True shall not override an inherited primitive operation of a tagged type whose Volatile_Function aspect is False. [The reverse is allowed.]

16. A protected object has at least the properties Async_Writers => True and Async_Readers => True. If and only if it has at least one Part_Of component with Effective_Writes => True or Effective_Reads => True, then the protected object also carries this property. [This is particularly relevant if a protected object is a constituent of an external state, or if a protected object is an input of a volatile function.]

7.1.3 External State - Variables

In Ada interfacing to an external device or subsystem normally entails using one or more effectively volatile objects to ensure that writes and reads to the device are not optimized by the compiler into internal register reads and writes.

SPARK 2014 refines the specification of volatility by introducing four new Boolean aspects which may be applied only to effectively volatile objects. The aspects may be specified in the aspect specification of an object declaration (this excludes effectively volatile objects that are formal parameters).

The new aspects are:

- Async_Readers - as described in *External State*.

- Async_Writers - as described in *External State*.

- Effective_Reads - as described in *External State*.

- Effective_Writes - as described in *External State*.

These four aspects are said to be the *volatility refinement* aspects. Ada's notion of volatility corresponds to the case where all four aspects are True. Specifying a volatility refinement aspect value of False for an object grants permission for the SPARK 2014 implementation to make additional assumptions about how the object in question is accessed; it is the responsibility of the user to ensure that these assumptions hold. In contrast, specifying a value of True imposes no such obligation on the user.

For example, consider

```
X : Integer with Volatile, Async_Writers => False;
...
procedure Proc with ... is
  Y : Integer;
begin
  X := 0;
  Y := X;
  pragma Assert (Y = 0);
end Proc;
```

The verification condition associated with the assertion can be successfully discharged but this success depends on the Async_Writers aspect specification.

Legality Rules

1. In the absence of an explicit aspect specification, the value of a volatility refinement aspect of an effectively volatile stand-alone object other than a formal parameter is True. The Effective_Reads aspect of an effectively volatile formal parameter of mode **in** is False; in all other cases, the value of a volatility refinement aspect of an effectively volatile formal parameter is True.

   The volatility refinement aspect values of a subcomponent of an object are those of the enclosing object.

2. The value of a volatility refinement aspect shall only be specified for an effectively volatile stand-alone object. [A formal parameter is not a stand-alone object; see Ada RM 3.3.1 .]

3. The declaration of an effectively volatile stand-alone object shall be a library-level declaration. [In particular, it shall not be declared within a subprogram.]

4. A constant object (other than a formal parameter of mode **in**) shall not be effectively volatile.

5. An effectively volatile type other than a protected type shall not have a discriminated part.

6. A type which is not effectively volatile shall not have an effectively volatile component.

7. An effectively volatile object shall not be used as an actual parameter in a generic instantiation.

8. A global_item of a nonvolatile function, or of a function which is nonvolatile for internal calls, shall not denote either an effectively volatile object or an external state abstraction.

9. A formal parameter (or result) of a nonvolatile function, or of a function which is nonvolatile for internal calls, shall not be of an effectively volatile type. [For a protected function, this rule does not apply to the notional parameter denoting the current instance of the associated protected unit described in section *Global Aspects*.]

10. If a procedure has an **in** mode parameter of an effectively volatile type, then the Effective_Reads aspect of any corresponding actual parameter shall be False. [This is because the parameter is passed by reference and the corresponding aspect of the formal parameter is False. In the 11 other cases, corresponding to the combination

of a parameter mode and a volatility refinement aspect, the volatility refinement aspect of the formal parameter is True and so the aspect of the corresponding actual parameter may be either True or False.]

11. An effectively volatile object shall only occur as an actual parameter of a subprogram if the corresponding formal parameter is of a non-scalar effectively volatile type or as an actual parameter in a call to an instance of Unchecked_Conversion.

12. Contrary to the general SPARK 2014 rule that expression evaluation cannot have side effects, a read of an effectively volatile object with the properties Async_Writers or Effective_Reads set to True is considered to have an effect when read. To reconcile this discrepancy, a name denoting such an object shall only occur in a *non-interfering context*. A name occurs in a non-interfering context if it is:

   - the name on the left-hand side of an assignment statement; or

   - the [right-hand side] expression of an assignment statement; or

   - the expression of an initialization expression of an object declaration; or

   - the `object_name` of an `object_renaming_declaration`; or

   - the actual parameter in a call to an instance of Unchecked_Conversion whose result is renamed [in an object renaming declaration]; or

   - an actual parameter in a call for which the corresponding formal parameter is of a non-scalar effectively volatile type; or

   - the (protected) prefix of a name denoting a protected operation; or

   - the return expression of a `simple_return_statement` which applies to a volatile function; or

   - the initial value expression of the `extended_return_object_declaration` of an `extended_return_statement` which applies to a volatile function; or

   - the prefix of a slice, `selected_component`, `indexed_component`, or `attribute_reference` which is itself a name occurring in a non-interfering context; or

   - the prefix of an `attribute_reference` whose `attribute_designator` is either Alignment, Component_Size, First_Bit, Last_Bit, Position, Size, or Storage_Size; or

   - the expression of a type conversion occurring in a non-interfering context; or

   - the expression in a `delay_statement`.

   [The attributes listed above all have the property that when their prefix denotes an object, evaluation of the attribute involves evaluation of only the name, not the value, of the object.]

   The same restrictions also apply to a call to a volatile function (except not in the case of an internal call to a protected function which is nonvolatile for internal calls) and to the evaluation of any attribute which is defined to introduce an implicit dependency on a volatile state abstraction [(these are the Callable, Caller, Count, and Terminated attributes; see section *Tasks and Synchronization*)]. [An internal call to a protected function is treated like a call to a nonvolatile function if the function's Volatile_Function aspect is False.]

Dynamic Semantics

13. There are no dynamic semantics associated with these aspects.

Verification Rules

14. An effectively volatile formal parameter of mode **out** shall not be read, even after it has been updated. [This is because the Async_Writers aspect of the parameter is True].

Examples

```
1   with System.Storage_Elements;
2
3   package Input_Port
4     with SPARK_Mode
5   is
6      Sensor : Integer
7        with Volatile,
8             Async_Writers,
9             Address => System.Storage_Elements.To_Address (16#ACECAF0#);
10  end Input_Port;
```

```
1   with System.Storage_Elements;
2
3   package Output_Port
4     with SPARK_Mode
5   is
6      Sensor : Integer
7        with Volatile,
8             Async_Readers,
9             Address => System.Storage_Elements.To_Address (16#ACECAF0#);
10  end Output_Port;
```

```
1   with System.Storage_Elements;
2
3   package Multiple_Ports
4     with SPARK_Mode
5   is
6      type Volatile_Type is record
7         I : Integer;
8      end record with Volatile;
9
10     --  This type declaration indicates all objects of this type will
11     --  be volatile. We can declare a number of objects of this type
12     --  with different properties.
13
14     --  V_In_1 is essentially an external input since it has
15     --  Async_Writers => True but Async_Readers => False. Reading a
16     --  value from V_In_1 is independent of other reads of the same
17     --  object. Two successive reads might not have the same value.
18     V_In_1 : Volatile_Type
19       with Async_Writers,
20            Address => System.Storage_Elements.To_Address (16#A1CAF0#);
21
22     --  V_In_2 is similar to V_In_1 except that each value read is
23     --  significant. V_In_2 can only be used as a Global with a
24     --  mode_Selector of Output or In_Out or as an actual parameter
25     --  whose corresponding formal parameter is of a Volatile type and
26     --  has mode out or in out.
27     V_In_2 : Volatile_Type
28       with Async_Writers,
29            Effective_Reads,
30            Address => System.Storage_Elements.To_Address (16#ABCCAF0#);
31
32
33     --  V_Out_1 is essentially an external output since it has
34     --  Async_Readers => True but Async_Writers => False. Writing the
35     --  same value successively might not have an observable effect.
```

```
36    V_Out_1 : Volatile_Type
37      with Async_Readers,
38           Address => System.Storage_Elements.To_Address (16#BBCCAF0#);
39
40    --  V_Out_2 is similar to V_Out_1 except that each write to
41    --  V_Out_2 is significant.
42    V_Out_2 : Volatile_Type
43      with Async_Readers,
44           Effective_Writes,
45           Address => System.Storage_Elements.To_Address (16#ADACAF0#);
46
47    --  This declaration defaults to the following properties:
48    --    Async_Readers     => True,
49    --    Async_Writers     => True,
50    --    Effective_Reads   => True,
51    --    Effective_Writes  => True;
52    --  That is the most comprehensive type of external interface which
53    --  is bi-directional and each read and write has an observable
54    --  effect.
55    V_In_Out : Volatile_Type
56      with Address => System.Storage_Elements.To_Address (16#BEECAF0#);
57
58    --  These volatile variable declarations may be used in specific
59    --  ways as global items and actual parameters of subprogram calls
60    --  depend on their properties.
61
62    procedure Read (Value : out Integer)
63      with Global  => (Input => V_In_1),
64           Depends => (Value => V_in_1);
65    --  V_In_1, V_Out_1 and V_Out_2 are compatible with a mode selector
66    --  of Input as this mode requires Effective_Reads => False.
67
68    procedure Write (Value : in Integer)
69      with Global  => (Output => V_Out_1),
70           Depends => (V_Out_1 => Value);
71    --  Any Volatile Global is compatible with a mode selector of
72    --  Output. A flow error will be raised if the subprogram attempts
73    --  to read a Volatile Global with Async_Writers and/or
74    --  Effective_Reads set to True.
75
76    procedure Read_With_Effect (Value : out Integer)
77      with Global  => (In_Out => V_In_2),
78           Depends => (Value   => V_In_2,
79                       V_In_2 => null);
80    --  Any Volatile Global is compatible with a mode selector of
81    --  In_Out. The Depends aspect is used to specify how the Volatile
82    --  Global is intended to be used and this is checked by flow
83    --  analysis to be compatible with the properties specified for the
84    --  Volatile Global.
85
86    --  When a formal parameter is volatile, assumptions have to be
87    --  made in the body of the subprogram as to the possible
88    --  properties that the actual volatile parameter might have
89    --  depending on the mode of the formal parameter.
90
91    procedure Read_Port (Port : in Volatile_Type; Value : out Integer)
92      with Depends => (Value => Port);
93    --  Port is Volatile and of mode in. Assume that the formal
```

```
94    --     parameter has the properties Async_Writers => True and
95    --     Effective_Reads => False. The actual parameter in a call of the
96    --     subprogram must have Async_Writers => True and
97    --     Effective_Reads => False and may have Async_Writers and/or
98    --     Effective_Writes set to True. As an in mode parameter it can
99    --     only be read by the subprogram.
100   --     Eg. Read_Port (V_In_1, Read_Value).
101
102   procedure Write_Port (Port : out Volatile_Type; Value : in Integer)
103     with Depends => (Port => Value);
104   --     Port is volatile and of mode out. Assume the formal parameter
105   --     has the properties Async_Readers => True and
106   --     Effective_Writes => True. The actual parameter in a call to the
107   --     subprogram must have Async_Readers and/or Effective_Writes
108   --     True, and may have Async_Writers and Effective_Reads True. As
109   --     the mode of the formal parameter is mode out, it is
110   --     incompatible with reading the parameter because this could read
111   --     a value from an Async_Writer. A flow error will be signalled if
112   --     a read of the parameter occurs in the subprogram.
113   --     Eg. Write_Port (V_Out_1, Output_Value) and
114   --         Write_Port (V_Out_2, Output_Value).
115
116   --     A Volatile formal parameter type of mode in out is
117   --     assumed to have all the properties True:
118   --        Async_Readers     => True,
119   --        Async_Writers     => True,
120   --        Effective_Reads   => True,
121   --        Effective_Writes  => True;
122   --     The corresponding actual parameter in a subprogram call must be
123   --     volatile with all of the properties set to True.
124   procedure Read_And_Ack (Port : in out Volatile_Type; Value : out Integer)
125     with Depends => (Value => Port,
126                      Port  => Port);
127   --     Port is Volatile and reading a value may require the sending of
128   --     an acknowledgement, for instance.
129   --     Eg. Read_And_Ack (V_In_Out, Read_Value).
130
131 end Multiple_Ports;
```

7.1.4 Abstract_State Aspects

State abstraction provides a mechanism for naming, in a package's visible part, state (typically a collection of variables) that will be declared within the package's body (its hidden state). For example, a package declares a visible procedure and we wish to specify the set of global variables that the procedure reads and writes as part of the specification of the subprogram. The variables declared in the package body cannot be named directly in the package specification. Instead, we introduce a state abstraction which is visible in the package specification and later, when the package body is declared, we specify the set of variables that *constitute* or *implement* the state abstraction.

If immediately within a package body, for example, a nested package is declared, then a state abstraction of the inner package may also be part of the implementation of the given state abstraction of the outer package.

The hidden state of a package may be represented by one or more state abstractions, with each pair of state abstractions representing disjoint sets of hidden variables.

If a subprogram P with a Global aspect is declared in the visible part of a package and P reads or updates any of the hidden state of the package then the state abstractions shall be denoted by P. If P has a Depends aspect then the state abstractions shall be denoted as inputs and outputs of P, as appropriate, in the `dependency_relation` of the Depends aspect.

SPARK 2014 facilitates the specification of a hierarchy of state abstractions by allowing a single state abstraction to contain visible declarations of package declarations nested immediately within the body of a package, private child or private sibling units and descendants thereof. Each visible state abstraction or variable of a private child or descendant thereof has to be specified as being *part of* a state abstraction of its parent or a public descendant of its parent.

The Abstract_State aspect is introduced by an `aspect_specification` where the `aspect_mark` is Abstract_State and the `aspect_definition` shall follow the grammar of `abstract_state_list` given below.

Syntax

```
abstract_state_list      ::= null
                           | state_name_with_options
                           | ( state_name_with_options { , state_name_with_options } )
state_name_with_options  ::= state_name
                           | ( state_name with option_list )
option_list              ::= option { , option }
option                   ::= simple_option
                           | name_value_option
simple_option            ::= Ghost | Synchronous
name_value_option        ::= Part_Of => abstract_state
                           | External [=> external_property_list]
external_property_list   ::= external_property
                           | ( external_property {, external_property} )
external_property        ::= Async_Readers [=> expression]
                           | Async_Writers [=> expression]
                           | Effective_Writes [=> expression]
                           | Effective_Reads  [=> expression]
                           | others => expression
state_name               ::= defining_identifier
abstract_state           ::= name
```

Legality Rules

1. An `option` shall not be repeated within a single `option_list`.

2. If External is specified in an `option_list` then there shall be at most one occurrence of each of Async_Readers, Async_Writers, Effective_Writes and Effective_Reads.

3. If an `option_list` contains one or more `name_value_option` items then they shall be the final options in the list. [This eliminates the possibility of a positional association following a named association in the property list.]

4. A package_declaration or generic_package_declaration that contains a non-null Abstract_State aspect shall have a completion (i.e., a body).

   [Ada RM 7.1's rule defining when a package "requires a completion" is unaffected by the presence of an Abstract_State aspect specification; such an aspect spec does not cause a package to "require a completion". This rule therefore implies that if an Abstract_State aspect specification occurs anywhere within the specification of a library unit package or generic package, then that library unit is going to have to contain a basic_declarative_item that requires a completion (or have an Elaborate_Body pragma) because otherwise it would be impossible to simultaneously satisfy this rule and Ada's rule that a library unit cannot have a package body unless it is required (Ada RM 7.2(4)). One could imagine a simpler rule that an Abstract_State aspect specification causes a package to "require a completion", but we want a SPARK program with its SPARK aspects removed (or ignored) to remain a legal Ada program.]

5. A function declaration that overloads a state abstraction has an implicit Global aspect denoting the state abstraction with a `mode_selector` of Input. An explicit Global aspect may be specified which replaces the implicit

one.

Static Semantics

6. Each `state_name` occurring in an Abstract_State aspect specification for a given package P introduces an implicit declaration of a state abstraction entity. This implicit declaration occurs at the beginning of the visible part of P. This implicit declaration shall have a completion and is overloadable.

   [The declaration of a state abstraction has the same visibility as any other declaration but a state abstraction shall only be named in contexts where this is explicitly permitted (e.g., as part of a Global aspect specification). A state abstraction is not an object; it does not have a type. The completion of a state abstraction declared in a package `aspect_specification` can only be provided as part of a Refined_State `aspect_specification` within the body of the package.]

7. A **null** `abstract_state_list` specifies that a package contains no hidden state.

8. An External state abstraction is one declared with an `option_list` that includes the External `option` (see *External State*).

9. If a state abstraction which is declared with an `option_list` that includes a Part_Of `name_value_option` whose `name` denote a state abstraction, this indicates that it is a constituent (see *State Refinement*) of the denoted state abstraction. [Alternatively, the name may denote a task or protected unit (see section *Tasks and Synchronization*).]

10. A state abstraction for which the `simple_option` Ghost is specified is said to be a ghost state abstraction. A state abstraction for which the `simple_option` Synchronous is specified is said to be a synchronized state abstraction. [The option name "Synchronous" is used instead of "Synchronized" to avoid unnecessary complications associated with the use of an Ada reserved word.] Every synchronized state abstraction is also (by definition) an external state abstraction. A synchronized state abstraction for which the `simple_option` External is not (explicitly) specified has (by definition) its Async_Readers and Async_Writers aspects specified to be True and its Effective_Writes and Effective_Reads aspects specified to be False.

Dynamic Semantics

There are no dynamic semantics associated with the Abstract_State aspect.

Verification Rules

There are no verification rules associated with the Abstract_State aspect.

Examples

```
1   package Q
2     with Abstract_State => State        -- Declaration of abstract state named State
3                                          -- representing internal state of Q.
4   is
5      function Is_Ready return Boolean    -- Function checking some property of the
    ↪State.
6         with Global => State;            -- State may be used in a global aspect.
7
8      procedure Init                       -- Procedure to initialize the internal state
    ↪of Q.
9         with Global => (Output => State), -- State may be used in a global aspect.
10            Post  => Is_Ready;
11
12     procedure Op_1 (V : Integer)         -- Another procedure providing some operation on
    ↪State
13        with Global => (In_Out => State),
14            Pre   => Is_Ready,
15            Post  => Is_Ready;
16  end Q;
```

```
1   package X
2     with Abstract_State => (A,
3                             B,
4                             (C with External => (Async_Writers,
5                                                  Effective_Reads => False))
6   --  Three abstract state names are declared A, B & C.
7   --  A and B are internal abstract states.
8   --  C is specified as external state which is an external input.
9   is
10     ...
11  end X;
```

```
1   package Mileage
2     with Abstract_State => (Trip,    -- number of miles so far on this trip (can be reset␣
    ↪to 0)
3                             Total) -- total mileage of vehicle since last factory-reset
4   is
5     function Trip  return Natural;   -- Has an implicit Global => Trip
6     function Total return Natural;   -- Has an implicit Global => Total
7
8     procedure Zero_Trip
9       with Global  => (Output => Trip),   -- In the Global and Depends aspects
10           Depends => (Trip => null),     -- Trip denotes the state abstraction.
11           Post    => Trip = 0;           -- In the Post condition Trip denotes
12                                          -- the function.
13    procedure Inc
14      with Global  => (In_Out => (Trip, Total)),
15           Depends => ((Trip, Total) =>+ null),
16           Post    => Trip = Trip'Old + 1 and Total = Total'Old + 1;
17
18    --  Trip and Old in the Post conditions denote functions but these
19    --  represent the state abstractions in Global and Depends specifications.
20
21  end Mileage;
```

7.1.5 Initializes Aspects

The Initializes aspect specifies the visible variables and state abstractions of a package that are initialized by the elaboration of the package. In SPARK 2014 a package shall only initialize variables declared immediately within the package.

If the initialization of a variable or state abstraction, *V*, during the elaboration of a package, *P*, is dependent on the value of a visible variable or state abstraction from another package, then this entity shall be denoted in the input list associated with *V* in the Initializes aspect of *P*.

The Initializes aspect is introduced by an aspect_specification where the aspect_mark is Initializes and the aspect_definition shall follow the grammar of initialization_spec given below.

Syntax

```
initialization_spec ::= initialization_list
                      | null

initialization_list ::= initialization_item
                      | ( initialization_item { , initialization_item } )

initialization_item ::= name [ => input_list]
```

Legality Rules

1. An Initializes aspect shall only appear in the `aspect_specification` of a `package_specification`.

2. The `name` of each `initialization_item` in the Initializes aspect definition for a package shall denote a state abstraction of the package or an entire object declared immediately within the visible part of the package. [For purposes of this rule, formal parameters of a generic package are not considered to be "declared in the package".]

3. Each `name` in the `input_list` shall denote an object, or a state abstraction but shall not denote an entity declared in the package with the `aspect_specification` containing the Initializes aspect.

4. Each entity in a single `input_list` shall be distinct.

5. An `initialization_item` with a **null** `input_list` is equivalent to the same `initialization_item` without an `input_list`. [That is Initializes => (A => **null**) is equivalent to Initializes => A.]

Static Semantics

6. The Initializes aspect of a package has visibility of the declarations occurring immediately within the visible part of the package.

7. The Initializes aspect of a package specification asserts which state abstractions and visible variables of the package are initialized by the elaboration of the package, both its specification and body, and any units which have state abstractions or variable declarations that are part (constituents) of a state abstraction declared by the package. [A package with a **null** `initialization_list`, or no Initializes aspect does not initialize any of its state abstractions or variables.]

8. An `initialization_item` shall have an `input_list` if and only if its initialization is dependent on visible variables and state anbstractions not declared within the package containing the Initializes aspect. Then the `names` in the `input_list` shall denote variables and state abstractions which are used in determining the initial value of the state abstraction or variable denoted by the `name` of the `initialization_item` but are not constituents of the state abstraction.

Dynamic Semantics

There are no dynamic semantics associated with the Initializes aspect.

Verification Rules

9. If the Initializes aspect is specified for a package, then after the body (which may be implicit if the package has no explicit body) has completed its elaboration, every (entire) variable and state abstraction denoted by a `name` in the Initializes aspect shall be initialized. A state abstraction is said to be initialized if all of its constituents are initialized. An entire variable is initialized if all of its components are initialized. Other parts of the visible state of the package shall not be initialized.

10. If an `initialization_item` has an `input_list` then the variables and state abstractions denoted in the input list shall be used in determining the initialized value of the entity denoted by the `name` of the `initialization_item`.

11. All variables and state abstractions which are not declared within the package but are used in the initialization of an `initialization_item` shall appear in an `input_list` of the `initialization_item`.

12. Any `initialization_item` that is a constant shall be a *constant with variable input*. Any entity in an `input_list` that is a constant shall be a parameter or *constant with variable input*.

[Note: these rules allow a variable or state abstraction to be initialized by the elaboration of a package but not be denoted in an Initializes aspect. In such a case the analysis tools will treat the variable or state abstraction as uninitialized when analyzing clients of the package.]

Examples

```
1   package Q
2     with Abstract_State => State,          -- Declaration of abstract state name State
3           Initializes    => (State,        -- Indicates that State
4                              Visible_Var)   -- and Visible_Var will be initialized
5                                             -- during the elaboration of Q.
6   is
7     Visible_Var : Integer;
8     ...
9   end Q;
```

```
1   with Q;
2   package R
3     with Abstract_State => S1,                     -- Declaration of abstract state name␣
    ↪S1
4           Initializes    => (S1 => Q.State,         -- Indicates that S1 will be␣
    ↪initialized
5                                                     -- dependent on the value of Q.State
6                              X  => Q.Visible_Var)   -- and X dependent on Q.Visible_Var
7                                                     -- during the elaboration of R.
8   is
9     X : Integer := Q.Visible_Var;
10    ...
11  end R;
```

```
1   package Y
2     with Abstract_State => (A, B, (C with External => (Async_Writers, Effective_
    ↪Reads))),
3           -- Three abstract state names are declared A, B & C
4           Initializes    => A
5           -- A is initialized during the elaboration of Y.
6           -- C is specified as external state with Async_Writers
7           -- and need not be explicitly initialized.
8           -- B is not initialized.
9   is
10    ...
11  end Y;
```

```
1   package Z
2     with Abstract_State => A,
3           Initializes    => null
4           -- Package Z has an abstract state name A declared but the
5           -- elaboration of Z and its private descendants do not
6           -- perform any initialization during elaboration.
7   is
8     ...
9   end Z;
```

7.1.6 Initial_Condition Aspects

The Initial_Condition aspect is introduced by an aspect_specification where the aspect_mark is Initial_Condition and the aspect_definition shall be a *Boolean*_expression.

Legality Rules

1. An Initial_Condition aspect shall only be placed in an `aspect_specification` of a `package_specification`.

Static Semantics

2. An Initial_Condition aspect is an assertion and behaves as a postcondition for the elaboration of both the specification and body of a package. If present on a package, then its assertion expression defines properties (a predicate) of the state of the package which can be assumed to be true immediately following the elaboration of the package. [The expression of the Initial_Condition cannot denote a state abstraction or hidden state. This means that to express properties of hidden state, functions declared in the visible part acting on the state abstractions of the package must be used.]

Dynamic Semantics

3. With respect to dynamic semantics, specifying a given expression as the Initial_Condition aspect of a package is equivalent to specifying that expression as the argument of an Assert pragma occurring at the end of the (possibly implicit) statement list of the (possibly implicit) body of the package. [This equivalence includes all interactions with pragma Assertion_Policy but does not extend to matters of static semantics, such as name resolution.] An Initial_Condition expression does not cause freezing until the point where it is evaluated [, at which point everything that it might freeze has already been frozen].

Verification Rules

4. [The Initial_Condition aspect gives a verification condition to show that the implementation of the `package_specification` and its body satisfy the predicate given in the Initial_Condition aspect.]

5. Each variable or indirectly referenced state abstraction in an Initial_Condition aspect of a package Q which is declared immediately within the visible part of Q shall be initialized during the elaboration of Q and be denoted by a `name` of an `initialization_item` of the Initializes aspect of Q.

Examples

```
1  package Q
2      with Abstract_State    => State,    -- Declaration of abstract state name State
3          Initializes        => State,    -- State will be initialized during␣
   ↪elaboration
4          Initial_Condition => Is_Ready   -- Predicate stating the logical state after
5                                          -- initialization.
6  is
7      function Is_Ready return Boolean
8          with Global => State;
9  end Q;
```

```
1  package X
2      with Abstract_State    => A,        -- Declares an abstract state named A
3          Initializes        => (A, B),   -- A and visible variable B are initialized
4                                          -- during package initialization.
5          Initial_Condition => A_Is_Ready and B = 0
6                                          -- The logical conditions that hold
7                                          -- after package elaboration.
8  is
9      ...
10     B : Integer;
11
12     function A_Is_Ready return Boolean
13         with Global => A;
14 end X;
```

7.2 Package Bodies

7.2.1 State Refinement

A `state_name` declared by an Abstract_State aspect in the specification of a package shall denote an abstraction representing all or part of its hidden state. The declaration must be completed in the package body by a Refined_State aspect. The Refined_State aspect defines a *refinement* for each `state_name`. The refinement shall denote the variables and subordinate state abstractions represented by the `state_name` and these are known as its *constituents*.

Constituents of each `state_name` have to be initialized consistently with that of their representative `state_name` as determined by its denotation in the Initializes aspect of the package.

A subprogram may have an *abstract view* and a *refined view*. The abstract view is a subprogram declaration in a package specification of a package where a subprogram may refer to private types and state abstractions whose details are not visible. A refined view of a subprogram is the body or body stub of the subprogram in the package body whose specification declares its abstract view.

In a refined view a subprogram has visibility of the full type declarations of any private types declared by the enclosing package and visibility of the refinements of state abstractions declared by the package. Refined versions of aspects are provided to express the contracts of a refined view of a subprogram.

7.2.2 Refined_State Aspects

The Refined_State aspect is introduced by an `aspect_specification` where the `aspect_mark` is Refined_State and the `aspect_definition` shall follow the grammar of `refinement_list` given below.

Syntax

```
refinement_list    ::= ( refinement_clause { , refinement_clause } )
refinement_clause  ::= state_name => constituent_list
constituent_list   ::= null
                     | constituent
                     | ( constituent { , constituent } )
```

where

> `constituent` ::= *object*_name | `state_name`

Name Resolution Rules

1. A Refined_State aspect of a `package_body` has visibility extended to the `declarative_part` of the body.

Legality Rules

2. A Refined_State aspect shall only appear in the `aspect_specification` of a `package_body`. [The use of `package_body` rather than package body allows this aspect to be specified for generic package bodies.]

3. If a `package_specification` has a non-null Abstract_State aspect its body shall have a Refined_State aspect.

4. If a `package_specification` does not have an Abstract_State aspect, then the corresponding `package_body` shall not have a Refined_State aspect.

5. Each `constituent` shall be either a variable, a constant, or a state abstraction.

6. An object which is a `constituent` shall be an entire object.

7. A `constituent` of a state abstraction of a package shall denote either an entity with no Part_Of `option` or aspect which is part of the hidden state of the package, or an entity whose declaration has a Part_Of `option` or aspect which denotes this state abstraction (see *Abstract_State, Package Hierarchy and Part_Of*).

8. Each *abstract_state_name* declared in the package specification shall be denoted exactly once as the `state_name` of a `refinement_clause` in the Refined_State aspect of the body of the package.

9. Every entity of the hidden state of a package shall be denoted as a `constituent` of exactly one *abstract_state_name* in the Refined_State aspect of the package and shall not be denoted more than once. [These `constituents` shall be either objects declared in the private part or body of the package, or the declarations from the visible part of nested packages declared immediately therein.]

10. In a package body where the refinement of a state abstraction is visible the `constituents` of the state abstraction must be denoted in aspect specifications rather than the state abstraction.

11. The legality rules related to a Refined_State aspect given in *Abstract_State, Package Hierarchy and Part_Of* also apply.

12. Each `constituent` of a ghost state abstraction shall be either a ghost variable or a ghost state abstraction. [The reverse situation (i.e., a ghost constituent of a non-ghost state abstraction) is permitted.]

13. A `constituent` of a synchronized state abstraction shall be either a synchronized object or another synchronized state abstraction. A `constituent` of a state abstraction which is neither external nor synchronized shall be not be an effectively volatile object, a synchronized state abstraction, or an external state abstraction.

Static Semantics

14. A Refined_State aspect of a `package_body` completes the declaration of the state abstractions occurring in the corresponding `package_specification` and defines the objects and each subordinate state abstraction that are the `constituents` of the *abstract_state_names* declared in the `package_specification`.

15. A **null** `constituent_list` indicates that the named abstract state has no constituents and termed a *null_refinement*. The state abstraction does not represent any actual state at all. [This feature may be useful to minimize changes to Global and Depends aspects if it is believed that a package may have some extra state in the future, or if hidden state is removed.]

Dynamic Semantics

There are no dynamic semantics associated with Refined_State aspect.

Verification Rules

16. Each `constituent` that is a constant shall be a constant *with variable inputs*.

17. If the Async_Writers aspect of a state abstraction is True and the Async_Writers aspect of a constituent of that state abstraction is False, then after the elaboration of the (possibly implicit) body of the package which declares the abstraction, the constituent shall be initialized.

Examples

```
1    -- Here, we present a package Q that declares two abstract states:
2    package Q
3       with Abstract_State => (A, B),
4            Initializes    => (A, B)
5    is
6       ...
7    end Q;
8
9    -- The package body refines
10   --   A onto three concrete variables declared in the package body
11   --   B onto the abstract state of a nested package
12   package body Q
13      with Refined_State => (A => (F, G, H),
14                             B => R.State)
15   is
16      F, G, H : Integer := 0; -- all initialized as required
```

```
17
18     package R
19        with Abstract_State => State,
20             Initializes   => State -- initialized as required
21     is
22        ...
23     end R;
24
25     ...
26  end Q;
```

7.2.3 Initialization Issues

Every state abstraction specified as being initialized in the Initializes aspect of a package has to have all of its constituents initialized. This may be achieved by initialization within the package, by assumed pre-initialization (in the case of external state) or, for constituents which reside in another package, initialization by their declaring package.

Verification Rules

1. For each state abstraction denoted by the name of an initialization_item of an Initializes aspect of a package, all the constituents of the state abstraction must be initialized by:

   • initialization within the package; or

   • assumed pre-initialization (in the case of external states); or

   • for constituents which reside in another unit [and have a Part_Of indicator associated with their declaration (see *Abstract_State, Package Hierarchy and Part_Of*)] by their declaring package. [It follows that such constituents will appear in the initialization clause of the declaring unit unless they are external states.]

7.2.4 Refined_Global Aspects

A subprogram declared in the specification of a package may have a Refined_Global aspect applied to its body or body stub. A Refined_Global aspect of a subprogram defines a *refinement* of the Global Aspect of the subprogram; that is, the Refined_Global aspect repeats the Global aspect of the subprogram except that references to state abstractions whose refinements are visible at the point of the subprogram_body are replaced with references to [some or all of the] constituents of those abstractions. References to a state abstraction whose refinement is not visible at the point of the subprogram_body may also be similarly replaced if Part_Of aspect specifications which are visible at the point of the subprogram body identify one or more constituents of the abstraction; such a state abstraction is said to be "optionally refinable" at the point of the subprogram body.

See section *Global Aspects* regarding how the rules given in this section apply to protected operations and to task bodies.

The Refined_Global aspect is introduced by an aspect_specification where the aspect_mark is Refined_Global and the aspect_definition shall follow the grammar of global_specification in *Global Aspects*.

Static Semantics

1. The static semantics are as for those of the Global aspect given in *Global Aspects*. [Differences between these two aspects for one subprogram stem from differences in state abstraction visibility between the points where the two aspects are specified.]

Legality Rules

2. A Refined_Global aspect is permitted on a body_stub (if one is present), subprogram body, entry body, or task body if and only if the stub or body is the completion of a declaration occurring in the specification of an enclosing package, the declaration has a Global aspect which denotes a state abstraction declared by the package and either the refinement of the state abstraction is visible or a Part_Of specification specifying a constituent of the state abstraction is visible.

3. A Refined_Global aspect specification shall *refine* the subprogram's Global aspect as follows:

   (a) For each `global_item` in the Global aspect which denotes a state abstraction whose non-**null** refinement is visible at the point of the Refined_Global aspect specification, the Refined_Global specification shall include one or more `global_items` which denote `constituents` of that state abstraction.

   (b) For each `global_item` in the Global aspect which denotes a state abstraction whose **null** refinement is visible at the point of the Refined_Global aspect specification, there are no corresponding `global_items` in the Refined_Global specification. If this results in a Refined_Global specification with no `global_items`, then the Refined_Global specification shall include a `null_global_specification`.

   (c) For each `global_item` in the Global aspect which does not denote a state abstraction whose refinement is visible and does not denote an optionally refinable state abstraction, the Refined_Global specification shall include exactly one `global_item` which denotes the same entity as the `global_item` in the Global aspect.

   (d) For each `global_item` in the Global aspect which designates a state abstraction which is optionally refinable, refinement of the abstraction is optional in the following sense: either the reference to the state abstraction may be replaced with references to its constituents (following the rules of case 'a' above) or not (in which case the rules of case 'c' above apply). However, only the latter option is available if the mode of the state abstraction in the Global specification is Output.

   (e) No other `global_items` shall be included in the Refined_Global aspect specification.

   (f) At least one state abstraction mentioned in the Global aspect specification shall be unmentioned in the Refined_Global aspect specification. [This usually follows as a consequence of other rules, but not in some cases involving optionally refinable state abstractions where the option is declined.]

4. `Global_items` in a Refined_Global `aspect_specification` shall denote distinct entities.

5. The mode of each `global_item` in a Refined_Global aspect shall match that of the corresponding `global_item` in the Global aspect unless that corresponding `global_item` denotes a state abstraction which is not mentioned in the Refined_Global aspect. In that case, the modes of the `global_items` in the Refined_Global aspect which denote (direct or indirect) constituents of that state abstraction collectively determine (as described below) an "effective mode" for the abstraction. If there is at least one such constituent, then that "effective mode" shall match that of the corresponding `global_item` in the Global aspect; it is determined as follows:

   (a) If the refinement of the abstraction is visible and every constituent of the abstraction is mentioned in the Refined_Global aspect with a mode of Output, then the effective mode is Output;

   (b) Otherwise, if at least one constituent of the abstraction is mentioned in the Refined_Global aspect with a mode of Output or In_Out, then the effective mode is In_Out;

   (c) Otherwise, if at least one constituent of the abstraction is mentioned in the Refined_Global aspect with a mode of Input, then the effective mode is Input;

   (d) Otherwise, the effective mode is Proof_In.

   [If there is no such consituent (e.g., because a *null* refinement is visible) then the mode of the state abstraction in the Global aspect plays no role in determining the legality of the Refined_Global aspect.]

6. The legality rules for *Global Aspects* and External states described in *Refined External States* also apply.

Dynamic Semantics

There are no dynamic semantics associated with a Refined_Global aspect.

Verification Rules

8. If a subprogram has a Refined_Global aspect it is used in the analysis of the subprogram body rather than its Global aspect.

9. The verification rules given for *Global Aspects* also apply.

Examples

```
package Refined_Global_Examples
  with SPARK_Mode,
       Abstract_State => (S1, S2),
       Initializes    => (S1, V1)
is
   V1 : Integer := 0;   -- Visible state variables

   procedure P1_1 (I : in Integer)
     with Global => (In_Out => S1);

   procedure P1_2 (I : in Integer)
     with Global => (In_Out => S1);

   procedure P1_3 (Result : out Integer)
     with Global => (Input => S1);

   procedure P1_4 (I : in Integer)
     with Global => (Output => S1);

   procedure P2
     with Global => (Input  => V1,
                     In_Out => S2);

   procedure P3 (J : in Integer)
     with Global => (Output => V1);

   procedure P4
     with Global => (Input  => (S1, V1),
                     In_Out => S2);
end Refined_Global_Examples;
```

```
package body Refined_Global_Examples
  with SPARK_Mode,
       Refined_State => (S1 => (A, B),
                         S2 => (X, Y, Z))
is
   A : Integer := 1;   -- The constituents of S1
   B : Integer := 2;   -- Initialized as promised

   X, Y, Z : Integer;  -- The constituents of S2
                       -- Not initialized

   procedure P1_1 (I : in Integer)
     with Refined_Global => (In_Out => A,   -- Refined onto constituents of S1
                             Output => B)   -- B is Output but A is In_Out and
                                            -- so Global S1 is also In_Out
   is
   begin
      B := A;
```

```
19       A := I;
20    end P1_1;
21
22    procedure P1_2 (I : in Integer)
23       with Refined_Global => (Output => A)   -- Not all of the constituents of
24                                               -- S1 are updated and so the Global
25                                               -- S1 must In_Out
26    is
27    begin
28       A := I;
29    end P1_2;
30
31    procedure P1_3 (Result : out Integer)
32       with Refined_Global => (Input => B)   -- Not all of the constituents of S1
33                                             -- are read but none of them are
34                                             -- updated so the Global S1 is Input
35    is
36    begin
37       Result := B;
38    end P1_3;
39
40    procedure P1_4 (I : in Integer)
41       with Refined_Global => (Output => (A, B))   -- The constituents of S1 are
42                                                   -- not read but they are all
43                                                   -- updated and so the mode
44                                                   -- selector of S1 is Output
45    is
46    begin
47       A := I;
48       B := A;
49    end P1_4;
50
51    procedure P2
52       with Refined_Global => (Input  => V1,   -- V1 has no constituents and is
53                                               -- not subject to refinement.
54                               Output => Z)    -- Only constituent Z of S2 is
55                                               -- updated and so mode selector of
56                                               -- Global S2 is In_Out.
57    is
58    begin
59       Z := V1;
60    end P2;
61
62    procedure P3 (J : in Integer)
63       -- No Refined_Global aspect here because V1 has no refinement.
64    is
65    begin
66       V1 := J;
67    end P3;
68
69    procedure P4
70       with Refined_Global => (Input  => (A, V1),   -- The refinment of both S1
71                                                    -- and S2 are visible and
72                               Output => (X, Y))    -- cannot be denoted here.
73                                                    -- Their constituents must be
74                                                    -- used instead.
75    is
76    begin
```

```
77        X := V1;
78        Y := A;
79     end P4;
80  end Refined_Global_Examples;
```

7.2.5 Refined_Depends Aspects

A subprogram declared in the specification of a package may have a Refined_Depends aspect applied to its body or body stub. A Refined_Depends aspect of a subprogram defines a *refinement* of the Depends aspect of the subprogram; that is, the Refined_Depends aspect repeats the Depends aspect of the subprogram except that references to state abstractions, whose refinements are visible at the point of the subprogram_body, are replaced with references to [some or all of the] constituents of those abstractions.

See section *Global Aspects* regarding how the rules given in this section apply to protected operations and to task bodies.

The Refined_Depends aspect is introduced by an `aspect_specification` where the `aspect_mark` is Refined_Depends and the `aspect_definition` shall follow the grammar of `dependency_relation` in *Depends Aspects*.

Static Semantics

1. The static semantics are as for those of the Depends aspect given in *Depends Aspects*. [Differences between these two aspects for one subprogram stem from differences in state abstraction visibility between the points where the two aspects are specified.]

Legality Rules

2. A Refined_Depends aspect is permitted on a body_stub (if one is present), subprogram body, entry body, or task body if and only if the stub or body is the completion of a declaration in the specification of an enclosing package and the declaration has a Depends aspect which denotes a state abstraction declared by the package and the refinement of the state abstraction is visible.

3. A Refined_Depends aspect specification is, in effect, a copy of the corresponding Depends aspect specification except that any references in the Depends aspect to a state abstraction, whose refinement is visible at the point of the Refined_Depends specification, are replaced with references to zero or more direct or indirect constituents of that state abstraction. A Refined_Depends aspect shall have a `dependency_relation` which is derivable from the original given in the Depends aspect as follows:

   (a) A *partially refined dependency relation* is created by first copying, from the Depends aspect, each `output` that is not state abstraction whose refinement is visible at the point of the Refined_Depends aspect, along with its `input_list`, to the partially refined dependency relation as an `output` denoting the same entity with an `input_list` denoting the same entities as the original. [The order of the `output`s and the order of `input`s within the `input_list` is insignificant.]

   (b) The partially refined dependency relation is then extended by replacing each `output` in the Depends aspect that is a state abstraction, whose refinement is visible at the point of the Refined_Depends, by zero or more `output`s in the partially refined dependency relation. It shall be zero only for a **null** refinement, otherwise all of the `output`s shall denote a `constituent` of the state abstraction.

   (c) If the `output` in the Depends aspect denotes a state abstraction which is not also an `input`, then each `constituent` of the state abstraction shall be denoted as an `output` of the partially refined dependency relation.

   (d) These rules may, for each `output` in the Depends aspect, introduce more than one `output` in the partially refined dependency relation. Each of these `output`s has an `input_list` that has zero or more of the `input`s from the `input_list` of the original `output`. The union of these `input`s and the original state abstraction, if it is an `input` in the `input_list`, shall denote the same `input`s that appear in the `input_list` of the original `output`.

(e) If the Depends aspect has a `null_dependency_clause`, then the partially refined dependency relation has a `null_dependency_clause` added with an `input_list` denoting the same `input`s as the original.

(f) The partially refined dependency relation is completed by replacing each `input` which is a state abstraction, whose refinement is visible at the point of the Refined_Depends aspect, by zero or more `input`s which are its constituents.

(g) If a state abstraction is denoted in an `input_list` of a `dependency_clause` of the original Depends aspect and its refinement is visible at the point of the Refined_Depends aspect (derived via the process described in the rules 3a - 3f above), then:

- at least one of its `constituent`s shall be denoted as an `input` in at least one of the `dependency_clauses` of the Refined_Depends aspect corresponding to the original `dependency_clause` in the Depends aspect; or

- at least one of its `constituent`s shall be denoted in the `input_list` of a `null_dependency_clause`; or

- the state abstraction is both an `input` and an `output` and not every `constituent` of the state abstraction is an `output` of the Refined_Depends aspect. [This rule does not exclude denoting a `constituent` of such a state abstraction in an `input_list`.]

4. These rules result in omitting each state abstraction whose **null** refinement is visible at the point of the Refined_Depends. If and only if required by the syntax, the state abstraction shall be replaced by a **null** symbol rather than being omitted.

5. No other `output`s or `input`s shall be included in the Refined_Depends aspect specification. `Output`s in the Refined_Depends aspect specification shall denote distinct entities. `Input`s in an `input_list` shall denote distinct entities.

6. [The above rules may be viewed from the perspective of checking the consistency of a Refined_Depends aspect with its corresponding Depends aspect. In this view, each `input` in the Refined_Depends aspect that is a `constituent` of a state abstraction, whose refinement is visible at the point of the Refined_Depends aspect, is replaced by its representative state abstraction with duplicate `input`s removed.

Each `output` in the Refined_Depends aspect, which is a `constituent` of the same state abstraction whose refinement is visible at the point of the Refined_Depends aspect, is merged along with its `input_list` into a single `dependency_clause` whose `output` denotes the state abstraction and `input_list` is the union of all of the `input`s replaced by their encapsulating state abstraction, as described above, and the state abstraction itself if not every `constituent` of the state abstraction appears as an `output` in the Refined_Depends aspect.]

7. The rules for *Depends Aspects* also apply.

Dynamic Semantics

There are no dynamic semantics associated with a Refined_Depends aspect as it is used purely for static analysis purposes and is not executed.

Verification Rules

8. If a subprogram has a Refined_Depends aspect it is used in the analysis of the subprogram body rather than its Depends aspect.

9. The verification rules given for *Depends Aspects* also apply.

Examples

```
1   package Refined_Depends_Examples
2     with SPARK_Mode,
3          Abstract_State => (S1, S2),
4          Initializes   => (S1, V1)
5   is
6      V1 : Integer := 0;  -- Visible state variables
7
8      procedure P1_1 (I : in Integer)
9        with Global  => (In_Out => S1),
10             Depends => (S1 =>+ I);
11
12     procedure P1_2 (I : in Integer)
13       with Global  => (In_Out => S1),
14            Depends => (S1 =>+ I);
15
16     procedure P1_3 (Result : out Integer)
17       with Global  => (Input => S1),
18            Depends => (Result => S1);
19
20     procedure P1_4 (I : in Integer)
21       with Global  => (Output => S1),
22            Depends => (S1 => I);
23
24     procedure P2
25       with Global  => (Input  => V1,
26                        In_Out => S2),
27            Depends => (S2 =>+ V1);
28
29     procedure P3 (J : in Integer)
30       with Global  => (Output => V1),
31            Depends => (V1 => J);
32
33     procedure P4
34       with Global  => (Input => (S1, V1),
35                        In_Out => S2),
36            Depends => (S2 =>+ (S1, V1));
37  end Refined_Depends_Examples;
```

```
1   package body Refined_Depends_Examples
2     with SPARK_Mode,
3          Refined_State => (S1 => (A, B),
4                            S2 => (X, Y, Z))
5   is
6      A : Integer := 1;  -- The constituents of S1
7      B : Integer := 2;  -- Initialized as promised
8
9      X, Y, Z : Integer; -- The constituents of S2
10                         -- Not initialized
11
12     procedure P1_1 (I : in Integer)
13       with Refined_Global  => (In_Out => A,
14                                Output => B),
15            Refined_Depends => (A => I,  -- A and B are constituents of S1 and
16                                         -- both are outputs.
17                                B => A)  -- A is dependent on I but A is also an
18                                         -- input and B depends on A. Hence the
19                                         -- Depends => (S1 =>+ I).
20     is
```

```
21   begin
22      B := A;
23      A := I;
24   end P1_1;
25
26   procedure P1_2 (I : in Integer)
27      with Refined_Global  => (Output => A),
28           Refined_Depends => (A => I)   -- One but not all of the constituents
29                                         -- of S1 is updated hence the
30                                         -- Depends => (S1 =>+ I)
31   is
32   begin
33      A := I;
34   end P1_2;
35
36   procedure P1_3 (Result : out Integer)
37      with Refined_Global  => (Input => B),
38           Refined_Depends => (Result => B)   -- Not all of the constituents of
39                                              -- S1 are read but none of them
40                                              -- are updated, hence
41                                              -- Depends => (Result => S1)
42   is
43   begin
44      Result := B;
45   end P1_3;
46
47   procedure P1_4 (I : in Integer)
48      with Refined_Global  => (Output => (A, B)),
49           Refined_Depends => ((A, B) => I)   -- The constituents of S1 are not
50                                              -- inputs but all constituents of
51                                              -- S1 are updated, hence,
52                                              -- Depends => (S1 => I)
53   is
54   begin
55      A := I;
56      B := I;
57   end P1_4;
58
59   procedure P2
60      with Refined_Global  => (Input  => V1,
61                               Output => Z),
62           Refined_Depends => (Z => V1)   -- Only constituent Z of S2 is an
63                                          -- output. The other constituents of
64                                          -- S2 are preserved, hence,
65                                          -- Depends => (S2 =>+ V1);
66   is
67   begin
68      Z := V1;
69   end P2;
70
71   procedure P3 (J : in Integer)
72      -- No Refined_Depends aspect here because V1 has no refinement.
73   is
74   begin
75      V1 := J;
76   end P3;
77
78   procedure P4
```

```
79       with Refined_Global   =>  (Input   =>  (A, V1),
80                                   Output  =>  (X, Y)),
81              Refined_Depends =>  (X =>  V1,  -- Only constituents X and Y of S2 are
82                                                -- updated.
83                                   Y =>  A)    -- Z is not updated and so S2 must have
84                                                -- a self-dependency. Constituent A of
85                                                -- S1 is read and no constituent of S1
86                                                -- is updated, hence,
87                                                -- Depends => (S2 =>+ (S1, V1))
88    is
89    begin
90       X := V1;
91       Y := A;
92    end P4;
93 end Refined_Depends_Examples;
```

7.2.6 Abstract_State, Package Hierarchy and Part_Of

In order to avoid aliasing-related problems (see *Anti-Aliasing*), SPARK 2014 must ensure that if a given piece of state (either an object or a state abstraction) is going to be a constituent of a given state abstraction, that relationship must be known at the point where the constituent is declared.

For a variable declared immediately within a package body, this is not a problem. The state refinement in which the variable is specified as a constituent precedes the declaration of the variable, and so there is no *window* between the introduction of the variable and its identification as a constituent. Similarly for a variable or state abstraction that is part of the visible state of a package that is declared immediately within the given package body.

For variable declared immediately within the private part of a package, such an unwanted window does exist (and similarly for a variable or state abstraction that is part of the visible state of a package that is declared immediately within the given private part).

In order to cope with this situation, the Part_Of aspect provides a mechanism for specifying at the point of a constituent's declaration the state abstraction to which it belongs, thereby closing the window. The state abstraction's refinement will eventually confirm this relationship. The Part_Of aspect, in effect, makes visible a preview of (some of) the state refinement that will eventually be provided in the package body.

This mechanism is also used in the case of the visible state of a private child unit (or a public descendant thereof).

The Part_Of aspect can also be used in a different way to indicate that an object or state abstraction is to be treated as though it were declared within a protected unit or task unit (see section *Tasks and Synchronization*).

Static Semantics

1. A *Part_Of indicator* is a Part_Of `option` of a state abstraction declaration in an Abstract_State aspect, a Part_Of aspect specification applied to a variable declaration or a Part_Of specification aspect applied to a generic package instantiation. The Part_Of indicator shall denote the *encapsulating* state abstraction of which the declaration is a constituent, or shall denote a task or protected unit (see section *Tasks and Synchronization*).

Legality Rules

2. A variable declared immediately within the private part of a given package or a variable or state abstraction that is part of the visible state of a package that is declared immediately within the private part of the given package shall have its Part_Of indicator specified; the Part_Of indicator shall denote a state abstraction declared by the given package.

3. A variable or state abstraction which is part of the visible state of a private child unit (or a public descendant thereof) shall have its Part_Of indicator specified; the Part_Of indicator shall denote a state abstraction declared by either the parent unit of the private unit or by a public descendant of that parent unit.

4. A Part_Of aspect specification for a package instantiation applies to each part of the visible state of the instantiation. More specifically, explicitly specifying the Part_Of aspect of a package instantiation implicitly specifies the Part_Of aspect of each part of the visible state of that instantiation. The legality rules for such an implicit specification are the same as for an explicit specification.

5. No other declarations shall have a Part_Of indicator which denotes a state abstraction. [Other declarations may have a Part_Of indicator which denotes a task or protected unit (see section *Tasks and Synchronization*).]

6. The refinement of a state abstraction denoted in a Part_Of indicator shall denote as `constituents` all of the declarations that have a Part_Of indicator denoting the state abstraction. [This might be performed once the package body has been processed.]

7. A state abstraction and a constituent (direct or indirect) thereof shall not both be denoted in one Global, Depends, Initializes, Refined_Global or Refined_Depends aspect specification. The denotation must be consistent between the Global and Depends or between Refined_Global and Refined_Depends aspects of a single subprogram.

Verification Rules

8. For flow analysis, where a state abstraction is visible as well as one or more of its `constituents`, its refinement is not visible and the Global and or Depends aspects of a subprogram denote the state abstraction, then in the implementation of the subprogram a direct or indirect

   - read of a `constituent` of the state abstraction shall be treated as a read of the encapsulating state abstraction of the `constituent`; or

   - update of a `constituent` of the state abstraction shall be treated as an update of the encapsulating state abstraction of the `constituent`. An update of such a `constituent` is regarded as updating its encapsulating state abstraction with a self dependency as it is unknown what other `constituents` the state abstraction encapsulates.

Examples

```
1    package P
2       --  P has no state abstraction
3    is
4       ...
5    end P;
6
7    --  P.Pub is the public package that declares the state abstraction
8    package P.Pub --  public unit
9      with Abstract_State => (R, S)
10   is
11      ...
12   end P.Pub;
13
14   --  State abstractions of P.Priv, A and B, plus the concrete variable X,
15   --  are split up among two state abstractions within P.Pub, R and S.
16   with P.Pub;
17   private package P.Priv --  private unit
18     with Abstract_State => ((A with Part_Of => P.Pub.R),
19                             (B with Part_Of => P.Pub.S))
20   is
21      X : T  --  visible variable which is a constituent of P.Pub.R.
22         with Part_Of => P.Pub.R;
23   end P.Priv;
24
25   with P.Priv; --  P.Priv has to be with'd because its state is part of
26               --  the refined state.
27   package body P.Pub
28     with Refined_State => (R => (P.Priv.A, P.Priv.X, Y),
```

```
29                         S => (P.Priv.B, Z))
30  is
31     Y : T2;   --  hidden state
32     Z : T3;   --  hidden state
33     ...
34  end P.Pub;
```

```
1   package Outer
2     with Abstract_State => (A1, A2)
3   is
4      procedure Init_A1
5        with Global  => (Output => A1),
6             Depends => (A1 => null);
7
8      procedure Init_A2
9        with Global  => (Output => A2),
10            Depends => (A2 => null);
11
12  private
13     -- A variable declared in the private part must have a Part_Of aspect
14     Hidden_State : Integer
15       with Part_Of => A2;
16
17     package Inner
18       with Abstract_state => (B1 with Part_Of => Outer.A1)
19       -- State abstraction declared in the private
20       -- part must have a Part_Of option.
21     is
22        -- B1 may be used in aspect specifications provided
23        -- Outer.A1 is not also used.
24       procedure Init_B1
25         with Global  => (Output => B1),
26              Depends => (B1 => null);
27
28       procedure Init_A2
29          -- We can only refer to Outer.Hidden_State which is a constituent
30          -- of Outer.A2 if the subprogram does not also refer to Outer.A2.
31         with Global  => (Output => Hidden_State),
32              Depends => (Hidden_State => null);
33     end Inner;
34  end Outer;
35
36  package body Outer
37    with Refined_State => (A1 => Inner.B1,
38                           A2 => (Hidden_State, State_In_Body))
39    -- A1 and A2 cannot be denoted in the body of Outer because their
40    -- refinements are visible.
41  is
42     State_In_Body : Integer;
43
44     package body Inner
45       with Refined_State => (B1 => null)  -- Oh, there isn't any state after all
46     is
47        procedure Init_B1
48          with Refined_Global  => null,  -- Refined_Global and
49               Refined_Depends => null   -- Refined_Depends of a null refinement
50        is
51        begin
```

```
52          null;
53       end Init_B1;
54
55       procedure Init_A2
56          --  The Global sparct is already in terms of the constituent
57          --  Hidden_State which is part of A2, so no refined
58          --  Global or Depends aspects are required.
59       is
60       begin
61          Outer.Hidden_State := 0;
62       end Init_A2;
63
64    end Inner;
65
66    procedure Init_A1
67      with Refined_Global  => (Output => Inner.B1),
68           Refined_Depends => (Inner.B1 => null)
69    is
70    begin
71       Inner.Init_B1;
72    end Init_A1;
73
74    procedure Init_A2
75      with Refined_Global  => (Output => (Hidden_State, State_In_Body)),
76           Refined_Depends => ((Hidden_State, State_In_Body) => null)
77    is
78    begin
79       State_In_Body := 42;
80       Inner.Init_A2;
81    end Init_A2;
82
83 end Outer;
84
85 package Outer.Public_Child is
86    --  Outer.A1 and Outer.A2 are visible but
87    --  Outer.Hidden_State is not (by the rules of Ada).
88    --  The Global and Depends Aspects are in terms
89    --  of the encapsulating state abstraction Outer.A2.
90    procedure Init_A2_With (Val : in Integer)
91      with Global  => (Output => Outer.A2),
92           Depends => (Outer.A2 => Val);
93 end Outer.Public_Child;
94
95 package body Outer.Public_Child is
96    --  Outer.Hidden is visible here but the
97    --  refinement of A2 is not so there are
98    --  no Refined_Global or Refined_Depends.
99    procedure Init_A2_With (Val : in Integer) is
100    begin
101       Outer.Init_A2;
102       Outer.Hidden_State := Val;
103    end Init_A2_With;
104 end Outer.Public_Child;
```

```
1 package Q
2   with Abstract_State => (Q1, Q2)
3 is
4    --  Q1 and Q2 may be denoted here
```

```
 5     procedure Init_Q1
 6       with Global   => (Output => Q1),
 7             Depends  => (Q1 => null);
 8
 9     procedure Init_Q2
10       with Global   => (Output => Q2),
11             Depends  => (Q2 => null);
12
13  private
14     Hidden_State : Integer
15       with Part_Of => Q2;
16  end Q;
17
18  private package Q.Child
19    with Abstract_State => (C1 with Part_Of => Q.Q1)
20  is
21     --  C1 rather than the encapsulating state abstraction
22     --  may be used in aspect specifications provided
23     --  Q.Q1 is not also denoted in the same aspect
24     --  specification.
25
26     --  Here C1 is used so Q1 cannot also be used in
27     --  the aspect specifications of this subprogram.
28     procedure Init_Q1
29       with Global   => (Output => C1),
30             Depends  => (C1 => null);
31
32     --  Q.Hidden_State which is a constituent of Q.Q2
33     --  is visible here so it can be used in a aspect
34     --  specification provided Q.Q2 is not also used.
35     procedure Init_Q2
36       with Global   => (Output => Q.Hidden_State),
37             Depends  => (Q.Hidden_State => null);
38  end Q.Child;
39
40  package body Q.Child
41    with Refined_State => (C1 => Actual_State)
42  is
43     --  C1 shall not be denoted here - only Actual_State
44     --  but Q.Q2 and Q.Hidden_State may be denoted.
45     Actual_State : Integer;
46
47     procedure Init_Q1
48       with Refined_Global  => (Output => Actual_State),
49             Refined_Depends => (Actual_State => null)
50     is
51     begin
52        Actual_State := 0;
53     end Init_Q1;
54
55     --  The refinement of Q2 is not visible and so Init_Q2
56     --  has no Refined_Global or Refined_Depends aspects.
57     procedure Init_Q2 is
58     begin
59        Q.Hidden_State := 0;
60     end Init_Q2;
61
62  end Q.Child;
```

```
63
64  with Q.Child;
65
66  package body Q
67    with Refined_State => (Q1 => Q.Child.C1,
68                           Q2 => (Hidden_State, State_In_Body))
69  is
70     -- Q1 and Q2 shall not be denoted here but the constituents
71     -- Q.Child.C1, State_In_Body and Hidden_State may be.
72     State_In_Body : Integer;
73
74     procedure Init_Q1
75       with Refined_Global  => (Output => Q.Child.C1),
76            Refined_Depends => (Q.Child.C1 => null)
77     is
78     begin
79        Q.Child.Init_Q1;
80     end Init_Q1;
81
82     procedure Init_Q2
83       with Refined_Global  => (Output => (Hidden_State, State_in_Body)),
84            Refined_Depends => ((Hidden_State, State_in_Body) => null)
85     is
86     begin
87        State_In_Body := 42;
88        Q.Child.Init_Q2;
89     end Init_Q2;
90  end Q;
```

```
1   package R
2     with Abstract_State => R1
3   is
4      -- R1 may be denoted here
5      procedure Init_R1
6        with Global  => (Output => R1),
7             Depends => (R1 => null);
8
9      procedure Op_1 (I : in Integer)
10       with Global  => (In_Out => R1),
11            Depends => (R1 =>+ I);
12  end Q;
13
14  private package R.Child
15    with Abstract_State => (R2 with Part_Of => R.R1)
16  is
17     -- Both R.R1 and R2 are visible.
18
19     -- Here more than just the R2 constituent of R.R1
20     -- will be updated and so we use R.R1 in the
21     -- aspect specifications rather than R2.
22     -- R2 cannot also be used in the aspect
23     -- specifications of this subprogram.
24     procedure Private_Op (I, J : in Integer)
25       with Global  => (In_Out => R.R1),
26            Depends => (R.R1 =>+ (I, J));
27  end R.Child;
28
29  package body R.Child
```

```
30    with Refined_State => (R2 => Actual_State)
31  is
32      -- R2 shall not be denoted here - only Actual_State
33      -- but R.R1 may be denoted.
34      Actual_State : Integer;
35
36      -- The Global and Depends aspects of Private_Op
37      -- are in terms of R.R1 and the refinement of
38      -- R.R1 is not visible and so Refined_Global
39      -- and Refined_Depends are not required.
40      procedure Private_Op (I, J : in Integer) is
41      begin
42         R.Op_1 (I);
43         Actual_State := J;
44      end Private_Op;
45  end R.Child;
```

7.2.7 Refined Postcondition Aspects

A subprogram declared in the specification of a package may have a Refined_Post aspect applied to its body or body stub. The Refined_Post aspect may be used to restate a postcondition given on the declaration of a subprogram in terms of the full view of a private type or the `constituents` of a refined `state_name`.

The Refined_Post aspect is introduced by an `aspect_specification` where the `aspect_mark` is "Refined_Post" and the `aspect_definition` shall be a Boolean `expression`.

Legality Rules

1. A Refined_Post aspect may only appear on a body_stub (if one is present) or the body (if no stub is present) of a subprogram or entry which is declared in the specification of a package, its abstract view. If the initial declaration in the visible part has no explicit postcondition, a postcondition of True is assumed for the abstract view.

2. A Refined_Post aspect is an assertion. The same legality rules apply to a Refined_Post aspect as for a postcondition (a Post aspect).

Static Semantics

3. [A Refined Postcondition of a subprogram defines a *refinement* of the postcondition of the subprogram and is intended for use by callers who can see the body of the subprogram.]

4. [Logically, the Refined Postcondition of a subprogram must imply its postcondition. This means that it is perfectly logical for the declaration not to have a postcondition (which in its absence defaults to True) but for the body or body stub to have a Refined Postcondition. It also means that a caller who sees the Refined Postcondition of a subprogram will always be able to prove at least as much about the results of the call as if the usual precondition were used instead.]

5. The static semantics are otherwise as for a postcondition.

Dynamic Semantics

6. When a subprogram or entry with a Refined Postcondition is called, the Refined Postcondition is evaluated immediately before the evaluation of the postcondition or, if there is no postcondition, immediately before the point at which a postcondition would have been evaluated. If the Refined Postcondition evaluates to False, then the exception Assertion.Assertion_Error is raised. Otherwise, the postcondition is then evaluated and checked as described in the Ada RM.

Verification Rules

7. If a subprogram has both a Refined_Post aspect and a Post (and/or Post'Class) aspect, then the verification condition associated with postcondition checking is discharged in two steps.

First, the success of the Refined_Post run-time check must be proven as usual (i.e., just like any other run-time check).

Next, an additional proof obligation is generated which relates the Refined_Post to to the Post (and Post'Class) aspects of the subprogram according to a "wrapper" model. Imagine two subprograms with the same parameter profile and Global and Depends aspects, but with different postconditions P1 and P2 (neither of these two subprograms has a Refined_Post aspect). Suppose further that the first subprogram is a "wrapper" for the second; that is, its implementation consists of nothing but a call to the second subprogram (for functions, the call would occur in a return statement). Consider the proof obligation generated for the postcondition check of that "wrapper" subprogram; roughly speaking, it is a check that P1 is implied by P2. In that sense of the word "implied", a verification condition is generated that any Post/Post'Class condition for a subprogram is implied by its Refined_Post condition. In particular, knowledge about the internals of the subprogram that was available in proving the Refined_Post condition is not available in proving this implication (just as, in the "wrapper" illustration, the internal details of the second subprogram are not available in proving the postcondition of the first).

8. If a Refined_Post aspect specification is visible at the point of a call to the subprogram, then the Refined_Post is used instead of the Postcondition aspect for purposes of formal analysis of the call. Similarly for using the Refined_Global aspect instead of the Global aspect and the Refined_Depends aspect instead of the Depends aspect. [Roughly speaking, the "contract" associated with a call is defined by using the Refined_* aspects of the callee instead of the corresponding non-refined aspects in the case where Refined_* aspect specifications are visible.]

Examples

These examples show the two ways in which the Refined_Post aspect is useful:

1. To write a postcondition in terms of the full view of a private type.

2. To write a postcondition in terms of the constituents of a state abstraction.

In either case a postcondition may be strengthened by the Refined_Post aspect by adding further constraints. The combination of these two types of usage in a single package is not necessarily common but is used here for brevity of the example.

```
1   package Stacks_1
2     with SPARK_Mode
3   is
4     type Stack_Type is private;
5
6     function Is_Empty (S : Stack_Type) return Boolean;
7     -- Default postcondition is True.
8
9     function Is_Full (S : Stack_Type) return Boolean;
10    -- Default postcondition is True.
11
12    procedure Push (S : in out Stack_Type; I : in Integer)
13      with Pre  => not Is_Full (S),
14           Post => not Is_Empty (S);
15
16    procedure Pop (S : in out Stack_Type)
17      with Post => not Is_Full (S);
18
19    function Top (S : Stack_Type) return Integer
20      with Pre => not Is_Empty (S);
21   private
22     -- Full type declaration of private type.
```

```
23      Stack_Size : constant := 100;
24
25      type Pointer_Type is range 0 .. Stack_Size;
26      subtype Stack_Index is Pointer_Type range 1 .. Pointer_Type'Last;
27      type Stack_Array is array (Stack_Index) of Integer;
28
29      --  All stack objects have default initialization.
30      type Stack_Type is record
31         Pointer : Pointer_Type := 0;
32         Vector  : Stack_Array := (others => 0);
33      end record;
34   end Stacks_1;
```

```
1    package body Stacks_1
2      with SPARK_Mode
3    is
4      function Is_Empty (S : Stack_Type) return Boolean is (S.Pointer = 0);
5      --  Default Refined_Post => Is_Empty'Result = S.Pointer = 0
6      --  refines the postcondition of True in terms of the full view of
7      --  Stack_Type.
8
9      function Is_Full (S : Stack_Type) return Boolean is
10       (S.Pointer = Stack_Size);
11      --  Default Refined_Post => Is_Full'Result = (S.Pointer = Stack_Size)
12      --  refines the postcondition of True in terms of the full view of
13      --  Stack_Type.
14
15      procedure Push (S : in out Stack_Type; I : in Integer)
16        with Refined_Post => S.Pointer = S.Pointer'Old + 1 and
17             S.Vector = S.Vector'Old'Update (S.Pointer => I)
18        --  Refined_Post in terms of full view of Stack_Type and a
19        --  further constraint added specifying what is required by the
20        --  implementation.
21      is
22      begin
23         S.Pointer := S.Pointer + 1;
24         S.Vector (S.Pointer) := I;
25      end Push;
26
27      procedure Pop (S : in out Stack_Type)
28        with Refined_Post => S.Pointer = S.Pointer'Old - 1
29        --  Refined_Post in terms of full view of Stack_Type and also
30        --  specifies what is required by the implementation.
31      is
32      begin
33         if S.Pointer > 0 then
34            S.Pointer := S.Pointer - 1;
35         end if;
36      end Pop;
37
38      function Top (S : Stack_Type) return Integer is (S.Vector (S.Pointer));
39      --  Default Refined_Post => Top'Result = S.Vector (S.Pointer)
40      --  refines the postcondition of True in terms of the full view of
41      --  Stack_Type.
42   end Stacks_1;
```

```
1   package Stacks_2
2     with SPARK_Mode,
3          Abstract_State => The_Stack,
4          Initializes   => The_Stack
5   is
6     function Is_Empty return Boolean
7       with Global => The_Stack;
8     -- Default postcondition is True.
9
10    function Is_Full return Boolean
11      with Global => The_Stack;
12    -- Default postcondition is True.
13
14    procedure Push (I : Integer)
15      with Global => (In_Out => The_Stack),
16           Pre    => not Is_Full,
17           Post   => not Is_Empty;
18
19    procedure Pop
20      with Global => (In_Out => The_Stack),
21      Post   => not Is_Full;
22
23    function Top return Integer
24      with Global => The_Stack,
25           Pre    => not Is_Empty;
26    -- Default postcondition is True.
27  private
28    -- Full type declaration of private type for usage (1).
29    Stack_Size : constant := 100;
30
31    type Pointer_Type is range 0 .. Stack_Size;
32    subtype Stack_Index is Pointer_Type range 1 .. Pointer_Type'Last;
33    type Stack_Array is array (Stack_Index) of Integer;
34
35    -- All stack objects have default initialization.
36    type Stack_Type is record
37      Pointer : Pointer_Type := 0;
38      Vector  : Stack_Array := (others => 0);
39    end record;
40  end Stacks_2;
```

```
1   package body Stacks_2
2     with SPARK_Mode,
3          Refined_State => (The_Stack => (A_Pointer, A_Vector))
4   is
5     -- Constituents of state abstraction The_Stack
6     -- We promised to initialize The_Stack
7     A_Pointer : Pointer_Type := 0;
8     A_Vector  : Stack_Array := (others => 0);
9
10    -- Is_Empty could have been written as a expression function as was done
11    -- for Is_Empty (S : Stack_Type) but is presented here as a subproram body
12    -- to contrast the two approaches
13    function Is_Empty return Boolean
14      with Refined_Global => A_Pointer,
15           Refined_Post   => Is_Empty'Result = (A_Pointer = 0)
16      -- Refines the postcondition of True in terms of the constituent A_Pointer.
17    is
```

```
18    begin
19       return A_Pointer = 0;
20    end Is_Empty;
21
22    --  Could be written as an expression function
23    function Is_Full return Boolean
24      with Refined_Global => A_Pointer,
25           Refined_Post   => Is_Full'Result = (A_Pointer = Stack_Size)
26      --  Refines the postcondition of True in terms of the constituent A_Pointer.
27    is
28    begin
29       return A_Pointer = Stack_Size;
30    end Is_Full;
31
32    procedure Push (I : Integer)
33      with Refined_Global => (In_Out => (A_Pointer, A_Vector)),
34           Refined_Post   => A_Pointer = A_Pointer'Old + 1 and
35                             A_Vector = A_Vector'Old'Update (A_Pointer => I)
36      --  Refined_Post in terms of constituents A_Pointer and A_Vector and a further
37      --  constraint added specifying what is required by the implementation.
38    is
39    begin
40       A_Pointer := A_Pointer + 1;
41       A_Vector (A_Pointer) := I;
42    end Push;
43
44    procedure Pop
45      with Refined_Global => (In_Out => A_Pointer),
46           Refined_Post   => A_Pointer = A_Pointer'Old - 1
47      --  Refined_Post in terms of constituents A_Pointer and also
48      --  specifies what is required by the implementation.
49    is
50    begin
51       A_Pointer := A_Pointer - 1;
52    end Pop;
53
54    function Top return Integer is (A_Vector (A_Pointer))
55      with Refined_Global => (A_Pointer, A_Vector);
56      --  Default Refined_Post => Top'Result = A_Vector (S.Pointer)
57      --  refines the postcondition of True in terms of the constituents
58      --  A_Pointer and A_Vector.
59 end Stacks_2;
```

7.2.8 Refined External States

External state which is a state abstraction requires a refinement as does any state abstraction. There are rules which govern refinement of a state abstraction on to external states which are given in this section.

Legality Rules

1. A state abstraction that is not specified as External shall not have `constituents` which are External states.

2. An External state abstraction shall have each of the properties set to True which are True for any of its `constituents`.

3. Refined_Global aspects must respect the rules related to external properties of constituents which are external states given in *External State* and *External State - Variables*.

4. All other rules for Refined_State, Refined_Global and Refined_Depends aspect also apply.

Examples

```
package Externals
  with SPARK_Mode,
       Abstract_State => ((Combined_Inputs with External => Async_Writers),
                          (Displays with External => Async_Readers),
                          (Complex_Device with External => (Async_Readers,
                                                            Effective_Writes,
                                                            Async_Writers))),
       Initializes   => Complex_Device
is
   procedure Read (Combined_Value : out Integer)
     with Global  => Combined_Inputs,  -- Combined_Inputs is an Input;
                                       -- it does not have Effective_Reads and
                                       -- may be an specified just as an
                                       -- Input in Global and Depends aspects.
          Depends => (Combined_Value => Combined_Inputs);

   procedure Display (D_Main, D_Secondary : in String)
     with Global  => (Output => Displays), -- Displays is an Output and may
                                           -- be specified just as an
                                           -- Output in Global and Depends
                                           -- aspects.
          Depends => (Displays => (D_Main, D_Secondary));

   function Last_Value_Sent return Integer
     with Volatile_Function,
          Global => Complex_Device;  -- Complex_Device is an External
                                     -- state.  It can be a global_item of
                                     -- a function provided the Refined_Global
                                     -- aspect only refers to non-volatile
                                     -- constituents and to external
                                     -- state abstractions via calls to
                                     -- functions defined on them.

   procedure Output_Value (Value : in Integer)
     with Global  => (In_Out => Complex_Device),
          Depends => (Complex_Device => (Complex_Device, Value));
   -- Output_Value only sends out a value if it is not the same
   -- as the last value sent.  When a value is sent it updates
   -- the saved value and has to check a status port.
   -- The subprogram must be a procedure.

end Externals;
```

```
private package Externals.Temperature
  with SPARK_Mode,
       Abstract_State => (State with External => Async_Writers,
                                      Part_Of  => Externals.Combined_Inputs)
is
   procedure Read (Temp : out Integer)
     with Global  => State,
          Depends => (Temp => State);
end Externals.Temperature;
```

```
1  private package Externals.Pressure
2    with SPARK_Mode,
3        Abstract_State => (State with External => Async_Writers,
4                                       Part_Of  => Externals.Combined_Inputs)
5  is
6    procedure Read (Press : out Integer)
7      with Global => State,
8           Depends => (Press => State);
9  end Externals.Pressure;
```

```
1  private package Externals.Main_Display
2    with SPARK_Mode,
3        Abstract_State => (State with External => Async_Readers,
4                                       Part_Of  => Externals.Displays)
5  is
6    procedure Display (Text: in String)
7      with Global => (Output => State),
8           Depends => (State => Text);
9  end Externals.Main_Display;
```

```
1  private package Externals.Secondary_Display
2    with SPARK_Mode,
3        Abstract_State => (State with External => Async_Readers,
4                                       Part_Of  => Externals.Displays)
5  is
6    procedure Display (Text: in String)
7      with Global => (Output => State),
8           Depends => (State => Text);
9  end Externals.Secondary_Display;
```

```
1  with System.Storage_Elements,
2       Externals.Temperature,
3       Externals.Pressure,
4       Externals.Main_Display,
5       Externals.Secondary_Display;
6
7  package body Externals
8    with SPARK_Mode,
9        Refined_State => (Combined_Inputs => (Externals.Temperature.State,
10                                              Externals.Pressure.State),
11                         -- Both Temperature and
12                         -- Pressure are inputs only.
13
14                         Displays => (Externals.Main_Display.State,
15                                      Externals.Secondary_Display.State),
16                         -- Both Main_Display and
17                         -- Secondary_Display are outputs only.
18
19                         Complex_Device => (Saved_Value,
20                                            Out_Reg,
21                                            In_Reg))
22                         -- Complex_Device is a mixture of inputs, outputs and
23                         -- non-volatile constituents.
24  is
25    Saved_Value : Integer := 0;  -- Initialized as required.
26
27    Out_Reg : Integer
```

```
28        with Volatile,
29             Async_Readers,
30             Effective_Writes, -- Every value written to the port is significant.
31             Address  => System.Storage_Elements.To_Address (16#ACECAFE0#);
32
33     In_Reg : Integer
34        with Volatile,
35             Async_Writers,
36             Address  => System.Storage_Elements.To_Address (16#A11CAFE0#);
37
38     procedure Read (Combined_Value : out Integer)
39        with Refined_Global  => (Temperature.State, Pressure.State),
40             Refined_Depends => (Combined_Value => (Temperature.State,
41                                                     Pressure.State))
42     is
43        Temp,
44        Press : Integer;
45        K : constant := 1234;
46     begin
47        Temperature.Read (Temp);
48        Pressure.Read (Press);
49        Combined_Value := Press + Temp * K; -- Some_Function_Of (Temp, Pressure);
50     end Read;
51
52     procedure Display (D_Main, D_Secondary : in String)
53        with Refined_Global  => (Output => (Main_Display.State,
54                                             Secondary_Display.State)),
55             Refined_Depends => (Main_Display.State      => D_Main,
56                                  Secondary_Display.State => D_Secondary)
57     is
58     begin
59        Main_Display.Display (D_Main);
60        Secondary_Display.Display (D_Secondary);
61     end Display;
62
63     function Last_Value_Sent return Integer
64        with Refined_Global => Saved_Value -- Refined_Global aspect only
65                                            -- refers to a non-volatile
66                                            -- constituent.
67     is
68     begin
69        return Saved_Value;
70     end Last_Value_Sent;
71
72     procedure Output_Value (Value : in Integer)
73        with Refined_Global  => (Input  => In_Reg,
74                                  Output => Out_Reg,
75                                  In_Out => Saved_Value),
76        -- Refined_Global aspect refers to both volatile
77        -- and non-volatile constituents.
78
79             Refined_Depends => ((Out_Reg,
80                                   Saved_Value) => (Saved_Value,
81                                                    Value),
82                                  null => In_Reg)
83     is
84        Ready  : constant Integer := 42;
85        Status : Integer;
```

```
86      begin
87         if Saved_Value /= Value then
88            loop
89               Status := In_Reg;    -- In_Reg has the property Async_Writers
90                                     -- and may appear on RHS of assignment
91                                     -- but not in a condition.
92               exit when Status = Ready;
93            end loop;
94
95            Out_Reg := Value;    -- Out_Reg has the property Async_Readers
96                                 -- and the assigned value will be consumed.
97            Saved_Value := Value;    -- Writing to the Out_Reg also results
98                                     -- in updating Saved_Value.
99         end if;
100      end Output_Value;
101   end Externals;
```

```
1    -- This is a hardware abstraction layer (HAL)
2    -- which handles input and output streams over serial interfaces
3    -- and monitors and resets an area of shared memory used
4    -- as a watchdog.
5    package HAL
6      with SPARK_Mode,
7           Abstract_State =>
8                    ((FIFO_Status
9                        with External => Async_Writers),
10                    (Serial_In
11                       with External => (Async_Writers,
12                                         Effective_Reads)),
13                       -- Each value received is significant
14                    (FIFO_Control
15                       with External => Async_Readers),
16                    (Serial_Out
17                       with External => (Async_Readers,
18                                         Effective_Writes)),
19                    (Wdog_State
20                       with External => (Async_Readers,
21                                         Async_Writers)))
22   is
23      type Byte_T is mod 256;
24
25      -- This procedure reads the next byte available on
26      -- the serial input port using a FIFO buffer.
27      procedure Get_Byte (A_Byte : out Byte_T)
28        with Global  => (In_Out => Serial_In),
29             Depends => (A_Byte    => Serial_In,
30                         Serial_In => Serial_In);
31
32      -- This procedure skips input bytes until
33      -- the byte matches the given pattern or the input
34      -- FIFO is empty.
35      procedure Skip_To (Pattern : in Byte_T; Found : out Boolean)
36        with Global  => (Input  => FIFO_Status,
37                         In_Out => Serial_In),
38             Depends => ((Found,
39                          Serial_In) => (FIFO_Status,
40                                         Pattern,
41                                         Serial_In));
```

```
42
43     -- This procedure reads the status of the input and output FIFOs.
44     procedure Get_FIFO_Status (A_Byte : out Byte_T)
45       with Global  => (Input  => FIFO_Status),
46            Depends => (A_Byte => FIFO_Status);
47
48     -- This procedure writes a byte to the serial
49     -- output port using a FIFO buffer.
50     procedure Put_Byte (A_Byte : Byte_T)
51       with Global  => (Output => Serial_Out),
52            Depends => (Serial_Out => A_Byte);
53
54
55     -- This procedure clears the input FIFO.
56     procedure Clear_In_FIFO
57       with Global  => (Output => FIFO_Control),
58            Depends => (FIFO_Control => null);
59
60
61     -- This procedure clears the output FIFO.
62     procedure Clear_Out_FIFO
63       with Global  => (Output => FIFO_Control),
64            Depends => (FIFO_Control => null);
65
66
67     -- This procedure checks and then resets the status of
68     -- the watchdog state.
69     procedure Wdog_Timed_Out (Result : out Boolean)
70       with Global  => (In_Out => Wdog_State),
71            Depends => (Result     => Wdog_State,
72                        Wdog_State => Wdog_State);
73  end HAL;
```

```
1   with System.Storage_Elements;
2
3   package body HAL
4     with SPARK_Mode,
5          Refined_State => (Serial_In    => Read_FIFO,
6                            Serial_Out   => Write_FIFO,
7                            FIFO_Status  => Status,
8                            FIFO_Control => Control,
9                            Wdog_State   => Wdog_Shared_memory)
10  is
11     -- Each byte read is significant, it is a sequence of bytes
12     -- and so Effective_Reads => True.
13     Read_FIFO: Byte_T
14       with Volatile,
15            Async_Writers,
16            Effective_Reads,
17            Address => System.Storage_Elements.To_Address(16#A1CAFE0#);
18
19     -- Each byte written is significant, it is a sequence of bytes
20     -- and so Effective_Writes => True.
21     Write_FIFO: Byte_T
22       with Volatile,
23            Async_Readers,
24            Effective_Writes,
25            Address => System.Storage_Elements.To_Address(16#A2CAFE0#);
```

```
26
27      -- The read of the FIFO status is a snap shot of the current status
28      -- individual reads are independent of other reads of the FIFO status
29      -- and so Effective_Reads => False.
30   Status: Byte_T
31     with Volatile,
32          Async_Writers,
33          Address => System.Storage_Elements.To_Address(16#A3CAFE0#);
34
35      -- The value written to the FIFO control register are independent
36      -- of other value written to the control register and so
37      -- Effective_Writes => False.
38   Control: Byte_T
39     with Volatile,
40          Async_Readers,
41          Address => System.Storage_Elements.To_Address(16#A4CAFE0#);
42
43      -- This is a bidirectional port but individual reads and writes
44      -- are independent and so Effective_Reads and Effective_Writes
45      -- are both False.
46   Wdog_Shared_Memory : Boolean
47     with Volatile,
48          Async_Writers,
49          Async_Readers,
50          Address => System.Storage_Elements.To_Address(16#A5CAFE0#);
51
52   procedure Get_Byte (A_Byte : out Byte_T)
53     with Refined_Global  => (In_Out    => Read_FIFO),
54          Refined_Depends => (A_Byte    => Read_FIFO,
55                              Read_FIFO => Read_FIFO)
56   is
57   begin
58      A_Byte := Read_FIFO;
59   end Get_Byte;
60
61   procedure Skip_To (Pattern : in Byte_T; Found : out Boolean)
62     with Refined_Global  => (Input  => Status,
63                              In_Out => Read_FIFO),
64          Refined_Depends => ((Found,
65                               Read_FIFO) => (Status,
66                                              Pattern,
67                                              Read_FIFO))
68   is
69      Read_FIFO_Empty : constant Byte_T := 16#010#;
70      Current_Status : Byte_T;
71      Next_Byte : Byte_T;
72   begin
73      Found := False;
74      loop
75         Get_FIFO_Status (Current_Status);
76         exit when Current_Status = Read_FIFO_Empty;
77         Get_Byte (Next_Byte);
78         if Next_Byte = Pattern then
79            Found := True;
80            exit;
81         end if;
82      end loop;
83   end Skip_To;
```

```
84
85      procedure Get_FIFO_Status (A_Byte : out Byte_T)
86        with Refined_Global  => (Input  => Status),
87             Refined_Depends => (A_Byte => Status)
88      is
89      begin
90         A_Byte := Status;
91      end Get_FIFO_Status;
92
93      procedure Put_Byte (A_Byte : Byte_T)
94        with Refined_Global  => (Output => Write_FIFO),
95             Refined_Depends => (Write_FIFO => A_Byte)
96      is
97      begin
98         Write_FIFO := A_Byte;
99      end Put_Byte;
100
101     procedure Clear_In_FIFO
102       with Refined_Global  => (Output => Control),
103            Refined_Depends => (Control => null)
104     is
105        In_FIFO_Clear : constant Byte_T := 16#010#;
106     begin
107        Control := In_FIFO_Clear;
108     end Clear_In_FIFO;
109
110     procedure Clear_Out_FIFO
111       with Refined_Global  => (Output => Control),
112            Refined_Depends => (Control => null)
113     is
114        Out_FIFO_Clear : constant Byte_T := 16#020#;
115     begin
116        Control := Out_FIFO_Clear;
117     end Clear_Out_FIFO;
118
119     procedure Wdog_Timed_Out (Result : out Boolean)
120       with Refined_Global  => (In_Out => Wdog_Shared_Memory),
121            Refined_Depends => (Result              => Wdog_Shared_Memory,
122                                Wdog_Shared_memory => Wdog_Shared_Memory)
123     is
124        Watch_Dog_OK : Boolean;
125     begin
126        Watch_Dog_OK := Wdog_Shared_Memory;
127        if Watch_Dog_OK then
128           -- Retrigger the watch dog timer
129           Wdog_shared_memory := True;
130           -- It has not timed out.
131           Result := False;
132        else
133           Result := True;
134        end if;
135     end Wdog_Timed_Out;
136
137  end HAL;
```

```
1  with HAL;
2  use type HAL.Byte_T;
3
```

```
 4  procedure Main_Hal
 5    with SPARK_Mode,
 6        Global  => (Input  => HAL.FIFO_Status,
 7                    In_Out => (HAL.Serial_In,
 8                               HAL.Wdog_State),
 9                    Output => (HAL.FIFO_Control,
10                               HAL.Serial_Out)),
11        Depends => (HAL.Serial_In   =>+ (HAL.FIFO_Status,
12                                         HAL.Wdog_State),
13                    HAL.Serial_Out  =>  (HAL.Serial_In,
14                                         HAL.FIFO_Status,
15                                         HAL.Wdog_State),
16                    HAL.Wdog_State  =>+ HAL.FIFO_Status,
17                    HAL.FIFO_Control => null)
18  is
19    Wdog_Timed_Out, Found : Boolean;
20    A_Byte                : HAL.Byte_T;
21  begin
22    HAL.Clear_Out_FIFO;
23
24    -- The start of the data is marked by the sequence 16#5555#
25    -- Skip until we find the start of the message or the FIFO is empty.
26    loop
27       HAL.Wdog_Timed_Out (Wdog_Timed_Out);
28       exit when Wdog_Timed_Out;
29       HAL.Skip_To (16#55#, Found);
30       exit when not Found;
31       HAL.Get_Byte (A_Byte);
32       exit when A_Byte = 16#55#;
33    end loop;
34
35    if Found and not Wdog_Timed_Out then
36       -- We have found the start of the data
37
38       -- As long as the watchdog doesn't time out, move data
39       -- from Serial_In to Serial_Out.
40       loop
41          HAL.Wdog_Timed_Out (Wdog_Timed_Out);
42
43          exit when Wdog_Timed_Out;
44
45          HAL.Get_Byte (A_Byte);
46          HAL.Put_Byte (A_Byte);
47       end loop;
48    end if;
49  end Main_Hal;
```

7.3 Private Types and Private Extensions

No extensions or restrictions.

7.3.1 Private Operations

No extensions or restrictions.

7.3.2 Type Invariants

[Type invariants are supported in SPARK, but are subject to restrictions which imply that if a type invariant is specified for a type T, then any new verification conditions which this introduces outside of the package which defines T are trivially satisfied. These restrictions ensure that any object or value of type T (or a descendant thereof) which can be named outside of that package will satisfy the invariant and so, for example, could not fail the runtime check associated with passing that object or value as a parameter in call to a procedure for which Ada requires runtime checking of the invariant (which, in turn, means that the verification condition corresponding to that runtime check is trivially satisfied). In order to accomplish this goal, verification conditions for type invariants are introduced in several contexts where Ada does not define corresponding runtime checks.]

[As a consequence of this approach, adding or deleting a type invariant for a private type should have little or no impact on users outside of the package defining the private type; on the other hand, such a change could have a great deal of impact on the verification conditions generated for the implementation of the private type and its operations.]

[Just as a reminder to the reader, text enclosed in square brackets is non-normative expository text. This is true everywhere in the SPARK RM, but there is a lot of such expository text in this section and we don't want anyone to be confused about what is strictly part of the language definition and what is not.]

Static Semantics

1. For a given type-invariant bearing type T, a *boundary* subprogram is a subprogram which is declared inside the immediate scope of type T, and visible outside the immediate scope of T.

   The point at which a generic is declared plays no role in determining whether a subprogram declared as or within an instantiation of that generic is a boundary subprogram.

Legality Rules

2. The aspect Type_Invariant may be specified in SPARK, but only for the completion of a private type. [In other words, the Type_Invariant aspect shall not be specified for a partial view of a type, nor for the completion of a private extension.] The aspect Type_Invariant'Class is not in SPARK.

3. [A Type_Invariant expression shall not have a variable input; see *Expressions* for the statement of this rule.]

Verification Rules

In Ada RM 7.3.2, Ada defines the points at which runtime checking of type invariants is performed. In SPARK, these rules (or, more precisely, the verification conditions corresponding to these Ada dynamic semantics rules) are extended in several ways. In effect, verification conditions are generated as if Ada defined additional dynamic type invariant checking at several points (described below) where, in fact, Ada defines no such checks. [This means that when we talk below about extending invariant checks, we are only talking about generating additional verification conditions; we are not talking about any changes in a program's behavior at run-time.]

4. The type invariant expression for a type T shall not include a call to a boundary function for type T. [This often means that a type invariant expression cannot contain calls to functions declared in the visible part of the package in question.]

Ramification: It is a consequence of other rules that upon entry to a boundary subprogram for a type T, every part of every input that is of type T can be assumed to satisfy T's invariant.

5. Upon returning from a boundary subprogram for a type T, a verification condition is introduced for every part of every output that is of type T (or a descendant thereof), to ensure that this part satisfies T's invariant.

6. For every subprogram declared inside the immediate scope of type T, the preceding rule [and ramification] also apply to [any parts of] any global input or output and to [any parts of] any tagged subprogram parameter.

7. When calling a boundary subprogram for a type T or a subprogram declared outside of the immediate scope of T, a verification condition is introduced for every part of every input that is of type T (or a descendant thereof), to ensure that this part satisfies T's invariant. [This verification condition is trivially satisfied if the caller is

outside of the immediate scope of T, or if the input in question is subject to rule 5 and constant for the caller. The idea here is to prevent invariant-violating values from "leaking out".]

Ramification: It is a consequence of other rules that upon return from a boundary subprogram for a type T or a subprogram declared outside of the immediate scope of T, every part of every output that is of type T (or a descendant thereof) can be assumed to satisfy T's invariant.

8. For every subprogram, the preceding rule [and ramification] also apply to [any parts of] any global input or output and to [any parts of] any tagged subprogram parameter. [The verification condition of rule 6 is trivially satisfied if the caller is outside of the immediate scope of T, or if the input in question is subject to rule 4 and constant for the caller.]

Ramification: In determining whether a dispatching call is a call to a boundary subprogram or to a subprogram declared outside of the immediate scope of T, the statically named callee is used. **Ramification:** It is possible that the underlying tag of a tagged object (at runtime) may differ from the tag of its nominal (compile time) type. Suppose that an object X is (statically) of type T1 (or T1'Class) but has T2'Tag as its underlying tag, and that T2 has one or more components which are not components of T1. Ada does not define runtime checking of type invariants for such "hidden" components of parameters. The rules about tagged inputs and outputs in rules 6 and 8 are introduced in order to deal with technical difficulties that would otherwise arise in the treatment of these hidden components.

7.3.3 Default_Initial_Condition Aspects

The Default_Initial_Condition aspect is introduced by an aspect_specification where the aspect_mark is Default_Initial_Condition. The aspect may be specified only as part of the aspect_specification of a `private_type_declaration`. The `aspect_definition`, if any, of such an aspect specification shall be either a null literal or a *Boolean*_expression.

The `aspect_definition` may be omitted; this is semantically equivalent to specifying a static *Boolean*_expression having the value True.

An aspect specification of "null" indicates that the partial view of the type does not define full default initialization (see *Declarations*). [The full view of the type might or might not define full default initialization.]

Conversely, an aspect specification of a *Boolean*_expression indicates that the partial view of the type does define full default initialization. In this case, the completion of the private type shall define full default initialization. [Implementations may provide a mechanism for suppressing enforcement of this rule as described; the burden is then on the user to ensure that this does not result in undetected uses of uninitialized variables.]

Unlike the null literal case, this case has associated dynamic semantics. The *Boolean*_expression (which might typically mention the current instance of the type, although this is not required) is an assertion which is checked (at run time) after any object of the given type (or of any descendant of the given type for which the specified aspect is inherited and not overridden), is "initialized by default" (see Ada RM 3.3.1).

The *Boolean*_expression, if any, causes freezing in the same way as the `default_expression` of a `component_declaration`. [If the expresion is non-static, this means that the expression does not cause freezing where it occurs, but instead when an object of the type is initialized by default.]

Default_Initial_Condition assertion is an assertion aspect, which means that it may be used in an Assertion_Policy pragma.

Within the Boolean expression of the Default_Initial_Condition aspect of a tagged type T, a name that denotes the current instance of the tagged type is interpreted as though it had a (notional) type NT that is a formal derived type whose ancestor type is T, with directly visible primitive operations. [This name resolution rule is similar to the "notional formal derived type" name resolution rule introduced in Ada RM 6.1.1 for certain subexpressions of class-wide precondition and postcondition expressions.] Any operations within a Default_Initial_Condition expression that were resolved in this way (i.e., as primitive operations of the (notional) formal derived type NT), are in the evaluation of the the expression (i.e., at run-time) bound to the corresponding operations of the type of the object being "initialized by default" (see Ada RM 3.3.1).

7.4 Deferred Constants

No extensions or restrictions.

7.5 Limited Types

No extensions or restrictions.

7.6 Assignment and Finalization

Legality Rules

1. Controlled types are not permitted in SPARK 2014.

7.7 Elaboration Issues

SPARK 2014 imposes a set of restrictions which ensure that a call to a subprogram cannot occur before the body of the subprogram has been elaborated. The success of the runtime elaboration check associated with a call is guaranteed by these restrictions and so the verification condition associated with such a check is trivially discharged. Similar restrictions are imposed to prevent the reading of uninitialized library-level variables during library unit elaboration, and to prevent instantiation of a generic before its body has been elaborated. Finally, restrictions are imposed in order to ensure that the Initial_Condition (and Initializes aspect) of a library-level package can be meaningfully used.

These restrictions are described in this section. Because all of these elaboration-related issues are treated similarly, they are discussed together in one section.

Note that throughout this section an implicit call (e.g., one associated with default initialization of an object or with a defaulted parameter in a call) is treated in the same way as an explicit call, and an explicit call which is unevaluated at the point where it (textually) occurs is ignored at that point (but is not ignored later at a point where it is evaluated). This is similar to the treatment of expression evaluation in Ada's freezing rules. This same principle applies to the rules about reading global variables discussed later in this section.

Static Semantics

1. A call which occurs within the same compilation_unit as the subprogram_body of the callee is said to be an *intra-compilation_unit call*.

2. A construct (specifically, a call to a subprogram or a read or write of a variable) which occurs in elaboration code for a library-level package is said to be *executable during elaboration*. If a subprogram call is executable during elaboration and the callee's body occurs in the same compilation_unit as the call, then any constructs occurring within that body are also executable during elaboration. [If a construct is executable during elaboration, this means that it could be executed during the elaboration of the enclosing library unit and is subject to certain restrictions described below.]

   For a given library unit L1 and a given distinct library unit's spec or body L2, the elaboration of the body of L1 is said to be *known to precede* the elaboration of L2 if either:

(a) L2 references L1 in an Elaborate or Elaborate_All pragma; or

(b) L1's Elaborate_Body aspect is True; or

(c) L1 does not require a body (the terminology is a little odd in this case because L1 has no body); or

(d) L1 is preelaborable and L2's library unit is not.

Legality Rules

3. SPARK 2014 requires that an intra-compilation_unit call which is executable during elaboration shall occur after a certain point in the unit (described below) where the subprogram's completion is known to have been elaborated. The portion of the unit following this point and extending to the start of the completion of the subprogram is defined to be the *early call region* for the subprogram. An intra-compilation_unit call which is executable during elaboration and which occurs (statically) before the start of the completion of the callee shall occur within the early call region of the callee.

4. The start of the early call region is obtained by starting at the subprogram's completion (typically a subprogram_body) and then traversing the preceding constructs in reverse elaboration order until a non-preelaborable statement/declarative_item/pragma is encountered. The early call region starts immediately after this non-preelaborable construct (or at the beginning of the enclosing block (or library unit package spec or body) if no such non-preelaborable construct is found).

   [The idea here is that once elaboration reaches the start of the early call region, there will be no further expression evaluation or statement execution (and, in particular, no further calls) before the subprogram_body has been elaborated because all elaborable constructs that will be elaborated in that interval will be preelaborable. Hence, any calls that occur statically after this point cannot occur dynamically before the elaboration of the subprogram body.]

   [These rules allow this example

```
package body Pkg is
   ...
   procedure P;
   procedure Q;
   X : Integer := Some_Function_Call;  -- not preelaborable
   procedure P is ... if Blap then Q; end if; ... end P;
   procedure Q is ... if Blaq then P; end if; ... end Q;
begin
   P;
end;
```

   even though the call to Q precedes the body of Q. The early call region for either P or Q begins immediately after the declaration of X. Note that because the call to P is executable during elaboration, so is the call to Q.]

5. For purposes of the above rules, a subprogram completed by a renaming-as-body is treated as though it were a wrapper which calls the renamed subprogram (as described in Ada RM 8.5.4(7.1/1)). [The notional "call" occuring in this wrapper is then subject to the above rules, like any other call.]

6. If an instance of a generic occurs in the same compilation_unit as the body of the generic, the body must precede the instance.

   [If this rule were only needed in order to avoid elaboration check failures, a similar rule to the rule for calls could be defined. This stricter rule is used in order to avoid having to cope with use-before-definition, as in

```
generic
package G is
   ...
end G;

procedure Proc is
```

```
    package I is new G; -- expansion of I includes references to X
begin ... ; end;

X : Integer;

package body G is
    ... <uses of X> ...
end G;
```

This stricter rule applies even if the declaration of the instantiation is not "executable during elaboration"].

7. In the case of a dispatching call, the subprogram_body mentioned in the above rules is that (if any) of the statically denoted callee.

8. The first freezing point of a tagged type shall occur within the early call region of each of its overriding primitive operations.

   [This rule is needed to prevent a dispatching call before the body of the (dynamic, not static) callee has been elaborated. The idea here is that after the freezing point it would be possible to declare an object of the type and then use it as a controlling operand in a dispatching call to a primitive operation of an ancestor type. No analysis is performed to identify scenarios where this is not the case, so conservative rules are adopted.]

   [Ada ensures that the freezing point of a tagged type will always occur after both the completion of the type and the declarations of each of its primitive subprograms; the freezing point of any type will occur before the declaration of any objects of the type or the evaluation of any expressions of the type. This is typically all that one needs to know about freezing points in order to understand how the above rule applies to a particular example.]

9. For purposes of defining the early call region, the specification and body of a library unit package whose Elaborate_Body aspect is True are treated as if they both belonged to some enclosing declaration list with the body immediately following the specification. This means that the early call region in which a call is permitted can span the specification/body boundary.

   This is important for tagged type declarations.

10. For each call that is executable during elaboration for a given library unit package spec or body, there are two cases: it is (statically) a call to a subprogram whose completion is in the current compilation_unit (or in a preelaborated unit), or it is not. In the latter case, an Elaborate_All pragma shall be provided to ensure that the given library unit spec or body will not be elaborated until after the complete semantic closure of the unit in which the (statically denoted) callee is declared.

11. For an instantiation of a generic package (excluding a bodiless generic package) which does not occur in the same compilation unit as the generic body, the same rules apply as described above for a call (i.e., an Elaborate_All pragma is required). For an instantiation of a generic subprogram which does not occur in the same compilation unit as the generic body, the same rules also apply except that only an Elaborate (as opposed to an Elaborate_All) pragma is required.

12. An implementation is permitted to accept constructs which violate the preceding rules in this section (e.g., an implementation might choose to behave, for purposes of defining an early call region, as though some non-preelaborable construct is preelaborable), but only if the implementation is able to statically ensure that accepting these constructs does not introduce the possibility of failing an elaboration check (either for a call or for an instantiation), reading an uninitialized variable, or unsafe reliance on a package's Initial_Condition. [If an implementation chooses to take advantage of this permission, then the burden is entirely on the implementation to "get it right".]

[These rules correctly prohibit the following example:

```
package P is
   function F return Boolean;
```

```
      Flag : Boolean := F; -- would fail elaboration checks
end; --]
```

Examples

```ada
1  function Times_2 (X : Integer) return Integer is
2  begin
3     return 2 * X;
4  end Times_2;
```

```ada
1  with Times_2;
2
3  package Intra_Unit_Elaboration_Order_Examples
4     with Initializes => (X, Y)
5  is
6     pragma Elaborate_Body;   -- Ensures body of package is elaborated
7                              --  immediately after its declaration
8     procedure P (I : in out Integer); -- P and hence Q are executable during
9     procedure Q (J : in out Integer); --  elaboration as P is called in the
10                                       --  package body
11
12    X : Integer := Times_2 (10);  -- Not preelaborable
13                                  -- The early call region begins here
14                                  -- and extends into the package body because
15                                  -- of the Elaborate_Body pragma.
16
17    Y : Integer;
18
19    procedure R (Z : in out Integer)
20       with Post => Z = G (Z'Old); -- The call to G is allowed here as it is in
21                                   --  the early call region
22
23    procedure S (A : in out Integer)
24       with Global => Y;           -- Global Y needs to be initialized.
25
26    function F (I : Integer) return Integer;
27    function G (J : Integer) return Integer is (2 * F (J));
28    -- The call to F is allowed here as it is in
29    -- early call region.
30 end Intra_Unit_Elaboration_Order_Examples;
```

```ada
1  package body Intra_Unit_Elaboration_Order_Examples is
2
3     function F (I : Integer) return Integer is (I + 1);
4     -- The early call region for F ends here as the body has been
5     -- declared. It can now be called using normal visibility rules.
6
7     procedure P (I : in out Integer) is
8     begin
9        if I > 10 then
10          Q (I);  -- Q is still in the early call region and so this call is
11                  --  allowed
12       end if;
13    end P;
14    -- The early call region for P ends here as the body has been
15    -- declared. It can now be called using normal visibility rules.
16
```

```
17    procedure Q (J : in out Integer) is
18    begin
19       if J > 20 then
20          J := J - 10;
21          P (J);  --  P can be called as its body is declared.
22       end if;
23    end Q;
24    --  The early call region for Q ends here as the body has been
25    --  declared. It can now be called using normal visibility rules.
26
27    procedure R (Z : in out Integer) is
28    begin
29       Z := G (Z);  --  The expression function G has been declared and
30                    --  so can be called
31    end R;
32
33    procedure S (A : in out Integer) is
34    begin
35       A := A + Y;  --  Reference to Y is ok because it is in the early call
36                    --  region and the Elaborate_Body pragma ensures it is
37                    --  initialized before it is used.
38    end S;
39
40 begin
41    Y := 42;
42    P (X);    --  Call to P and hence Q during the elaboration of the package.
43 end Intra_Unit_Elaboration_Order_Examples;
```

```
1 package Inter_1 is
2    function F (I : Integer) return Integer;
3 end Inter_1;
```

```
1 package body Inter_1 is
2    function F (I : Integer) return Integer is (I);
3 end Inter_1;
```

```
1 package Inter_2 is
2    function G (I : Integer) return Integer;
3 end Inter_2;
```

```
1 package body Inter_2 is
2    function G (I : Integer) return Integer is (I);
3 end Inter_2;
```

```
1  with Inter_1;
2  pragma Elaborate_All (Inter_1);  --  Ensure the body of the called function F
3                                    --  has been elaborated.
4
5  package Inter_Unit_Elaboration_Examples with Elaborate_Body is
6     X : Integer := Inter_1.F (10);  --  The call to F is ok because its body is
7                                     --  sure to have been elaborated.
8     Y : Integer;
9
10    procedure P (I : in out Integer);  --  P is declared so that the package
11                                       --  requires a body for this example.
12 end Inter_Unit_Elaboration_Examples;
```

```
1  with Inter_2;
2  pragma Elaborate_All (Inter_2);  --  Ensure body of called function G has
3                                    --  been elaborated.
4
5  package body Inter_Unit_Elaboration_Examples is
6     procedure P (I : in out Integer) is
7     begin
8        I := 2 * I;
9     end P;
10 begin
11    Y := Inter_2.G (20);  --  Call to G is ok because the body of
12                          --  G is sure to have been elaborated.
13 end Inter_Unit_Elaboration_Examples;
```

7.7.1 Use of Initial_Condition and Initializes Aspects

Static Semantics

To ensure the correct semantics of the Initializes and Initial_Condition aspects, when applied to library units, language restrictions (described below) are imposed in SPARK 2014 which have the following consequences:

1. During the elaboration of a library unit package (spec or body), library-level variables declared outside of that package cannot be modified and library-level variables declared outside of that package can only be read if

    (a) the variable (or its state abstraction) is mentioned in the Initializes aspect of its enclosing package (from *Initializes Aspects*); and

    (b) either the variable is declared and initialized during the elaboration of the specification of its enclosing library unit package or the elaboration of the body of that library unit is known to precede the elaboration of the spec or body which reads the variable.

2. From the end of the elaboration of a library package's body to the invocation of the main program (i.e., during subsequent library unit elaboration), variables declared in the package (and constituents of state abstractions declared in the package) remain unchanged. The Initial_Condition aspect is an assertion which is checked at the end of the elaboration of a package body (but occurs textually in the package spec; see *Initial_Condition Aspects*). The initial condition of a library-level package will remain true from this point until the invocation of the main subprogram (because none of the inputs used in computing the condition can change during this interval). This means that a package's initial condition can be assumed to be true both upon entry to the main subprogram itself and during elaboration of any other unit (spec or body) whose elaboration is known to follow that of the body of the package (see preceding definition of "known to precede"; *known to follow* is, by definition, the inverse relationship). An Initial_Condition which depends on no variable inputs can also be assumed to be true throughout the execution of the main subprogram.

3. If a package's Initializes aspect mentions a state abstraction whose refinement includes constituents declared outside of that package, then the elaboration of bodies of the enclosing packages of those constituents will precede the elaboration of the body of the package declaring the abstraction (as a consequence of the rules given in *Elaboration Issues*). The idea here is that all constituents of a state abstraction whose initialization has been promised are in fact initialized by the end of the elaboration of the body of the abstraction's unit - we don't have to wait for the elaboration of other units (e.g., private children) which contribute to the abstraction.

Verification Rules

4. If a read of a variable (or state abstraction, in the case of a call to a subprogram which takes an abstraction as an input) declared in another library unit is executable during elaboration (as defined above), then either

    • the entity being read shall be a variable (i.e., not a state abstraction) and shall be initialized (perhaps by default) during the elaboration of its enclosing library unit specification; or

- the elaboration of the compilation unit which performs the read shall be known to follow that of the body of the unit declaring the variable or state abstraction.

In either case, the variable or state abstraction shall be specified as being initialized in the Initializes aspect of the declaring package. [This is needed to ensure that the variable has been initialized at the time of the read.]

5. If a variable is declared (immediately or not) within a library unit package specification, and if that variable is initialized (perhaps by default) during the elaboration of that specification, and if any part of that variable is also assigned to during the elaboration of the corresponding library unit package body, then that library unit's Elaborate_Body aspect shall be True. [This is needed to ensure that the variable remains unread between the elaboration of the specification and of the body of its enclosing library unit.]

6. The elaboration of a package's specification and body shall not write to a variable (or state abstraction, in the case of a call to a procedure which takes an abstraction as an output) declared outside of the package. The output associated with a read of an external state with the property Effective_Reads is permitted. [This rule applies to all packages: library-level or not, instantiations or not.] The inputs and outputs of a package's elaboration (including the elaboration of any private descendants of a library unit package) shall be as described in the Initializes aspect of the package.

Legality Rules

7. The elaboration of a package body shall be known to follow the elaboration of the body of each of the library units [(typically private children)] which provide constituents for a state abstraction denoted in the Initializes aspect of the given package.

Examples

```
1  package P
2    with Initializes => VP
3  is
4    pragma Elaborate_Body;    --  Needed because VP is
5    VP : Integer;             --  Initialized in the body
6  end P;
```

```
1  with P;
2  pragma Elaborate_All (P);   --  P.VP is used in initialization of V
3
4  package Initialization_And_Elaboration
5    with Abstract_State    => State,
6         Initializes       => (State,
7                               V => P.VP),   -- Initializing V depends on P.VP
8         Initial_Condition => V = P.VP and Get_It = 0
9  is
10    V : Integer := P.VP;
11
12    procedure Do_It (I : in Integer)
13      with Global => (In_Out => State);
14
15    function Get_It return Integer
16      with Global => State;
17  end Initialization_And_Elaboration;
```

```
1  private package Initialization_And_Elaboration.Private_Child
2    with Abstract_State    => (State with Part_Of =>
3                               Initialization_And_Elaboration.State),
4         Initializes       => State,
5         Initial_Condition => Get_Something = 0
6  is
7    procedure Do_Something (I : in Integer)
```

```
 8          with Global => (In_Out => State);
 9
10       function Get_Something return Integer
11          with Global => State;
12    end Initialization_And_Elaboration.Private_Child;
```

```
 1    with Initialization_And_Elaboration.Private_Child;
 2    pragma Elaborate (Initialization_And_Elaboration.Private_Child);
 3    --  pragma Elaborate for the private child is required because it is a
 4    --  constituent of the state abstraction
 5    --  Initialization_And_Elaboration.State, which is mentioned in the
 6    --  Initializes aspect of the package.
 7
 8    package body Initialization_And_Elaboration
 9      with Refined_State => (State => Private_Child.State)
10      --  State is initialized
11      --  Private child must be elaborated.
12    is
13       procedure Do_It (I : in Integer)
14         with Refined_Global => (In_Out => Private_Child.State)
15       is
16       begin
17          Private_Child.Do_Something (I);
18       end Do_It;
19
20       function Get_It return Integer
21         with Refined_Global => Private_Child.State
22       is
23       begin
24          return Private_Child.Get_Something;
25       end Get_It;
26    end Initialization_And_Elaboration;
```

VISIBILITY RULES

8.1 Declarative Region

No extensions or restrictions.

8.2 Scope of Declarations

No extensions or restrictions.

8.3 Visibility

No extensions or restrictions.

8.3.1 Overriding Indicators

No extensions or restrictions.

8.4 Use Clauses

Legality Rules

1. Use clauses are always in SPARK 2014, even if the unit mentioned is not completely in SPARK 2014.

8.5 Renaming Declarations

8.5.1 Object Renaming Declarations

Legality Rules

1. [An expression or range occurring as part of an `object_renaming_declaration` shall not have a variable input; see *Expressions* for the statement of this rule.] [This rule can apply to an index of an indexed_component and the range of a slice.]

8.5.2 Exception Renaming Declarations

No extensions or restrictions.

8.5.3 Package Renaming Declarations

No extensions or restrictions.

8.5.4 Subprogram Renaming Declarations

From the point of view of both static and dynamic verification, a *renaming-as-body* is treated as a one-line subprogram that "calls through" to the renamed unit.

Legality Rules

1. The `aspect_specification` on a `subprogram_renaming_declaration` shall not include any of the SPARK 2014-defined aspects introduced in this document.

8.5.5 Generic Renaming Declarations

No extensions or restrictions.

8.6 The Context of Overload Resolution

No extensions or restrictions.

TASKS AND SYNCHRONIZATION

Tasks and protected types are in SPARK 2014, but are subject to the restrictions of the Ravenscar profile (see Ada RM D.13) or the more permissive Extended Ravenscar profile (see http://docs.adacore.com/gnathie_ug-docs/html/gnathie_ug/gnathie_ug/the_predefined_profiles.html#the-extended-ravenscar-profiles). In particular, task entry declarations are never in SPARK 2014.

Tasks may communicate with each other via synchronized objects; these include protected objects, suspension objects, atomic objects, constants, and "constant after elaboration" objects (described later).

Other objects are said to be unsynchronized and may only be referenced (directly or via intermediate calls) by a single task (including the environment task) or by the protected operations of a single protected object.

These rules statically eliminate the possibility of erroneous concurrent access to shared data (i.e., "data races").

Tagged task types, tagged protected types, and the various forms of synchronized interface types are in SPARK 2014. Subject to the restrictions of (extended) Ravenscar, delay statements and protected procedure handlers are in SPARK 2014. The attributes Callable, Caller, Identity and Terminated are in SPARK 2014.

Static Semantics

1. A type is said to *yield synchronized objects* if it is

    - a task type; or

    - a protected type; or

    - a synchronized interface type; or

    - an array type whose element type yields synchronized objects; or

    - a record type or type extension whose discriminants, if any, lack default values, which has at least one nondiscriminant component (possibly inherited), and all of whose nondiscriminant component types yield synchronized objects; or

    - a descendant of the type Ada.Synchronous_Task_Control.Suspension_Object.

    An object is said to be *synchronized* if it is

    - of a type which yields synchronized objects; or

    - an atomic object whose Async_Writers aspect is True; or

    - a variable which is "constant after elaboration" (see section *Object Declarations*); or

    - a constant.

    [Synchronized objects may be referenced by multiple tasks without causing erroneous execution. The declaration of a synchronized stand-alone variable shall be a library-level declaration.]

Legality Rules

2. Task and protected units are in SPARK 2014, but their use requires the (extended) Ravenscar profile. [In other words, a task or protected unit is not in SPARK 2014 if neither the Ravenscar profile nor the Extended Ravenscar profile apply to the enclosing compilation unit.] Similarly, the use of task or protected units also requires a Partition_Elaboration_Policy of Sequential. [This is to prevent data races during library unit elaboration.] Similarly, the use of any subprogram which references the predefined state abstraction Ada.Task_Identification.Tasking_State (described below) as a global requires the (extended) Ravenscar profile.

3. If the declaration of a variable or a package which declares a state abstraction follows (within the same immediately enclosing declarative region) a `single_task_declaration` or a `single_protected_declaration`, then the Part_Of aspect of the variable or state abstraction may denote the task or protected unit. This indicates that the object or state abstraction is not part of the visible state or private state of its enclosing package. [Loosely speaking, flow analysis will treat the object as though it were declared within its "owner". This can be useful if, for example, a protected object's operations need to reference an object whose Address aspect is specified. The protected (as opposed to task) case corresponds to the previous notion of "virtual protected elements" in RavenSPARK.]

An object or state abstraction which "belongs" to a task unit in this way is treated as a local object of the task (e.g., it cannot be named in a Global aspect specification occurring outside of the body of the task unit, just as an object declared immediately within the task body could not be). An object or state abstraction which "belongs" to a protected unit in this way is treated as a component of the (anonymous) protected type (e.g., it can never be named in any Global aspect specification, just as a protected component could not be). [There is one obscure exception to these rules, described in the next paragraph: a subprogram which is declared within the statement list of the body of the immediately enclosing package (this is possible via a block statement).]

Any name denoting such an object or state abstraction shall occur within either

- the body of the "owning" task or protected unit; or
- the statement list of the object's immediately enclosing package; or
- an Initializes or Initial_Condition aspect specification for the object's immediately enclosing package.

[Roughly speaking, such an object can only be referenced from within the "owning" unit or during the execution of the statement list of its enclosing package].

The notional equivalences described above break down in the case of package elaboration. The presence or absence of such a Part_Of aspect specification is ignored in determining the legality of an Initializes or Initial_Condition aspect specification. [Very roughly speaking, the restrictions implied by such a Part_Of aspect specification are not really "in effect" during library unit elaboration; or at least that's one way to view it. For example such an object can be accessed from within the elaboration code of its immediately enclosing package. On the other hand, it could not be accessed from within a subprogram unless the subprogram is declared within either the task unit body in question (in the task case) or within the statement list of the body of the immediately enclosing package (in either the task or the protected case).]

4. A protected type shall define full default initialization. A variable whose Part_Of aspect specifies a task unit or protected unit shall be of a type which defines full default initialization, or shall be declared with an initial value expression, or shall be imported.

5. A type which does not yield synchronized objects shall not have a component type which yields synchronized objects. [Roughly speaking, no mixing of synchronized and unsynchronized component types.] In enforcing this rule, privacy of types is ignored (that is, any partial views of types are ignored and the corresponding full view is unconditionally used instead). [TBD: add an aspect to allow this property to be expressed explicitly when a partial view of a type is declared.]

6. A constituent of a synchronized state abstraction shall be a synchronized object or a synchronized state abstraction.

Verification Rules

7. A `global_item` occurring in a Global aspect specification of a task unit or of a protected operation shall not denote an object or state abstraction which is not synchronized.

8. A `global_item` occurring in the Global aspect specification of the main subprogram shall not denote an object or state abstraction whose Part_Of aspect denotes a task or protected unit. [In other words, the environment task cannot reference objects which "belong" to other tasks.]

9. A state abstraction whose Part_Of aspect specifies a task unit or protected unit shall be named in the Initializes aspect of its enclosing package.

10. The precondition of a protected operation shall not reference a global variable, unless it is *constant after elaboration*.

11. The Ravenscar profile includes "Max_Entry_Queue_Length => 1" and "Max_Protected_Entries => 1" restrictions. The Extended Ravenscar profile does not, but does allow use of pragma Max_Queue_Length to specify the maximum entry queue length for a particular entry. If the maximum queue length for some given entry of some given protected object is specified (via either mechanism) to have the value N, then at most N distinct tasks (including the environment task) shall ever call (directly or via intermediate calls) the given entry of the given protected object. [Roughly speaking, each such protected entry can be statically identified with a set of at most N "caller tasks" and no task outside that set shall call the entry. This rule is enforced via (potentially conservative) flow analysis, as opposed to by introducing verification conditions.]

   For purposes of this rule, Ada.Synchronous_Task_Control.Suspension_Object is assumed to be a protected type having one entry and the procedure Suspend_Until_True is assumed to contain a call to the entry of its parameter. [This rule discharges the verification condition associated with the Ada rule that two tasks cannot simultaneously suspend on one suspension object (see Ada RM D.10(10)).]

12. The verification condition associated with the Ada rule that it is a bounded error to invoke an operation that is potentially blocking (including due to cyclic locking) during a protected action (see Ada RM 9.5.1(8)) is discharged via (potentially conservative) flow analysis, as opposed to by introducing verification conditions. [Support for the "Potentially_Blocking" aspect discussed in AI12-0064 may be incorporated into SPARK 2014 at some point in the future.]

   The verification condition associated with the Ada rule that it is a bounded error to call the Current_Task function from an entry_body, or an interrupt handler (see Ada RM C.7.1(17/3)) is discharged similarly.

   The verification condition associated with the Ada rule that the active priority of a caller of a protected operation is not higher than the ceiling of the corresponding protected object (see Ada RM D.3(13)) is dependent on (potentially conservative) flow analysis. This flow analysis is used to determine which tasks potentially call (directly or indirectly) a protected operation of which protected objects, and similarly which protected objects have protected operations that potentially perform calls (directly or indirectly) on the operations of other protected objects. A verification condition is created for each combination of potential (task or protected object) caller and called protected object to ensure that the (task or ceiling) priority of the potential caller is no greater than the ceiling priority of the called protected object.

13. The end of a task body shall not be reachable. [This follows from from (extended) Ravenscar's No_Task_Termination restriction.]

14. A nonvolatile function shall not be potentially blocking. [Strictly speaking this rule is already implied by other rules of SPARK 2014, notably the rule that a nonvolatile function cannot depend on a volatile input.] [A dispatching call which statically denotes a primitive subprogram of a tagged type T is a potentially blocking operation if the corresponding primitive operation of any descendant of T is potentially blocking.]

15. The package Ada.Task_Identification declares (and initializes) a synchronized external state abstraction named Tasking_State. The packages Ada.Real_Time and Ada.Calendar declare (and initialize) synchronized external state abstractions named Clock_Time. The Async_Readers and Async_Writers aspects of all those state abstractions are True, and their Effective_Reads and Effective_Writes aspects are False. Each is listed in the Initializes aspect of its respective package. For each of the following language-defined functions, the Volatile_Function

aspect of the function is defined to be True and the Global aspect of the function specifies that one of these two state abstractions is referenced as an Input global:

- Ada.Real_Time.Clock references Ada.Real_Time.Clock_Time;

- Ada.Execution_Time.Clock references Ada.Real_Time.Clock_Time;

- Ada.Execution_Time.Clock_For_Interrupts references Ada.Real_Time.Clock_Time;

- Ada.Execution_Time.Interrupts.Clock references Ada.Real_Time.Clock_Time;

- Ada.Calendar.Clock (which is excluded by the Ravenscar profile but not by the Extended Ravenscar profile) references Ada.Real_Time.Clock_Time;

- Ada.Task_Identification.Current_Task references Ada.Task_Identification.Tasking_State;

- Ada.Task_Identification.Is_Terminated references Ada.Task_Identification.Tasking_State;

- Ada.Task_Identification.Is_Callable references Ada.Task_Identification.Tasking_State;

- Ada.Task_Identification.Activation_Is_Complete references Ada.Task_Identification.Tasking_State;

- Ada.Dispatching.EDF.Get_Deadline references Ada.Task_Identification.Tasking_State;

- Ada.Interrupts.Is_Reserved references Ada.Task_Identification.Tasking_State;

- Ada.Interrupts.Is_Attached references Ada.Task_Identification.Tasking_State;

- Ada.Interrupts.Detach_Handler references Ada.Task_Identification.Tasking_State;

- Ada.Interrupts.Get_CPU references Ada.Task_Identification.Tasking_State;

- Ada.Synchronous_Task_Control.Current_State references Ada.Task_Identification.Tasking_State.

[Functions excluded by the Extended Ravenscar profile (and therefore also by the Ravenscar profile) are not on this list.]

16. For each of the following language-defined procedures, the Global aspect of the procedure specifies that the state abstraction Ada.Task_Identification.Tasking_State is referenced as an In_Out global:

- Ada.Interrupts.Detach_Handler.

17. For purposes of determining global inputs and outputs, a delay statement is considered to reference the state abstraction Ada.Real_Time.Clock_Time as an input. [In other words, a delay statement can be treated like a call to a procedure which takes the delay expression as an actual parameter and references the Clock_Time state abstraction as an Input global.]

18. For purposes of determining global inputs and outputs, a use of any of the Callable, Caller, Count, or Terminated attributes is considered to reference the state abstraction Ada.Task_Identification.Tasking_State as an Input. [In other words, evaluation of one of these attributes can be treated like a call to a volatile function which takes the attribute prefix as a parameter (in the case where the prefix denotes an object or value) and references the Tasking_State state abstraction as an Input global.] [On the other hand, use of the Identity or Storage_Size attributes introduces no such dependency.]

19. Preconditions are added to suprogram specifications as needed in order to avoid the failure of language-defined runtime checks for the following subprograms:

- for Ada.Execution_Time.Clock, T does not equal Task_Identification.Null_Task_Id.

- for Ada.Execution_Time.Clock_For_Interrupts, Interrupt_Clocks_Supported is True.

- for Ada.Execution_Time.Interrupts.Clock, Separate_Interrupt_Clocks_Supported is True.

- for Ada.Execution_Time's arithmetic and conversion operators (including Time_Of), preconditions are defined to ensure that the result belongs to the result type.

- for Ada.Real_Time's arithmetic and conversion operators (including Time_Of), preconditions are defined to ensure that the result belongs to the result type.

20. All procedures declared in the visible part of Ada.Synchronous_Task_Control have a dependency "(S => null)" despite the fact that S has mode **in out**.

PROGRAM STRUCTURE AND COMPILATION ISSUES

SPARK 2014 supports constructive, modular analysis. This means that analysis may be performed before a program is complete based on unit interfaces. For instance, to analyze a subprogram which calls another all that is required is a specification of the called subprogram including, at least, its `global_specification` and if formal verification of the calling program is to be performed, then the Pre and Postcondition of the called subprogram need to be provided. The body of the called subprogram does not need to be implemented to analyze the caller. The body of the called subprogram is checked to be conformant with its specification when its implementation code is available and analyzed.

The separate compilation of Ada `compilation_units` is consistent with SPARK 2014 modular analysis except where noted in the following subsections but, particularly with respect to incomplete programs, analysis does not involve the execution of the program.

10.1 Separate Compilation

Legality Rules

1. A program unit cannot be a task unit, a protected unit or a protected entry.

10.1.1 Compilation Units - Library Units

No restrictions or extensions.

10.1.2 Context Clauses - With Clauses

Legality Rules

1. With clauses are always in SPARK 2014, even if the unit mentioned is not completely in SPARK 2014.

Abstract Views

State abstractions are visible in the limited view of packages in SPARK 2014. The notion of an *abstract view* of an object declaration is also introduced, and the limited view of a package includes the abstract view of any objects declared in the visible part of that package. The only allowed uses of an abstract view of an object are where the use of a state abstraction would be allowed (for example, in a Global `aspect_specification`).

Legality Rules

2. A name denoting the abstract view of an object shall occur only:

   (a) as a `global_item` in a Global or Refined_Global aspect specification; or

(b) as an `input` or `output` in a Depends or Refined_Depends aspect specification; or

(c) in an `input_list` of an Initializes aspect.

Static Semantics

3. Any state abstractions declared within a given package are present in the limited view of the package. [This means that, for example, a Global `aspect_specification` for a subprogram declared in a library unit package *P1* could refer to a state abstraction declared in a package *P2* if *P1* has a limited with of *P2*.]

4. For every object declared by an `object_declaration` occurring immediately within the visible part of a given package, the limited view of the package contains an *abstract view* of the object.

10.1.3 Subunits of Compilation Units

No restrictions or extensions.

10.1.4 The Compilation Process

The analysis process in SPARK 2014 is similar to the compilation process in Ada except that the `compilation_units` are analyzed, that is flow analysis and formal verification is performed, rather than compiled.

10.1.5 Pragmas and Program Units

No restrictions or extensions.

10.1.6 Environment-Level Visibility Rules

No restrictions or extensions.

10.2 Program Execution

SPARK 2014 analyses do not involve program execution. However, SPARK 2014 programs are executable including those new language defined aspects and pragmas where they have dynamic semantics given.

10.2.1 Elaboration Control

No extensions or restrictions.

EXCEPTIONS

11.1 Exception Declarations

No additions or restrictions

11.2 Exception Handlers

Legality Rules

1. Exception handlers are not permitted in SPARK 2014.

11.3 Raise Statements

Raise statements are in SPARK 2014, but must (as described below) be provably never executed.

Verification Rules

1. A `raise_statement` introduces an obligation to prove that the statement will not be executed, much like the verification condition associated with

   ```
   pragma Assert (False);
   ```

   [In other words, the verification conditions introduced for a raise statement are the same as those introduced for a run-time check which fails unconditionally.]

11.4 Exception Handling

No additions or restrictions but exception handlers are not permitted in SPARK 2014.

11.4.1 The Package Exceptions

11.4.2 Pragmas Assert and Assertion_Policy

Legality Rules

1. The pragmas `Assertion_Policy`, `Suppress`, and `Unsuppress` are allowed in SPARK 2014, but have no effect on the generation of verification conditions. [For example, an array index value must be shown to be in bounds regardless of whether Index_Check is suppressed at the point of the array indexing.]

2. The following SPARK 2014 defined aspects and pragmas are assertions and their *Boolean*_expressions are assertion expressions:

- Assert_And_Cut;

- Assume;

- Contract_Cases;

- Default_Initial_Condition;

- Initial_Condition;

- Loop_Invariant;

- Loop_Variant; and

- Refined_Post.

There is an *assertion*_aspect_mark for each of these aspects and pragmas with the same identifier as the corresponding aspect or pragma. In addition, Ghost is a SPARK 2014 defined *assertion*_aspect_mark.

An implementation may introduce further implementation defined *assertion*_aspect_marks some of which may apply to groups of these assertions.

GENERIC UNITS

Enforcement of SPARK 2014's rules within a generic unit is not guaranteed. Violations might not be reported until an instance of the generic unit is analyzed. If an instance of a generic unit occurs within another generic unit, this principle is applied recursively.

12.1 Generic Instantiation

Legality Rules

1. An instantiation of a generic is or is not in SPARK 2014 depending on whether the instance declaration and the instance body (described in section 12.3 of the Ada reference manual) are in SPARK 2014 [(i.e., when considered as a package (or, in the case of an instance of a generic subprogram, as a subprogram)].

2. [A generic actual parameter corresponding to a generic formal object having mode **in** shall not have a variable input; see *Expressions* for the statement of this rule.]

[For example, a generic which takes a formal limited private type would be in SPARK 2014. An instantiation which passes in an access type as the actual type would not be in SPARK 2014; another instantiation of the same generic which passes in, for example, Standard.Integer, might be in SPARK 2014.]

[Ada has a rule that legality rules are not enforced in an instance body (and, in some cases, in the private part of an instance of a generic package). No such rule applies to the restrictions defining which Ada constructs are in SPARK 2014. For example, a goto statement in an instance body would cause the instantiation to not be in SPARK 2014.]

[Consider the problem of correctly specifying the Global and Depends aspects of a subprogram declared within an instance body which contains a call to a generic formal subprogram (more strictly speaking, to the corresponding actual subprogram of the instantiation in question). These aspects are simply copied from the corresponding aspect specification in the generic, so this implies that we have to "get them right" in the generic (where "right" means "right for all instantiations"). One way to do this is to assume that a generic formal subprogram references no globals (or, more generally, references any fixed set of globals) and to only instantiate the generic with actual subprograms that meet this requirement.]

REPRESENTATION ISSUES

13.1 Operational and Representation Aspects

SPARK 2014 defines several Boolean-valued aspects. These include the Async_Readers, Async_Writers, Constant_After_Elaboration, Effective_Reads, Effective_Writes, Extensions_Visible, Ghost, and Volatile_Function aspects. [Note that this list does not include expression-valued aspects, such as Default_Initial_Condition or Initial_Condition.]

The following rules apply to each of these aspects unless specified otherwise for a particular aspect:

1. In the absence of an aspect specification (explicit or inherited), the default value of the given aspect is False.

2. If the given aspect is specified via an aspect_specification [(as opposed to via a pragma)] then the aspect_definition (if any) shall be a static Boolean expression. [Omitting the aspect_definition in an aspect_specification is equivalent to specifying a value of True as described in Ada RM 13.1.1(15).]

3. The usage names in an aspect_definition for the given aspect are resolved at the point of the associated declaration. [This supersedes the name resolution rule given in Ada RM 13.1.1 that states that such names are resolved at the end of the enclosing declaration list.]

[One case where the "unless specified otherwise" clause applies is illustrated by

X : Integer with Volatile;

where the Async_Readers aspect of X is True, not False.]

Ada allows aspect specifications for package declarations and package bodies but does not define any aspects which can be specified in this way. SPARK 2014 defines, for example, the Initial_Condition and Refined_State aspects (the former can be specified for a package declaration; the latter for a package body). Ada's usual rule that

The usage names in an aspect_definition [are not resolved at the point of the associated declaration, but rather] are resolved at the end of the immediately enclosing declaration list.

is applied for such aspects as though "the immediately enclosing declaration list" is that of the visible part (in the former case) or of the body (in the latter case). [For example, the Initial_Condition expression of a package which declares a variable in its visible part can (directly) name that variable. Simlarly, the Refined_State aspect specification for a package body can name variables declared within the package body.]

13.2 Packed Types

No restrictions or additions.

13.3 Operational and Representation Attributes

No restrictions or additions.

13.4 Enumeration Representation Clauses

No restrictions or additions.

13.5 Record Layout

13.6 Change of Representation

No restrictions or additions.

13.7 The Package System

Legality Rules

1. The use of the operators defined for type Address are not permitted in SPARK 2014 except for use within representation clauses.

13.8 Machine Code Insertions

Legality Rules

1. Machine code insertions are not in SPARK 2014.

13.9 Unchecked Type Conversions

The validity of unchecked type conversions is not currently checked by SPARK 2014 the onus is on the user to ensure that the value read from an unchecked type conversion is valid (see *Data Validity*).

13.9.1 Data Validity

Currently SPARK 2014 does not check for data validity. It is therefore up to users to ensure that data read from external sources and values from unchecked type conversions are valid.

Validity can be ensured by using a type for the target of the data read from an external source or an unchecked type conversion which is sufficient to encompass all possible values of the source. Alternatively the X'Valid (or X'Valid_Scalars for composite types) may be used to determine the validity of an object.

The use of invalid values in a program (other than in a Valid, or Valid_Scalars attribute) may invalidate any proofs performed on the program.

13.10 Unchecked Access Value Creation

Legality Rules

1. As access types are not supported in SPARK 2014, neither is this attribute.

13.11 Storage Management

Legality Rules

1. These features are related to access types and not in SPARK 2014.

13.12 Pragma Restrictions and Pragma Profile

Restrictions and Profiles will be available with SPARK 2014 to provide profiles suitable for different application environments.

13.13 Streams

Legality Rules

1. Stream types and operations are not in SPARK 2014.

13.14 Freezing Rules

No restrictions or additions.

PREDEFINED LANGUAGE ENVIRONMENT (ANNEX A)

This chapter describes how SPARK 2014 treats the Ada predefined language environment and standard libraries, corresponding to appendices A through H of the Ada RM.

SPARK 2014 programs are able to use much of the Ada predefined language environment and standard libraries. The standard libraries are not necessarily mathematically, formally proven in any way, unless specifically stated, and should be treated as tested code.

In addition many standard library subprograms have checks on the consistency of the actual parameters when they are called. If they are inconsistent in some way they will raise an exception. It is strongly recommended that each call of a standard library subprogram which may raise an exception due to incorrect actual parameters should be immediately preceded by a pragma Assert to check that the actual parameters meet the requirements of the called subprogram. Alternatively the called subprogram may be wrapped in a user defined subprogram with a suitable precondition. Examples of these approaches are given in *The Package Strings.Maps (A.4.2)*.

No checks or warnings are given that this protocol is followed. The onus is on the user to ensure that a library subprogram is called with consistent actual parameters.

14.1 The Package Standard (A.1)

SPARK 2014 supports all of the types, subtypes and operators declared in package Standard. The predefined exceptions are considered to be declared in Standard, but their use is constrained by other language restrictions.

14.2 The Package Ada (A.2)

No additions or restrictions.

14.3 Character Handling (A.3)

14.3.1 The Packages Characters, Wide_Characters, and Wide_Wide_Characters (A.3.1)

No additions or restrictions. As in Ada, the wide character sets provided are SPARK 2014 tool, compiler and platform dependent.

14.3.2 The Package Characters.Handling (A.3.2)

No additions or restrictions.

14.3.3 The Package Characters.Latin_1 (A.3.3)

No additions or restrictions.

14.3.4 The Package Characters.Conversions (A.3.4)

No Additions or restrictions.

14.3.5 The Package Wide_Characters.Handling (A.3.5)

No additions or restrictions.

14.3.6 The Package Wide_Wide_Characters.Handling (A.3.6)

No additions or restrictions.

14.4 String Handling (A.4)

No additions or restrictions.

14.4.1 The Package Strings (A.4.1)

No additions or restrictions.

The predefined exceptions are considered to be declared in Stings, but their use is constrained by other language restrictions.

14.4.2 The Package Strings.Maps (A.4.2)

1. The type declaration Character_Mapping_Function is not in SPARK 2014 and cannot be referenced within SPARK 2014 program text.

The function To_Mapping may raise the exception Translation_Error if its actual parameters are inconsistent. To guard against this exception each call of To_Mapping should be immediately preceded by an assert statement checking that the actual parameters are correct.

Examples

```
--  From the Ada RM for To_Mapping: "To_Mapping produces a
--  Character_Mapping such that each element of From maps to the
--  corresponding element of To, and each other character maps to
--  itself. If From'Length /= To'Length, or if some character is
--  repeated in From, then Translation_Error is propagated".

--  Each call should be preceded with a pragma Assert, checking the
```

```
--  actual parameters, of the form:
pragma Assert (Actual_From'Length = Actual_To'Length and then
                (for all I in Actual_From'Range =>
                  (for all J in Actual_From'Range =>
                    (if I /= J then Actual_From (I) /= Actual_From (J)))));
CM := To_Mapping (From => Actual_From,
                  To   => Actual_To);

--  Alternatively To_Mapping could be wrapped in a user defined
--  subprogram with a suitable precondition and used to call
--  To_Mapping indirectly.  For example:
function My_To_Mapping (From, To : in Character_Sequence)
                        return Character_Mapping
  with Pre => (From'Length = To'Length and then
                (for all I in From'Range =>
                  (for all J in From'Range =>
                    (if I /= J then From (I) /= From (J)))));
is
begin
   return Ada.Strings.Maps.To_Mapping (From, To);
end My_To_Mapping;
```

14.4.3 Fixed-Length String Handling (A.4.3)

1. Translate (with Maps.Character_Mapping_Function formal parameter) is not callable from SPARK 2014 as it has a an access to function type parameter.

All other subprograms may be called but the subprograms Move, Index, Count (with a mapping formal parameter), Find_Token, Replace_Slice, Insert, Overwrite, Head (with Justify formal parameter), Tail (with Justify formal parameter) may raise an exception if they are called with inconsistent actual parameters. Each call of these subprograms should be preceded with a pragma Assert to check that the actual parameters are consistent.

14.4.4 Bounded-Length String Handling (A.4.4)

1. The subprograms Index, Count and Translate with Maps.Character_Mapping_Function formal parameters are not callable from SPARK 2014.

The other subprograms in Bounded-Length String Handling are callable from SPARK 2014 program texts but many of them may raise an exception if they are called with inconsistent actual parameters. Each call of these subprograms should be preceded with a pragma Assert to check that the actual parameters are consistent.

14.4.5 Unbounded-Length String Handling (A.4.5)

1. The type String_Access and the procedure Free are not in SPARK 2014 as they require access types and cannot be denoted in SPARK 2014 program text.

2. The subprograms Index, Count and Translate with Maps.Character_Mapping_Function formal parameters are not callable from SPARK 2014.

The function and procedure Unbounded_Slice both may propagate Index_Error if Low > Length(Source)+1 or High > Length(Source) and so every call to each of these subprograms should be immediately preceded by a pragma Assert of the form:

```
pragma Assert (Actual_Low  <= Length (Actual_Source) and
               Actual_High <= Length (Actual_Source));
```

14.4.6 String-Handling Sets and Mappings (A.4.6)

No additions or restrictions.

14.4.7 Wide_String Handling (A.4.7)

1. The types Wide_String_Access and Wide_Character_Mapping_Function are not in SPARK 2014 nor are the subprograms which have formal parameters of these types and cannot be denoted in SPARK 2014 program texts.

Each call of a subprogram which may raise an exception if it is called with inconsistent actual parameters should be immediately preceded by a pragma Assert checking the consistency of the actual parameters.

14.4.8 Wide_Wide_String Handling (A.4.8)

1. The types Wide_Wide_String_Access and Wide_Wide_Character_Mapping_Function are not in SPARK 2014 nor are the subprograms which have formal parameters of these types and cannot be denoted in SPARK 2014 program texts.

Each call of a subprogram which may raise an exception if it is called with inconsistent actual parameters should be immediately preceded by a pragma Assert checking the consistency of the actual parameters.

14.4.9 String Hashing (A.4.9)

No additions or restrictions.

14.4.10 String Comparison (A.4.10)

No additions or restrictions.

14.4.11 String Encoding (A.4.11)

The subprograms of this package are callable from SPARK 2014 but those that may raise an exception due to inconsistent parameters should have a pragma Assert confirming that the actual parameters are consistent immediately preceding each call of such a subprogram.

14.5 The Numerics Packages (A.5)

No additions or restrictions

14.5.1 Elementary Functions (A.5.1)

Most of the elementarty functions may raise an exception. The functions have no preconditions to guard against an exception being raised. The functions should be treated as tested code and call of an elementary function should be immediately preceded by a pragma assert in lieu of a precondition.

For instance a call to Log (X, Base) should be immediately preceded by the assert statement:

```
pragma Assert (X > 0  and Base > 1);
```

Even with such a guard certain elementary functions may raise a constraint error. The onus is on the user to ensure this does not happen or is handled in non-SPARK 2014 text in a manner compatible with SPARK 2014.

14.5.2 Random Number Generation (A.5.2)

The package Ada.Numerics.Float_Random and an instantiation of package Ada.Numerics.Discrete_Random is ostensibly in SPARK 2014 but the functions have side effects and should not be called from SPARK 2014 text.

14.6 Input-Output (A.6)

No additions or restrictions.

14.7 External Files and File Objects (A.7)

No additions or restrictions.

14.8 Sequential and Direct Files (A.8)

No additions or restrictions.

14.8.1 The Generic Package Sequential_IO (A.8.1)

An instantiation of Sequential_IO will ostensibly be in SPARK 2014 but in use it may give rise to flow-errors as the effect of reads and writes is not captured in the subprogram contracts. Calls to its subprograms may raise IO_Exceptions based on external events.

14.8.2 File Management (A.8.2)

No additions or restrictions.

14.8.3 Sequential Input-Output Operations (A.8.3)

No additions or restrictions.

14.8.4 The Generic Package Direct_IO (A.8.4)

An instantiation of Direct_IO will ostensibly be in SPARK 2014 but in use it may give rise to flow-errors as the effect of reads and writes is not captured in the subprogram contracts. Calls to its subprograms may raise IO_Exceptions based on external events.

14.8.5 Direct Input-Output Operations (A.8.5)

No additions or restrictions.

14.9 The Generic Package Storage_IO (A.9)

An instantiation of Storage_IO will ostensibly be in SPARK 2014 but in use it may give rise to flow-errors as the effect of reads and writes is not captured in the subprogram contracts. Calls to its subprograms may raise IO_Exceptions based on external events.

14.10 Text Input-Output (A.10)

No additions or restrictions.

14.10.1 The Package Text_IO (A.10.1)

Ada.Text_IO is ostensibly in SPARK 2014 except for the type File_Access and the functions which return this type. The use Ada.Text_IO may give rise to flow-errors as the effect of reads and writes is not captured in the subprogram contracts. The Ada.Text_IO.Get_Line functions should not be called as they have a side effect of reading data from a file and updating its file pointers. The subprograms Set_Input, Set_Output and Set_Error should not be called as they introduce an alias to the file passed as a parameter. Calls to the subprograms of Ada.Text_IO may raise IO_Exceptions based on external events.

14.10.2 Text File Management (A.10.2)

No additions or restrictions.

14.10.3 Default Input, Output and Error Files (A.10.3)

The subprograms Ada.Text_IO.Set_Input, Ada.Text_IO.Set_Output and Ada.Text_IO.Set_Error should not be called from SPARK 2014 program text as they introduce an alias of the file parameter.

14.10.4 Specification of Line and Page Lengths (A.10.4)

No additions or restrictions.

14.10.5 Operations on Columns, Lines and Pages (A.10.5)

No additions or restrictions.

14.10.6 Get and Put Procedures (A.10.6)

No additions or restrictions.

14.10.7 Input-Output of Characters and Strings (A.10.7)

The functions Ada.Text_IO.Get_Line should not be called from SPARK 2014 program text as the functions have a side effect of reading from a file.

14.10.8 Input-Output for Integer Types (A.10.8)

No additions or restrictions.

14.10.9 Input-Output for Real Types (A.10.9)

No additions or restrictions.

14.10.10 Input-Output for Enumeration Types (A.10.10)

No additions or restrictions.

14.10.11 Input-Output for Bounded Strings (A.10.11)

An instantiation of Bounded_IO will ostensibly be in SPARK 2014 but in use it may give rise to flow-errors as the effect of reads and writes is not captured in the subprogram contracts. Calls to its subprograms may raise IO_Exceptions based on external events.

14.10.12 Input-Output of Unbounded Strings (A.10.12)

Ada.Text_IO.Unbounded_IO is ostensibly in SPARK 2014 but in use it may give rise to flow-errors as the effect of reads and writes is not captured in the subprogram contracts. Calls to its subprograms may raise IO_Exceptions based on external events.

The functions Ada.Text_IO.Unbounded_IO.Get_Line should not be called from SPARK 2014 program text as the functions have a side effect of reading from a file.

14.11 Wide Text Input-Output and Wide Wide Text Input-Output (A.11)

These packages have the same constraints as was discussed for Ada.Text_IO.

14.12 Stream Input-Output (A.12)

Stream input and output is not supported by SPARK 2014 and the use of the package Ada.Streams.Stream_IO and the child packages of Ada.Text_IO concerned with streams is not permitted in SPARK 2014 program text.

14.13 Exceptions in Input-Output (A.13)

The exceptions declared in package Ada.IO_Exceptions which are raised by the Ada input-output subprograms are in SPARK 2014 but the exceptions cannot be handled in SPARK 2014 program text.

14.14 File Sharing (A.14)

File sharing is not permitted in SPARK 2014, since it may introduce an alias.

14.15 The Package Command_Line (A.15)

The package Command_Line is in SPARK 2014 except that the function Argument may propagate Constraint_Error. To avoid this exception each call to Argument should be immediately preceded by the assertion:

```
pragma Assert (Number <= Argument_Count);
```

where Number represents the actual parameter to the function Argument.

14.16 The Package Directories (A.16)

The package Directories is ostensibly in SPARK 2014 but in use it may give rise to flow-errors as the effect of reads and writes is not captured in the subprogram contracts. Calls to its subprograms may raise IO_Exceptions based on external events.

14.17 The Package Environment_Variables (A.17)

The package Environment_Variables is ostensibly mostly in SPARK 2014 but in use it may give rise to flow-errors as the effect of reads and writes is not captured in the subprogram contracts. Calls to its subprograms may raise IO_Exceptions based on external events.

The procedure Iterate is not in SPARK 2014.

14.18 Containers (A.18)

The standard Ada container libraries are not supported in SPARK 2014.

An implementation may choose to provide alternative container libraries whose specifications are in SPARK 2014 and are intended to support formal verification.

14.19 The Package Locales (A.19)

No additions or restrictions.

14.20 Interface to Other Languages (Annex B)

This section describes features for mixed-language programming in SPARK 2014, covering facilities offered by Ada's Annex B.

Package `Interfaces` can be used in SPARK 2014, including its intrinsic "Shift" and "Rotate" functions.

Other packages are not directly supported.

The pragma `Unchecked_Union` is not permitted in SPARK 2014.

14.21 Systems Programming (Annex C)

This section describes features for systems programming in SPARK 2014, covering facilities offered by Ada's Annex C.

Almost all of the facilities offered by this Annex are out of scope for SPARK 2014 and so are not supported.

14.21.1 Pragma Discard_Names (C.5)

Pragma Discard_Names is not permitted in SPARK 2014, since its use can lead to implementation defined behaviour at run time.

14.21.2 Shared Variable Control (C.6)

The following restrictions are applied to the declaration of volatile types and objects in SPARK 2014:

Legality Rules

1. A volatile representation aspect may only be applied to an `object_declaration` or a `full_type_declaration`.

2. A type which is not effectively volatile shall not have a volatile subcomponent.

3. A discriminant shall not be volatile.

4. Neither a discriminated type nor an object of such a type shall be volatile.

5. Neither a tagged type nor an object of such a type shall be volatile.

6. An effectively volatile object shall only be declared at library-level.

14.22 Real-Time Systems (Annex D)

SPARK 2014 supports the parts of the real-time systems annex that comply with the Ravenscar profile (see Ada RM D.13) or the Extended Ravenscar profile (see docs.adacore.com/gnathie_ug-docs/html/gnathie_ug/gnathie_ug/the_predefined_profiles.html#the-extended-ravenscar-profiles). See section *Tasks and Synchronization*.

14.23 Distributed Systems (Annex E)

SPARK 2014 does not support the distributed systems annex.

14.24 Information Systems (Annex F)

The `Machine_Radix` aspect and attribute are permitted in SPARK 2014.

The package `Ada.Decimal` may be used, although it declares constants whose values are implementation defined.

The packages `Ada.Text_IO.Editing` and its "Wide" variants are not directly supported in SPARK 2014.

14.25 Numerics (Annex G)

This section describes features for numerical programming in SPARK 2014, covering facilities offered by Ada's Annex G.

Packages declared in this Annex are usable in SPARK 2014, although many details are implementation defined.

Implementations (both compilers and verification tools) should document how both *strict mode* and *relaxed mode* are implemented and their effect on verification and performance.

14.26 High Integrity Systems (Annex H)

SPARK 2014 fully supports the requirements of Ada's Annex H.

LANGUAGE-DEFINED ASPECTS AND ATTRIBUTES (ANNEX K)

15.1 Language-Defined Aspects

1. Ada language aspects are permitted as shown in the following table:

Aspect	Allowed in SPARK 2014	Comment
Address	Yes	
Alignment (object)	Yes	
Alignment (subtype)	Yes	
All_Calls_Remote	No	
Asynchronous	No	
Atomic	Yes	
Atomic_Components	Yes	
Attach_Handler	Yes	
Bit_Order	Yes	
Coding	Yes	
Component_Size	Yes	
Constant_Indexing	No	
Convention	Yes	
CPU	Yes	
Default_Component_Value	Yes	
Default_Iterator	No	
Default_Storage_Pool	No	
Default_Value	Yes	
Default_Storage_Pool	No	Restricted access types
Dispatching_Domain	No	Ravenscar
Dynamic_Predicate	Yes	
Elaborate_Body	Yes	
Export	Yes	
External_Name	Yes	
External_Tag	No	No tags
Implicit_Dereference	No	Restricted access types
Import	Yes	
Independent	Yes	
Independent_Components	Yes	
Inline	Yes	
Interrupt_Handler	Yes	
Interrupt_Priority	Yes	
Iterator_Element	No	
		Continued on next page

Table 15.1 – continued from previous page

Aspect	Allowed in SPARK 2014	Comment
Layout (record)	Yes	
Link_Name	Yes	
Machine_Radix	Yes	
No_Return	Yes	
Output	No	No streams
Pack	Yes	
Pre	Yes	
Pre'Class	Yes	
Post	Yes	
Post'Class	Yes	
Predicate_Failure	Yes	
Preelaborate	Yes	
Priority	Yes	
Pure	Yes	
Relative_Deadline	Yes	
Remote_Call_Interface	No	
Remote_Types	No	
Shared_Passive	No	
Size (object)	Yes	
Size (subtype)	Yes	
Small	Yes	
Static_Predicate	Yes	
Storage_Pool	No	Restricted access types
Storage_Size (access)	No	Restricted access types
Storage_Size (task)	Yes	
Stream_Size	No	No streams
Synchronization	Yes	
Type_Invariant	Yes	
Type_Invariant'Class	No	
Unchecked_Union	No	
Variable_Indexing	No	
Volatile	Yes	
Volatile_Components	Yes	
Write	No	No streams

2. SPARK 2014 defines the following aspects:

Aspect	Allowed in SPARK 2014	Comment
Abstract_State	Yes	
Async_Readers	Yes	
Async_Writers	Yes	
Constant_After_Elaboration	Yes	
Contract_Cases	Yes	
Default_Initial_Condition	Yes	
Depends	Yes	
Depends'Class	Yes	
Effective_Reads	Yes	
Effective_Writes	Yes	
Extensions_Visible	Yes	
Ghost	Yes	
Global	Yes	
Global'Class	Yes	
Initial_Condition	Yes	
Initializes	Yes	
Part_Of	Yes	
Refined_Depends	Yes	
Refined_Global	Yes	
Refined_Post	Yes	
Refined_State	Yes	
SPARK_Mode	Yes	Language defined but implementation dependent
Volatile_Function	Yes	

15.2 Language-Defined Attributes

1. The following attributes are in SPARK 2014.

Attribute	Allowed in SPARK 2014	Comment
P'Access	No	Restricted access types
X'Access	Yes	
X'Address	No	Only allowed in representation clauses
S'Adjacent	Yes	Implicit precondition (Ada RM A.5.3(50))
S'Aft	Yes	
S'Alignment	Warn	Warning in pedantic mode
X'Alignment	Warn	Warning in pedantic mode
S'Base	Yes	
S'Bit_Order	Warn	Warning in pedantic mode
P'Body_Version	Yes	
T'Callable	Yes	
E'Caller	Yes	
S'Ceiling	Yes	
S'Class	Yes	
X'Component_Size	Warn	Warning in pedantic mode
S'Compose	No	
A'Constrained	Yes	
S'Copy_Sign	Yes	
E'Count	No	
S'Definite	Yes	

Continued on next page

Table 15.2 – continued from previous page

Attribute	Allowed in SPARK 2014	Comment
S'Delta	Yes	
S'Denorm	Yes	
S'Digits	Yes	
S'Exponent	No	
S'External_Tag	No	No tags
A'First	Yes	
S'First	Yes	
A'First(N)	Yes	
R.C'First_Bit	Warn	Warning in Pedantic mode
S'First_Valid	Yes	
S'Floor	Yes	
S'Fore	Yes	
S'Fraction	No	
X'Has_Same_Storage	No	
E'Identity	No	
T'Identity	Yes	
S'Image	Yes	
S'Class'Input	No	No streams
S'Input	No	No streams
A'Last	Yes	
S'Last	Yes	
A'Last(N)	Yes	
R.C'Last_Bit	Warn	Warning in pedantic mode
S'Last_Valid	Yes	
S'Leading_Part	No	
A'Length	Yes	
A'Length(N)	Yes	
X'Loop_Entry	Yes	
S'Machine	Yes	
S'Machine_Emax	Yes	
S'Machine_Emin	Yes	
S'Machine_Mantissa	Yes	
S'Machine_Overflows	Yes	
S'Machine_Radix	Yes	
S'Machine_Rounding	Yes	
S'Machine_Rounds	Yes	
S'Max	Yes	
S'Max_Alignment_For_Allocation	No	Restricted access types
S'Max_Size_In_Storage_Elements	No	Restricted access types
S'Min	Yes	
S'Mod	Yes	
S'Model	Yes	
S'Model_Emin	Yes	
S'Model_Epsilon	Yes	
S'Model_Mantissa	Yes	
S'Model_Small	Yes	
S'Modulus	Yes	
X'Old	Yes	
S'Class'Output	No	No streams

Continued on next page

Table 15.2 – continued from previous page

Attribute	Allowed in SPARK 2014	Comment
S'Output	No	No streams
X'Overlaps_Storage	No	
D'Partition_Id	Yes	
S'Pos	Yes	
R.C'Position	Warn	Warning in pedantic mode
S'Pred	Yes	Implicit precondition (Ada RM 3.5(27))
P'Priority	No	Ravenscar
A'Range	Yes	
S'Range	Yes	
A'Range(N)	Yes	
S'Class'Read	No	No streams
S'Read	No	No streams
S'Remainder	Yes	
F'Result	Yes	
S'Round	Yes	
S'Rounding	Yes	
S'Safe_First	Yes	
S'Safe_Last	Yes	
S'Scale	Yes	
S'Scaling	Yes	
S'Size	Warn	Warning in pedantic
X'Size	Warn	Warning in pedantic
S'Small	Yes	
S'Storage_Pool	No	Restricted access types
S'Storage_Size	No	Restricted access types
T'Storage_Size	Yes	
S'Stream_Size	No	No streams
S'Succ	Yes	Implicit precondition (Ada RM 3.5(24))
S'Tag	No	No tags
X'Tag	No	No tags
T'Terminated	Yes	
System'To_Address	Yes	
S'Truncation	Yes	
S'Truncation	Yes	
X'Unchecked_Access	No	
X'Update	Yes	
S'Val	Yes	Implicit precondition (Ada RM 3.5.5(7))
X'Valid	Yes	Assumed to be True at present
S'Value	Yes	Implicit precondition (Ada RM 3.5(55/3))
P'Version	Yes	
S'Wide_Image	Yes	
S'Wide_Value	Yes	Implicit precondition (Ada RM 3.5(43/3))
S'Wide_Wide_Image	Yes	
S'Wide_Wide_Value	Yes	Implicit precondition (Ada RM 3.5(39.12/3))
S'Wide_Wide_Width	Yes	
S'Wide_Width	Yes	
S'Width	Yes	
S'Class'Write	No	No streams
S'Write	No	No streams

LANGUAGE-DEFINED PRAGMAS (ANNEX L)

16.1 Ada Language-Defined Pragmas

The following Ada language-defined pragmas are supported as follows:

Pragma	Allowed in SPARK 2014	Comment
All_Calls_Remote	No	
Assert	Yes	
Assertion_Policy	Yes	
Asynchronous	No	
Atomic	Yes	
Atomic_Components	Yes	
Attach_Handler	Yes	
Convention	Yes	
CPU	Yes	
Default_Storage_Pool	No	No access types
Detect_Blocking	Yes	
Discard_Names	No	
Dispatching_Domain	No	Ravenscar
Elaborate	Yes	
Elaborate_All	Yes	
Elaborate_Body	Yes	
Export	Yes	
Import	Yes	
Independent	Yes	
Independent_Components	Yes	
Inline	Yes	
Inspection_Point	Yes	
Interrupt_Handler	Yes	
Interrupt_Priority	Yes	
Linker_Options	Yes	
List	Yes	
Locking_Policy	Yes	
No_Return	Yes	
Normalize_Scalars	Yes	
Optimize	Yes	
Pack	Yes	
Page	Yes	
Partition_Elaboration_Policy	Yes	Ravenscar
	Continued on next page	

Table 16.1 – continued from previous page

Pragma	Allowed in SPARK 2014	Comment
Preelaborable_Initialization	Yes	
Preelaborate	Yes	
Priority	Yes	
Priority_Specific_Dispatching	No	Ravenscar
Profile	Yes	
Pure	Yes	
Queuing_Policy	Yes	Ravenscar
Relative_Deadline	Yes	
Remote_Call_Interface	No	Distributed systems
Remote_Types	No	Distributed systems
Restrictions	Yes	
Reviewable	Yes	
Shared_Passive	No	Distributed systems
Storage_Size	Yes/No	tasks, not access types
Suppress	Yes	
Task_Dispatching_Policy	No	Ravenscar
Unchecked_Union	Yes	
Unsuppress	Yes	
Volatile	Yes	
Volatile_Components	Yes	

16.2 SPARK 2014 Language-Defined Pragmas

The following SPARK 2014 language-defined pragmas are defined:

Pragma	Allowed in SPARK 2014	Comment
Abstract_State	Yes	
Assert_And_Cut	Yes	
Assume	Yes	
Async_Readers	Yes	
Async_Writers	Yes	
Constant_After_Elaboration	Yes	
Contract_Cases	Yes	
Default_Initial_Condition	Yes	
Depends	Yes	
Effective_Reads	Yes	
Effective_Writes	Yes	
Extensions_Visible	Yes	
Ghost	Yes	
Global	Yes	
Initial_Condition	Yes	
Initializes	Yes	
Loop_Invariant	Yes	
Loop_Variant	Yes	
Part_Of	Yes	
Post	Yes	
Pre	Yes	
Refined_Depends	Yes	
Refined_Global	Yes	
Refined_Post	Yes	
Refined_State	Yes	
SPARK_Mode	Yes	Language defined but implementation dependent
Volatile_Function	Yes	

16.3 GNAT Implementation-Defined Pragmas

The following GNAT implementation-defined pragmas are permitted in SPARK 2014:

Pragma	Allowed in SPARK 2014	Comment
Ada_83	Yes	
Ada_95	Yes	
Ada_05	Yes	
Ada_2005	Yes	
Ada_12	Yes	
Ada_2012	Yes	
Annotate	Yes	
Check	Yes	
Check_Policy	Yes	
Debug	Yes	Ignored (replaced by null statement)
Default_Scalar_Storage_Order	Yes	
Inline_Always	Yes	
Linker_Section	Yes	
Max_Queue_Length	Yes	Extended Ravenscar
No_Elaboration_Code_All	Yes	
No_Heap_Finalization	Yes	
Overflow_Mode	Yes	
Predicate_Failure	Yes	
Pure_Function	Yes	
Restriction_Warnings	Yes	
Secondary_Stack_Size	Yes	
Style_Checks	Yes	
Test_Case	Yes	
Unmodified	Yes	
Unreferenced	Yes	
Unused	Yes	
Validity_Checks	Yes	
Warnings	Yes	
Weak_External	Yes	

GLOSSARY

The SPARK 2014 Reference Manual uses a number of technical terms to describe its features and rules. Some of these terms are well known others are less well known or have been defined within this document. In the glossary given here the less well known terms and those defined by SPARK 2014 are listed with a brief explanation to their meaning.

- Data-Flow analysis is the process of collecting information about the way the variables are used and defined in the program. In particular, in SPARK 2014 it is used to detect the use of uninitialized variables and state abstractions.

- Executable semantics

- Flow analysis is a term used to cover both data-flow and information-flow analysis.

- Formal Analysis is a term used to cover flow analysis and formal verification.

- Formal Verification, in the context of hardware and software systems, is the act of proving or disproving the correctness of intended algorithms underlying a system with respect to a certain formal specification or property, using formal methods of mathematics. In SPARK 2014 this entails proving the implementation of a subprogram against its specification given its precondition using an automatic theorem prover (which may be part of the SPARK 2014 toolset. The specification may be given by a postcondition or assertions or may be implicit from the definition of Ada when proving absence of run-time exceptions (robustness property).

- Formal verification of functional properties is the proof that an implementation meets its specification given as an assertion expression such as a postcondition.

- Formal verification of robustness properties, in Ada terminology, is the proof that certain predefined checks such as the ones that raise Constraint_Error will never fail at run-time.

- Information-Flow analysis in an information theoretical context is the transfer of information from a variable x to a variable y in a given process, that is x depends on y. Not all flows may be desirable. For example, a system shouldn't leak any secret (partially or not) to public observers. In SPARK 2014 information-flow analysi is used to detect ineffective statements and check that the implementation of a subprogram satisfies its Global aspect and Depends aspect (if it is present). It may also be used for security analysis in SPARK 2014.

- Refinement

- State abstraction

SPARK 2005 TO SPARK 2014 MAPPING SPECIFICATION

This appendix defines the mapping between SPARK 2005 and SPARK 2014. It is intended as both a completeness check for the SPARK 2014 language design, and as a guide for projects upgrading from SPARK 2005 to SPARK 2014.

A.1 SPARK 2005 Features and SPARK 2014 Alternatives

Nearly every SPARK 2005 feature has a SPARK 2014 equivalent or there is an alternative way of providing the same feature in SPARK 2014. The only SPARK 2005 (not including RavenSPARK) features that do not have a direct alternative are:

- the 'Always_Valid attribute;

- the ability to add pre and postconditions to an instantiation of a generic subprogram, e.g., Unchecked_Conversion; and

- a precondition on the body of a subprogram refining the one on the specification - this is not usually required in SPARK 2014, it is normally replaced by the use of expression functions.

At the moment the first two features have to be accomplished using pragma Assume.

The following subsections of this appendix demonstrate how many SPARK 2005 idioms map into SPARK 2014. As a quick reference the table below shows, for each SPARK 2005 annotation or SPARK 2005 specific feature, a reference to the equivalent or alternative in SPARK 2014. In the table headings 2014 RM is the SPARK 2014 Reference Manual and Mapping is this appendix, the SPARK 2005 to SPARK 2014 mapping specification.

SPARK 2005	SPARK 2014	2014 RM	Mapping
~ in post	'Old attribute - see Ada RM 6.1.1		A.2.2
~ in body	'Loop_Entry attribute	5.5.3	A.7
<->	=		
A -> B	(if A then B) - see Ada RM 4.5.7		A.2.2
%	not needed		A.7
always_valid	not supported		A.4.1
assert	pragma Assert_And_Cut	5.9	A.4.2
assert in loop	pragma Loop_Invariant	5.5.3	A.4.1
assume	pragma Assume	5.9	A.4.1
check	pragma Assert - see Ada RM 11.4.2		A.4.1
derives on spec	Depends aspect	6.1.5	A.2.1
derives on body	No separate spec - Depends aspect		
derives on body	Separate spec - Refined_Depends aspect	7.2.5	A.3.2
for all	quantified_expression - see Ada RM 4.5.8		A.2.3
for some	quantified_expression - See Ada RM 4.5.8		A.4.1
	Continued on next page		

SPARK 2005	SPARK 2014	2014 RM	Mapping
global on spec	Global aspect	6.1.4	A.2.1
global on body	No separate spec - Global aspect		
global on body	Separate spec - Refined_Global aspect	7.2.4	A.2.4
hide	pragma SPARK_Mode - see User Guide		
inherit	not needed		A.3.4
initializes	Initializes aspect	7.1.5	A.2.4
main_program	not needed		
object assertions	rule declarations are not needed		A.5.3
own on spec	Abstract_State aspect	7.1.4	A.3.2
own on body	Refined_State aspect	7.2.2	A.3.2
post on spec	postcondition - see Ada RM 6.1.1	6.1.1	A.2.2
post on body	No separate spec - postcondition		
post on body	Separate spec - Refined_Post aspect	7.2.7	
pre	precondition - see Ada RM 6.1.1	6.1.1	
proof functions	Ghost functions	6.9	A.5.3
proof types	Ada types		A.5.5
return	'Result attribute - see Ada RM 6.1.1		A.2.2
update	'Update attribute	4.4.1	A.6

A.2 Subprogram patterns

A.2.1 Global and Derives

This example demonstrates how global variables can be accessed through procedures/functions and presents how the SPARK 2005 *derives* annotation maps over to *depends* in SPARK 2014. The example consists of one procedure (*Swap*) and one function (*Add*). *Swap* accesses two global variables and swaps their contents while *Add* returns their sum.

Specification in SPARK 2005:

```
1   package Swap_Add_05
2   --# own X, Y: Integer;
3   is
4      X, Y: Integer;
5
6      procedure Swap;
7      --# global in out X, Y;
8      --# derives X from Y &
9      --#         Y from X;
10
11     function Add return Integer;
12     --# global in X, Y;
13
14  end Swap_Add_05;
```

body in SPARK 2005:

```
1   package body Swap_Add_05
2   is
3      procedure Swap
4      is
```

```
5        Temporary: Integer;
6     begin
7        Temporary := X;
8        X          := Y;
9        Y          := Temporary;
10    end Swap;
11
12    function Add return Integer
13    is
14    begin
15       return X + Y;
16    end Add;
17
18 end Swap_Add_05;
```

Specification in SPARK 2014:

```
1  package Swap_Add_14
2    with SPARK_Mode
3  is
4    -- Visible variables are not state abstractions.
5    X, Y: Integer;
6
7    procedure Swap
8      with Global  => (In_Out => (X, Y)),
9           Depends => (X => Y,    -- to be read as "X depends on Y"
10                      Y => X);   -- to be read as "Y depends on X"
11
12   function Add return Integer
13     with Global  => (Input => (X, Y));
14 end Swap_Add_14;
```

Body in SPARK 2014:

```
1  package body Swap_Add_14
2    with SPARK_Mode
3  is
4    procedure Swap is
5       Temporary: Integer;
6    begin
7       Temporary := X;
8       X          := Y;
9       Y          := Temporary;
10    end Swap;
11
12   function Add return Integer is (X + Y);
13 end Swap_Add_14;
```

A.2.2 Pre/Post/Return contracts

This example demonstrates how the *Pre/Post/Return* contracts are restructured and how they map from SPARK 2005 to SPARK 2014. Procedure *Swap* and function *Add* perform the same task as in the previous example, but the global variables have been replaced by parameters (this is not necessarry for proof) and they have been augmented by pre and post annotations. Two additional functions (*Max* and *Divide*) and one additional procedure (*Swap_Array_Elements*) have also been included in this example in order to demonstrate further features. *Max* returns the maximum of the two parameters. *Divide* returns the division of the two parameters after having ensured that the divisor is not equal to zero. The *Swap_Array_Elements* procedure swaps the contents of two elements of an array.

Specification in SPARK 2005:

```
1   package Swap_Add_Max_05 is
2
3      subtype Index      is Integer range 1..100;
4      type    Array_Type is array (Index) of Integer;
5
6      procedure Swap (X , Y : in out Integer);
7      --# post X = Y~ and Y = X~;
8
9      function Add (X, Y : Integer) return Integer;
10     --# pre ((X >= 0 and Y >= 0) -> (X + Y <= Integer'Last)) and
11     --#     ((X <  0 and Y <  0) -> (X + Y >= Integer'First));
12     --# return X + Y;
13
14     function Max (X, Y : Integer) return Integer;
15     --# return Z => (X >= Y -> Z = X) and
16     --#             (Y >  X -> Z = Y);
17
18     function Divide (X , Y : Integer) return Integer;
19     --# pre Y /= 0 and X > Integer'First;
20     --# return X / Y;
21
22     procedure Swap_Array_Elements(I, J : Index; A: in out Array_Type);
23     --# post A = A~[I => A~(J); J => A~(I)];
24
25  end Swap_Add_Max_05;
```

Body in SPARK 2005:

```
1   package body Swap_Add_Max_05
2   is
3      procedure Swap (X, Y: in out Integer)
4      is
5         Temporary: Integer;
6      begin
7         Temporary := X;
8         X         := Y;
9         Y         := Temporary;
10     end Swap;
11
12     function Add (X, Y : Integer) return Integer
13     is
14     begin
15        return X + Y;
16     end Add;
17
18     function Max (X, Y : Integer) return Integer
19     is
20        Result: Integer;
21     begin
22        if X >= Y then
23           Result := X;
24        else
25           Result := Y;
26        end if;
```

```
27      return Result;
28   end Max;
29
30   function Divide (X, Y : Integer) return Integer
31   is
32   begin
33      return X / Y;
34   end Divide;
35
36   procedure Swap_Array_Elements(I, J : Index; A: in out Array_Type)
37   is
38      Temporary: Integer;
39   begin
40      Temporary := A(I);
41      A(I)      := A(J);
42      A(J)      := Temporary;
43   end Swap_Array_Elements;
44
45 end Swap_Add_Max_05;
```

Specification in SPARK 2014:

```
1  package Swap_Add_Max_14
2    with SPARK_Mode
3  is
4     subtype Index      is Integer range 1..100;
5     type    Array_Type is array (Index) of Integer;
6
7     procedure Swap (X, Y : in out Integer)
8       with Post => (X = Y'Old and Y = X'Old);
9
10    function Add (X, Y : Integer) return Integer
11      with Pre  => (if X >= 0 and Y >= 0 then X <= Integer'Last - Y
12                    elsif X < 0 and Y < 0 then X >= Integer'First - Y),
13           -- The precondition may be written as X + Y in Integer if
14           -- an extended arithmetic mode is selected
15           Post => Add'Result = X + Y;
16
17    function Max (X, Y : Integer) return Integer
18      with Post => Max'Result = (if X >= Y then X else Y);
19
20    function Divide (X, Y : Integer) return Integer
21      with Pre  => Y /= 0 and X > Integer'First,
22           Post => Divide'Result = X / Y;
23
24    procedure Swap_Array_Elements(I, J : Index; A: in out Array_Type)
25      with Post => A = A'Old'Update (I => A'Old (J),
26                                     J => A'Old (I));
27 end Swap_Add_Max_14;
```

Body in SPARK 2014:

```
1  package body Swap_Add_Max_14
2    with SPARK_Mode
3  is
4     procedure Swap (X, Y : in out Integer) is
5        Temporary: Integer;
6     begin
```

```
7      Temporary := X;
8      X        := Y;
9      Y        := Temporary;
10  end Swap;
11
12  function Add (X, Y : Integer) return Integer is (X + Y);
13
14  function Max (X, Y : Integer) return Integer is
15    (if X >= Y then X
16     else Y);
17
18  function Divide (X, Y : Integer) return Integer is (X / Y);
19
20  procedure Swap_Array_Elements(I, J : Index; A: in out Array_Type) is
21     Temporary: Integer;
22  begin
23     Temporary := A(I);
24     A(I)      := A(J);
25     A(J)      := Temporary;
26  end Swap_Array_Elements;
27 end Swap_Add_Max_14;
```

A.2.3 Attributes of unconstrained out parameter in precondition

The following example illustrates the fact that the attributes of an unconstrained formal array parameter of mode "out" are permitted to appear in a precondition. The flow analyzer also needs to be smart about this, since it knows that X'First and X'Last are well-defined in the body, even though the content of X is not.

Specification in SPARK 2005:

```
1  package P
2  is
3     type A is array (Positive range <>) of Integer;
4
5     -- Shows that X'First and X'Last _can_ be used in
6     -- precondition here, even though X is mode "out"...
7     procedure Init (X : out A);
8     --# pre X'First = 1  and
9     --#     X'Last  >= 20;
10    --# post for all I in Positive range X'Range =>
11    --#        ((I /= 20 -> (X (I) = 0)) and
12    --#         (I = 1 -> (X (I) = X'Last)) and
13    --#         (I = 20 -> (X (I) = -1)));
14
15 end P;
```

Body in SPARK 2005:

```
1  package body P is
2
3     procedure Init (X : out A) is
4     begin
5        X := (others => 0);
6        X (1) := X'Last;
7        X (20) := -1;
8     end Init;
```

```
 9
10   end P;
```

Specification in SPARK 2014:

```
 1   package P
 2     with SPARK_Mode
 3   is
 4      type A is array (Positive range <>) of Integer;
 5
 6      -- Shows that X'First, X'Last and X'Length _can_ be used
 7      -- in precondition here, even though X is mode "out"...
 8      procedure Init (X : out A)
 9        with Pre  => X'First = 1 and X'Last >= 20,
10             Post => (for all I in X'Range =>
11                        (if I = 1 then X (I) = X'Last
12                         elsif I = 20 then X (I) = -1
13                         else X (I) = 0));
14   end P;
```

Body in SPARK 2014:

```
 1   package body P
 2     with SPARK_Mode
 3   is
 4      procedure Init (X : out A) is
 5      begin
 6         X := (1 => X'Last, 20 => -1, others => 0);
 7      end Init;
 8   end P;
```

A.2.4 Data Abstraction, Refinement and Initialization

This example demonstrates data abstraction and refinement. It also shows how abstract data is shown to be initialized during package elaboration (it need not be - it could be initialized through an explicit subprogram call, in which case the Initalizes annotation should not be given). There is also a demonstration of how procedures and functions can be nested within other procedures and functions. Furthermore, it illustrates how global variable refinement can be performed.

Specification in SPARK 2005:

```
 1   package Nesting_Refinement_05
 2   --# own State;
 3   --# initializes State;
 4   is
 5      procedure Operate_On_State;
 6      --# global in out State;
 7   end Nesting_Refinement_05;
```

Body in SPARK 2005:

```
 1   package body Nesting_Refinement_05
 2   --# own State is X, Y;        -- Refined State
 3   is
 4      X, Y: Integer;
 5
```

```
6     procedure Operate_On_State
7     --# global in out X;      -- Refined Global
8     --#           out Y;
9     is
10        Z: Integer;
11
12        procedure Add_Z_To_X
13        --# global in out X;
14        --#           in     Z;
15        is
16        begin
17           X := X + Z;
18        end Add_Z_To_X;
19
20        procedure Overwrite_Y_With_Z
21        --# global    out Y;
22        --#           in     Z;
23        is
24        begin
25           Y := Z;
26        end Overwrite_Y_With_Z;
27     begin
28        Z := 5;
29        Add_Z_To_X;
30        Overwrite_Y_With_Z;
31     end Operate_On_State;
32
33  begin -- Promised to initialize State
34        -- (which consists of X and Y)
35     X := 10;
36     Y := 20;
37  end Nesting_Refinement_05;
```

Specification in **SPARK 2014**:

```
1  package Nesting_Refinement_14
2    with SPARK_Mode,
3         Abstract_State => State,
4         Initializes    => State
5  is
6     procedure Operate_On_State
7        with Global   => (In_Out => State);
8  end Nesting_Refinement_14;
```

Body in **SPARK 2014**:

```
1  package body Nesting_Refinement_14
2    -- State is refined onto two concrete variables X and Y
3    with SPARK_Mode,
4         Refined_State => (State => (X, Y))
5  is
6     X, Y: Integer;
7
8     procedure Operate_On_State
9        with Refined_Global => (In_Out => X,
10                                Output => Y)
11     is
12        Z: Integer;
```

```
13
14    procedure Add_Z_To_X
15      with Global => (In_Out => X,
16                      Input  => Z)
17    is
18    begin
19       X := X + Z;
20    end Add_Z_To_X;
21
22    procedure Overwrite_Y_With_Z
23      with Global => (Output => Y,
24                      Input  => Z)
25    is
26    begin
27       Y := Z;
28    end Overwrite_Y_With_Z;
29 begin
30    Z := 5;
31    Add_Z_To_X;
32    Overwrite_Y_With_Z;
33 end Operate_On_State;
34
35 begin
36    -- Promised to initialize State
37    -- (which consists of X and Y)
38    X := 10;
39    Y := 20;
40 end Nesting_Refinement_14;
```

A.3 Package patterns

A.3.1 Abstract Data Types (ADTs)

Visible type

The following example adds no mapping information. The SPARK 2005 and SPARK 2014 versions of the code are identical. Only the specification of the SPARK 2005 code will be presented. The reason why this code is being provided is to allow for a comparison between a package that is purely public and an equivalent one that also has private elements.

Specification in SPARK 2005:

```
1 package Stacks_05 is
2    Stack_Size : constant := 100;
3    type Pointer_Range is range 0 .. Stack_Size;
4    subtype Index_Range is Pointer_Range range 1 .. Stack_Size;
5    type Vector is array(Index_Range) of Integer;
6
7    type Stack is
8      record
9         Stack_Vector : Vector;
10        Stack_Pointer : Pointer_Range;
11     end record;
12
13    function Is_Empty(S : Stack) return Boolean;
```

```
14      function Is_Full(S : Stack) return Boolean;
15
16      procedure Clear(S : out Stack);
17      procedure Push(S : in out Stack; X : in Integer);
18      procedure Pop(S : in out Stack; X : out Integer);
19   end Stacks_05;
```

Private type

Similarly to the previous example, this one does not contain any annotations either. Due to this, the SPARK 2005 and SPARK 2014 versions are exactly the same. Only the specification of the 2005 version shall be presented.

Specification in SPARK 2005:

```
1   package Stacks_05 is
2
3      type Stack is private;
4
5      function Is_Empty(S : Stack) return Boolean;
6      function Is_Full(S : Stack) return Boolean;
7
8      procedure Clear(S : out Stack);
9      procedure Push(S : in out Stack; X : in Integer);
10     procedure Pop(S : in out Stack; X : out Integer);
11
12  private
13     Stack_Size : constant := 100;
14     type Pointer_Range is range 0 .. Stack_Size;
15     subtype Index_Range is Pointer_Range range 1 .. Stack_Size;
16     type Vector is array(Index_Range) of Integer;
17
18     type Stack is
19        record
20           Stack_Vector : Vector;
21           Stack_Pointer : Pointer_Range;
22        end record;
23   end Stacks_05;
```

Private type with pre/post contracts

This example demonstrates how *pre* and *post* conditions of subprograms may be specified in terms of functions declared in the same package specification. The function declarations are completed in the body and the postconditions of the completed functions are used to prove the implementations of the other subprograms. In SPARK 2014 explicit postconditions do not have to be specified on the bodies of the functions as they are implemented as expression functions and the expression, E, of the function acts as a default refined postcondition, i.e., F'Result = E. Note that the SPARK 2014 version is proven entirely automatically whereas the SPARK 2005 version requires user defined proof rules.

Specification in SPARK 2005:

```
1   package Stacks_05
2   is
3
4      type Stack is private;
5
```

```
6      function Is_Empty(S : Stack) return Boolean;
7      function Is_Full(S : Stack) return Boolean;
8
9      procedure Clear(S : in out Stack);
10     --# post Is_Empty(S);
11     procedure Push(S : in out Stack; X : in Integer);
12     --# pre  not Is_Full(S);
13     --# post not Is_Empty(S);
14     procedure Pop(S : in out Stack; X : out Integer);
15     --# pre  not Is_Empty(S);
16     --# post not Is_Full(S);
17
18  private
19     Stack_Size : constant := 100;
20     type    Pointer_Range is range 0 .. Stack_Size;
21     subtype Index_Range   is Pointer_Range range 1 .. Stack_Size;
22     type    Vector        is array(Index_Range) of Integer;
23
24     type Stack is
25        record
26           Stack_Vector  : Vector;
27           Stack_Pointer : Pointer_Range;
28        end record;
29  end Stacks_05;
```

Body in SPARK 2005:

```
1   package body Stacks_05 is
2
3      function Is_Empty (S : Stack) return Boolean
4      --# return S.Stack_Pointer = 0;
5      is
6      begin
7         return S.Stack_Pointer = 0;
8      end Is_Empty;
9
10     function Is_Full (S : Stack) return Boolean
11     --# return S.Stack_Pointer = Stack_Size;
12     is
13     begin
14        return S.Stack_Pointer = Stack_Size;
15     end Is_Full;
16
17     procedure Clear (S : in out Stack)
18     --# post Is_Empty(S);
19     is
20     begin
21        S.Stack_Pointer := 0;
22     end Clear;
23
24     procedure Push (S : in out Stack; X : in Integer)
25     is
26     begin
27        S.Stack_Pointer := S.Stack_Pointer + 1;
28        S.Stack_Vector (S.Stack_Pointer) := X;
29     end Push;
30
31     procedure Pop (S : in out Stack; X : out Integer)
```

```
32     is
33     begin
34        X := S.Stack_Vector (S.Stack_Pointer);
35        S.Stack_Pointer := S.Stack_Pointer - 1;
36     end Pop;
37  end Stacks_05;
```

Specification in SPARK 2014:

```
1   package Stacks_14
2     with SPARK_Mode
3   is
4      type Stack is private;
5
6      function Is_Empty(S : Stack) return Boolean;
7      function Is_Full(S : Stack) return Boolean;
8
9      procedure Clear(S : in out Stack)
10       with Post => Is_Empty(S);
11
12     procedure Push(S : in out Stack; X : in Integer)
13       with Pre  => not Is_Full(S),
14            Post => not Is_Empty(S);
15
16     procedure Pop(S : in out Stack; X : out Integer)
17       with Pre  => not Is_Empty(S),
18            Post => not Is_Full(S);
19
20  private
21     Stack_Size : constant := 100;
22     type     Pointer_Range is range 0 .. Stack_Size;
23     subtype Index_Range   is Pointer_Range range 1 .. Stack_Size;
24     type     Vector        is array(Index_Range) of Integer;
25
26     type Stack is record
27        Stack_Vector  : Vector;
28        Stack_Pointer : Pointer_Range;
29     end record;
30  end Stacks_14;
```

Body in SPARK 2014:

```
1   package body Stacks_14
2     with SPARK_Mode
3   is
4      -- Expression function has default refined postcondition of
5      -- Is_Empty'Result = (S.Stack_Pointer = 0)
6      function Is_Empty(S : Stack) return Boolean is (S.Stack_Pointer = 0);
7
8      -- Expression function has default refined postcondition of
9      -- Is_Empty'Result = (S.Stack_Pointer = Stack_Size)
10     function Is_Full(S : Stack) return Boolean is (S.Stack_Pointer = Stack_Size);
11
12     procedure Clear(S : in out Stack) is
13     begin
14        S.Stack_Pointer := 0;
15     end Clear;
16
```

```
17    procedure Push(S : in out Stack; X : in Integer) is
18    begin
19       S.Stack_Pointer := S.Stack_Pointer + 1;
20       S.Stack_Vector(S.Stack_Pointer) := X;
21    end Push;
22
23    procedure Pop(S : in out Stack; X : out Integer) is
24    begin
25       X := S.Stack_Vector(S.Stack_Pointer);
26       S.Stack_Pointer := S.Stack_Pointer - 1;
27    end Pop;
28 end Stacks_14;
```

Private/Public child visibility

The following example demonstrates visibility rules that apply between public children, private children and their parent in SPARK 2005. More specifically, it shows that:

- Private children are able to see their private siblings but not their public siblings.

- Public children are able to see their public siblings but not their private siblings.

- All children have access to their parent but the parent can only access private children.

Applying the SPARK tools on the following files will produce certain errors. This was intentionally done in order to illustrate both legal and illegal access attempts.

SPARK 2014 shares Ada2012's visibility rules. No restrictions have been applied in terms of visibility. Note that SPARK 2014 code does not require Inherit annotations.

Specification of parent in SPARK 2005:

```
1 package Parent_05
2 is
3    function F (X : Integer) return Integer;
4    function G (X : Integer) return Integer;
5 end Parent_05;
```

Specification of private child A in SPARK 2005:

```
1 --#inherit Parent_05; -- OK
2 private package Parent_05.Private_Child_A_05
3 is
4    function F (X : Integer) return Integer;
5 end Parent_05.Private_Child_A_05;
```

Specification of private child B in SPARK 2005:

```
1 --#inherit Parent_05.Private_Child_A_05, -- OK
2 --#          Parent_05.Public_Child_A_05;  -- error, public sibling
3 private package Parent_05.Private_Child_B_05
4 is
5    function H (X : Integer) return Integer;
6 end Parent_05.Private_Child_B_05;
```

Specification of public child A in SPARK 2005:

```
1  --#inherit Parent_05,                        -- OK
2  --#          Parent_05.Private_Child_A_05;  -- error, private sibling
3  package Parent_05.Public_Child_A_05
4  is
5     function G (X : Integer) return Integer;
6  end Parent_05.Public_Child_A_05;
```

Specification of public child B in SPARK 2005:

```
1  --#inherit Parent_05.Public_Child_A_05; -- OK
2  package Parent_05.Public_Child_B_05
3  is
4     function H (X : Integer) return Integer;
5  end Parent_05.Public_Child_B_05;
```

Body of parent in SPARK 2005:

```
1  with Parent_05.Private_Child_A_05,      -- OK
2       Parent_05.Public_Child_A_05;       -- error, public children not visible
3  package body Parent_05
4  is
5     function F (X : Integer) return Integer is
6     begin
7        return Private_Child_A_05.F (X);
8     end F;
9
10    function G (X : Integer) return Integer is
11    begin
12       return Public_Child_A_05.G (X);
13    end G;
14
15 end Parent_05;
```

Body of public child A in SPARK 2005:

```
1  package body Parent_05.Public_Child_A_05
2  is
3     function G (X : Integer) return Integer is
4        Result : Integer;
5     begin
6        if X <= 0 then
7           Result := 0;
8        else
9           Result := Parent_05.F (X);   -- OK
10       end if;
11       return Result;
12    end G;
13 end Parent_05.Public_Child_A_05;
```

Body of public child B in SPARK 2005:

```
1  with Parent_05.Private_Child_B_05;
2  package body Parent_05.Public_Child_B_05
3  is
4     function H (X : Integer) return Integer is
5     begin
6        return Parent_05.Private_Child_B_05.H (X);
```

```
7         end H;
8     end Parent_05.Public_Child_B_05;
```

Body of private child B in SPARK 2005:

```
1     package body Parent_05.Private_Child_B_05
2     is
3        function H (X : Integer) return Integer is
4           Result : Integer;
5        begin
6           if X <= 10 then
7              Result := 10;
8           else
9              Result := Parent_05.F (X);   -- Illegal in SPARK 2005
10          end if;
11          return Result;
12       end H;
13    end Parent_05.Private_Child_B_05;
```

Specification of parent in SPARK 2014:

```
1     package Parent_14
2       with SPARK_Mode
3     is
4        function F (X : Integer) return Integer;
5        function G (X : Integer) return Integer;
6     end Parent_14;
```

Specification of private child A in SPARK 2014:

```
1     private package Parent_14.Private_Child_A_14
2       with SPARK_Mode
3     is
4        function F (X : Integer) return Integer;
5     end Parent_14.Private_Child_A_14;
```

Specification of private child B in SPARK 2014:

```
1     private package Parent_14.Private_Child_B_14
2       with SPARK_Mode
3     is
4        function H (X : Integer) return Integer;
5     end Parent_14.Private_Child_B_14;
```

Specification of public child A in SPARK 2014:

```
1     package Parent_14.Public_Child_A_14
2       with SPARK_Mode
3     is
4        function G (X : Integer) return Integer;
5     end Parent_14.Public_Child_A_14;
```

Specification of public child B in SPARK 2014:

```
1     package Parent_14.Public_Child_B_14
2       with SPARK_Mode
3     is
```

```
4      function H (X : Integer) return Integer;
5   end Parent_14.Public_Child_B_14;
```

Body of parent in SPARK 2014:

```
1   with Parent_14.Private_Child_A_14,    -- OK
2       Parent_14.Public_Child_A_14;     -- OK
3
4   package body Parent_14
5     with SPARK_Mode
6   is
7      function F (X : Integer) return Integer is (Private_Child_A_14.F (X));
8
9      function G (X : Integer) return Integer is (Public_Child_A_14.G (X));
10  end Parent_14;
```

Body of public child A in SPARK 2014:

```
1   package body Parent_14.Public_Child_A_14
2     with SPARK_Mode
3   is
4      function G (X : Integer) return Integer is
5        (if X <= 0 then 0
6         else Parent_14.F (X));   -- OK
7   end Parent_14.Public_Child_A_14;
```

Body of public child B in SPARK 2014:

```
1   with Parent_14.Private_Child_B_14;
2
3   package body Parent_14.Public_Child_B_14
4     with SPARK_Mode
5   is
6      function H (X : Integer) return Integer is
7        (Parent_14.Private_Child_B_14.H (X));
8   end Parent_14.Public_Child_B_14;
```

Body of private child B in SPARK 2014:

```
1   package body Parent_14.Private_Child_B_14
2     with SPARK_Mode
3   is
4      function H (X : Integer) return Integer is
5        (if X <= 10 then 10
6         else Parent_14.F (X));   -- Legal in SPARK 2014
7   end Parent_14.Private_Child_B_14;
```

A.3.2 Abstract State Machines (ASMs)

Visible, concrete state

Initialized by declaration

The example that follows presents a way in SPARK 2005 of initializing a concrete own variable (a state that is not refined) at the point of the declaration of the variables that compose it. Generally it is not good practice to declare several concrete own variables, data abstraction should be used but here we are doing it for the point of illustration.

In SPARK 2014 the client's view of package state is either visible (declared in the visible part of the package) or a state abstraction representing hidden state. A variable cannot overload the name of a state abstraction and therefore a state abstraction must be completed by a refinement given in the body of the package - there is no concept of a concrete state abstraction. The constituents of a state abstraction may be initialized at their declaration.

Specification in SPARK 2005:

```
1  package Stack_05
2  --# own S, Pointer;       -- concrete state
3  --# initializes S, Pointer;
4  is
5     procedure Push(X : in Integer);
6     --# global in out S, Pointer;
7
8     procedure Pop(X : out Integer);
9     --# global in S; in out Pointer;
10 end Stack_05;
```

Body in SPARK 2005:

```
1  package body Stack_05
2  is
3     Stack_Size : constant := 100;
4     type    Pointer_Range is range 0 .. Stack_Size;
5     subtype Index_Range   is Pointer_Range range 1..Stack_Size;
6     type    Vector        is array(Index_Range) of Integer;
7
8     S : Vector := Vector'(Index_Range => 0);   -- Initialization of S
9     Pointer : Pointer_Range := 0;               -- Initialization of Pointer
10
11    procedure Push(X : in Integer)
12    is
13    begin
14       Pointer := Pointer + 1;
15       S(Pointer) := X;
16    end Push;
17
18    procedure Pop(X : out Integer)
19    is
20    begin
21       X := S(Pointer);
22       Pointer := Pointer - 1;
23    end Pop;
24
25 end Stack_05;
```

Specification in SPARK 2014:

```
1  package Stack_14
2    with SPARK_Mode,
3         Abstract_State => (S_State, Pointer_State),
4         Initializes    => (S_State, Pointer_State)
5  is
6     procedure Push(X : in Integer)
7       with Global => (In_Out => (S_State, Pointer_State));
8
9     procedure Pop(X : out Integer)
```

```
10      with Global => (Input   => S_State,
11                      In_Out => Pointer_State);
12   end Stack_14;
```

Body in SPARK 2014:

```
1    package body Stack_14
2      with SPARK_Mode,
3          Refined_State => (S_State       => S,
4                            Pointer_State => Pointer)
5    is
6       Stack_Size : constant := 100;
7       type    Pointer_Range is range 0 .. Stack_Size;
8       subtype Index_Range   is Pointer_Range range 1..Stack_Size;
9       type    Vector        is array(Index_Range) of Integer;
10
11      S : Vector := Vector'(Index_Range => 0);   -- Initialization of S
12      Pointer : Pointer_Range := 0;               -- Initialization of Pointer
13
14      procedure Push (X : in Integer)
15        with Refined_Global => (In_Out => (S, Pointer))
16      is
17      begin
18         Pointer := Pointer + 1;
19         S (Pointer) := X;
20      end Push;
21
22      procedure Pop(X : out Integer)
23        with Refined_Global => (Input  => S,
24                                In_Out => Pointer)
25      is
26      begin
27         X := S (Pointer);
28         Pointer := Pointer - 1;
29      end Pop;
30   end Stack_14;
```

Initialized by elaboration

The following example presents how a package's concrete state can be initialized at the statements section of the body. The specifications of both SPARK 2005 and SPARK 2014 are not presented since they are identical to the specifications of the previous example.

Body in SPARK 2005:

```
1    package body Stack_05
2    is
3       Stack_Size : constant := 100;
4       type    Pointer_Range is range 0 .. Stack_Size;
5       subtype Index_Range   is Pointer_Range range 1..Stack_Size;
6       type    Vector        is array(Index_Range) of Integer;
7
8       S : Vector;
9       Pointer : Pointer_Range;
10
11      procedure Push(X : in Integer)
```

```
12    is
13    begin
14       Pointer := Pointer + 1;
15       S(Pointer) := X;
16    end Push;
17
18    procedure Pop(X : out Integer)
19    is
20    begin
21       X := S(Pointer);
22       Pointer := Pointer - 1;
23    end Pop;
24
25 begin  -- initialization
26    Pointer := 0;
27    S := Vector'(Index_Range => 0);
28 end Stack_05;
```

Body in SPARK 2014:

```
1  package body Stack_14
2    with SPARK_Mode,
3         Refined_State => (S_State       => S,
4                           Pointer_State => Pointer)
5  is
6     Stack_Size : constant := 100;
7     type    Pointer_Range is range 0 .. Stack_Size;
8     subtype Index_Range   is Pointer_Range range 1..Stack_Size;
9     type    Vector        is array(Index_Range) of Integer;
10
11    S : Vector;
12    Pointer : Pointer_Range;
13
14    procedure Push (X : in Integer)
15      with Refined_Global => (In_Out => (S, Pointer))
16    is
17    begin
18       Pointer := Pointer + 1;
19       S (Pointer) := X;
20    end Push;
21
22    procedure Pop(X : out Integer)
23      with Refined_Global => (Input  => S,
24                              In_Out => Pointer)
25    is
26    begin
27       X := S (Pointer);
28       Pointer := Pointer - 1;
29    end Pop;
30 begin
31    -- initialization
32    Pointer := 0;
33    S := Vector'(Index_Range => 0);
34 end Stack_14;
```

Private, concrete state

In SPARK 2005 variables declared in the private part of a package are considered to be concrete own variables. In SPARK 2014 they are hidden state and must be constituents of a state abstraction.

The SPARK 2005 body has not been included since it does not contain any annotations.

Specification in SPARK 2005:

```
1   package Stack_05
2   --# own S, Pointer;
3   is
4      procedure Push(X : in Integer);
5      --# global in out S, Pointer;
6
7      procedure Pop(X : out Integer);
8      --# global in      S;
9      --#        in out Pointer;
10  private
11     Stack_Size : constant := 100;
12     type    Pointer_Range is range 0 .. Stack_Size;
13     subtype Index_Range   is Pointer_Range range 1..Stack_Size;
14     type    Vector        is array(Index_Range) of Integer;
15
16     S : Vector;
17     Pointer : Pointer_Range;
18  end Stack_05;
```

Specification in SPARK 2014:

```
1   package Stack_14
2     with SPARK_Mode,
3          Abstract_State => (S_State, Pointer_State)
4   is
5      procedure Push(X : in Integer)
6        with Global => (In_Out => (S_State, Pointer_State));
7
8      procedure Pop(X : out Integer)
9        with Global => (Input  => S_State,
10                        In_Out => Pointer_State);
11
12  private
13     Stack_Size : constant := 100;
14     type    Pointer_Range is range 0 .. Stack_Size;
15     subtype Index_Range   is Pointer_Range range 1..Stack_Size;
16     type    Vector        is array(Index_Range) of Integer;
17
18     S       : Vector with Part_Of => S_State;
19     Pointer : Pointer_Range with Part_Of => Pointer_State;
20  end Stack_14;
```

Body in SPARK 2014:

```
1   package body Stack_14
2     with SPARK_Mode,
3          Refined_State => (S_State       => S,
4                            Pointer_State => Pointer)
5   is
6      procedure Push(X : in Integer)
```

```
7        with Refined_Global => (In_Out => (S, Pointer))
8     is
9     begin
10       Pointer := Pointer + 1;
11       S (Pointer) := X;
12    end Push;
13
14    procedure Pop (X : out Integer)
15       with Refined_Global => (Input  => S,
16                               In_Out => Pointer)
17    is
18    begin
19       X := S (Pointer);
20       Pointer := Pointer - 1;
21    end Pop;
22 end Stack_14;
```

Private, abstract state, refining onto concrete states in body

Initialized by procedure call

In this example, the abstract state declared at the specification is refined at the body. Procedure *Init* can be invoked by users of the package, in order to initialize the state.

Specification in **SPARK 2005**:

```
1  package Stack_05
2  --# own State;
3  is
4     procedure Push(X : in Integer);
5     --# global in out State;
6
7     procedure Pop(X : out Integer);
8     --# global in out State;
9
10    procedure Init;
11    --# global     out State;
12
13 end Stack_05;
```

Body in **SPARK 2005**:

```
1  package body Stack_05
2  --# own State is S, Pointer;
3  is
4     Stack_Size : constant := 100;
5     type    Pointer_Range is range 0 .. Stack_Size;
6     subtype Index_Range   is Pointer_Range range 1..Stack_Size;
7     type    Vector        is array(Index_Range) of Integer;
8
9     Pointer : Pointer_Range;
10    S       : Vector;
11
12    procedure Push(X : in Integer)
13    --# global in out Pointer, S;
14    is
```

```
15    begin
16        Pointer := Pointer + 1;
17        S(Pointer) := X;
18    end Push;
19
20    procedure Pop(X : out Integer)
21    --# global in      S;
22    --#          in out Pointer;
23    is
24    begin
25        X := S(Pointer);
26        Pointer := Pointer - 1;
27    end Pop;
28
29    procedure Init
30    --# global    out Pointer, S;
31    is
32    begin
33        Pointer := 0;
34        S := Vector'(Index_Range => 0);
35    end Init;
36 end Stack_05;
```

Specification in **SPARK 2014**:

```
1  package Stack_14
2    with SPARK_Mode,
3         Abstract_State => State
4  is
5     procedure Push(X : in Integer)
6        with Global => (In_Out => State);
7
8     procedure Pop(X : out Integer)
9        with Global => (In_Out => State);
10
11    procedure Init
12       with Global => (Output => State);
13 end Stack_14;
```

Body in **SPARK 2014**:

```
1  package body Stack_14
2    with SPARK_Mode,
3         Refined_State => (State => (Pointer, S))
4  is
5     Stack_Size : constant := 100;
6     type    Pointer_Range is range 0 .. Stack_Size;
7     subtype Index_Range   is Pointer_Range range 1..Stack_Size;
8     type    Vector        is array(Index_Range) of Integer;
9
10    Pointer : Pointer_Range;
11    S       : Vector;
12
13    procedure Push(X : in Integer)
14       with Refined_Global => (In_Out => (Pointer, S))
15    is
16    begin
17        Pointer := Pointer + 1;
```

```
18        S (Pointer) := X;
19     end Push;
20
21     procedure Pop (X : out Integer)
22        with Refined_Global => (In_Out => Pointer,
23                                 Input  => S)
24     is
25     begin
26        X := S (Pointer);
27        Pointer := Pointer - 1;
28     end Pop;
29
30     procedure Init
31        with Refined_Global => (Output => (Pointer, S))
32     is
33     begin
34        Pointer := 0;
35        S := (Index_Range => 0);
36     end Init;
37  end Stack_14;
```

Initialized by elaboration of declaration

The example that follows introduces an abstract state at the specification and refines it at the body. The constituents of the abstract state are initialized at declaration.

Specification in **SPARK 2005**:

```
1  package Stack_05
2  --# own State;
3  --# initializes State;
4  is
5     procedure Push(X : in Integer);
6     --# global in out State;
7
8     procedure Pop(X : out Integer);
9     --# global in out State;
10
11 end Stack_05;
```

Body in **SPARK 2005**:

```
1  package body Stack_05
2  --# own State is Pointer, S; -- refinement of state
3  is
4     Stack_Size : constant := 100;
5     type    Pointer_Range is range 0 .. Stack_Size;
6     subtype Index_Range   is Pointer_Range range 1..Stack_Size;
7     type    Vector        is array(Index_Range) of Integer;
8
9     S : Vector := Vector'(others => 0);
10    Pointer : Pointer_Range := 0;
11    -- initialization by elaboration of declaration
12
13    procedure Push(X : in Integer)
14    --# global in out Pointer, S;
```

```
15      is
16      begin
17          Pointer := Pointer + 1;
18          S(Pointer) := X;
19      end Push;
20
21      procedure Pop(X : out Integer)
22      --# global in      S;
23      --#          in out Pointer;
24      is
25      begin
26          X := S(Pointer);
27          Pointer := Pointer - 1;
28      end Pop;
29  end Stack_05;
```

Specification in **SPARK 2014**:

```
1   package Stack_14
2     with SPARK_Mode,
3          Abstract_State => State,
4          Initializes    => State
5   is
6     procedure Push(X : in Integer)
7       with Global => (In_Out => State);
8
9     procedure Pop(X : out Integer)
10      with Global => (In_Out => State);
11  end Stack_14;
```

Body in **SPARK 2014**:

```
1   package body Stack_14
2     with SPARK_Mode,
3          Refined_State => (State => (Pointer, S)) -- refinement of state
4   is
5     Stack_Size : constant := 100;
6     type    Pointer_Range is range 0 .. Stack_Size;
7     subtype Index_Range   is Pointer_Range range 1..Stack_Size;
8     type    Vector        is array(Index_Range) of Integer;
9
10    S : Vector := (others => 0);
11    Pointer : Pointer_Range := 0;
12    -- initialization by elaboration of declaration
13
14    procedure Push(X : in Integer)
15      with Refined_Global => (In_Out => (Pointer, S))
16    is
17    begin
18        Pointer := Pointer + 1;
19        S (Pointer) := X;
20    end Push;
21
22    procedure Pop(X : out Integer)
23      with Refined_Global => (In_Out => Pointer,
24                              Input  => S)
25    is
26    begin
```

```
27        X := S (Pointer);
28        Pointer := Pointer - 1;
29     end Pop;
30  end Stack_14;
```

Initialized by package body statements

This example introduces an abstract state at the specification and refines it at the body. The constituents of the abstract state are initialized at the statements part of the body. The specifications of the SPARK 2005 and SPARK 2014 versions of the code are as in the previous example and have thus not been included.

Body in SPARK 2005:

```
1   package body Stack_05
2   --# own State is Pointer, S;   -- refinement of state
3   is
4      Stack_Size : constant := 100;
5      type      Pointer_Range is range 0 .. Stack_Size;
6      subtype Index_Range    is Pointer_Range range 1..Stack_Size;
7      type      Vector          is array(Index_Range) of Integer;
8
9      S : Vector;
10     Pointer : Pointer_Range;
11
12     procedure Push(X : in Integer)
13     --# global in out Pointer, S;
14     is
15     begin
16        Pointer := Pointer + 1;
17        S(Pointer) := X;
18     end Push;
19
20     procedure Pop(X : out Integer)
21     --# global in out Pointer;
22     --#            in      S;
23     is
24     begin
25        X := S(Pointer);
26        Pointer := Pointer - 1;
27     end Pop;
28  begin  -- initialized by package body statements
29     Pointer := 0;
30     S := Vector'(Index_Range => 0);
31  end Stack_05;
```

Body in SPARK 2014:

```
1   package body Stack_14
2     with SPARK_Mode,
3          Refined_State => (State => (Pointer, S))   -- refinement of state
4   is
5      Stack_Size : constant := 100;
6      type      Pointer_Range is range 0 .. Stack_Size;
7      subtype Index_Range    is Pointer_Range range 1..Stack_Size;
8      type      Vector          is array(Index_Range) of Integer;
9
```

```
10    S        : Vector;
11    Pointer : Pointer_Range;
12
13    procedure Push(X : in Integer)
14      with Refined_Global => (In_Out => (Pointer, S))
15    is
16    begin
17        Pointer := Pointer + 1;
18        S (Pointer) := X;
19    end Push;
20
21    procedure Pop(X : out Integer)
22      with Refined_Global => (In_Out => Pointer,
23                              Input  => S)
24    is
25    begin
26        X := S (Pointer);
27        Pointer := Pointer - 1;
28    end Pop;
29 begin
30    -- initialized by package body statements
31    Pointer := 0;
32    S := (Index_Range => 0);
33 end Stack_14;
```

Initialized by mixture of declaration and statements

This example introduces an abstract state at the specification and refines it at the body. Some of the constituents of the abstract state are initialized during their declaration and the rest at the statements part of the body.

Specification in **SPARK 2005**:

```
1  package Stack_05
2  --# own Stack;
3  --# initializes Stack;
4  is
5     procedure Push(X : in Integer);
6     --# global in out Stack;
7
8     procedure Pop(X : out Integer);
9     --# global in out Stack;
10
11 end Stack_05;
```

Body in **SPARK 2005**:

```
1  package body Stack_05
2  --# own Stack is S, Pointer; -- state refinement
3  is
4     Stack_Size : constant := 100;
5     type    Pointer_Range is range 0 .. Stack_Size;
6     subtype Index_Range   is Pointer_Range range 1..Stack_Size;
7     type    Vector        is array(Index_Range) of Integer;
8     S : Vector;
9
10    Pointer : Pointer_Range := 0;
```

```
11     -- initialization by elaboration of declaration
12
13     procedure Push(X : in Integer)
14     --# global in out S, Pointer;
15     is
16     begin
17        Pointer := Pointer + 1;
18        S(Pointer) := X;
19     end Push;
20
21     procedure Pop(X : out Integer)
22     --# global in      S;
23     --#           in out Pointer;
24     is
25     begin
26        X := S(Pointer);
27        Pointer := Pointer - 1;
28     end Pop;
29  begin  -- initialization by body statements
30     S := Vector'(Index_Range => 0);
31  end Stack_05;
```

Specification in **SPARK 2014**:

```
1   package Stack_14
2     with SPARK_Mode,
3          Abstract_State => Stack,
4          Initializes    => Stack
5   is
6      procedure Push(X : in Integer)
7        with Global => (In_Out => Stack);
8
9      procedure Pop(X : out Integer)
10       with Global => (In_Out => Stack);
11  end Stack_14;
```

Body in **SPARK 2014**:

```
1   package body Stack_14
2     with SPARK_Mode,
3          Refined_State => (Stack => (S, Pointer)) -- state refinement
4   is
5      Stack_Size : constant := 100;
6      type    Pointer_Range is range 0 .. Stack_Size;
7      subtype Index_Range   is Pointer_Range range 1..Stack_Size;
8      type    Vector        is array(Index_Range) of Integer;
9
10     S       : Vector; -- left uninitialized
11     Pointer : Pointer_Range := 0;
12     -- initialization by elaboration of declaration
13
14     procedure Push(X : in Integer)
15       with Refined_Global => (In_Out => (S, Pointer))
16     is
17     begin
18        Pointer := Pointer + 1;
19        S (Pointer) := X;
20     end Push;
```

```
21
22      procedure Pop (X : out Integer)
23        with Refined_Global => (Input  => S,
24                                In_Out => Pointer)
25      is
26      begin
27         X := S (Pointer);
28         Pointer := Pointer - 1;
29      end Pop;
30  begin
31      -- partial initialization by body statements
32      S := (Index_Range => 0);
33  end Stack_14;
```

Initial condition

This example introduces a new SPARK 2014 feature that did not exist in SPARK 2005. On top of declaring an abstract state and promising to initialize it, we also illustrate certain conditions that will be valid after initialization. There is a verification condition to show that immediately after the elaboration of the package that the specified Initial_Condition is True. Checks will be generated that have to be proven (or executed at run-time) to show that the initial condition is True.

Specification in SPARK 2014:

```
1   package Stack_14
2     with SPARK_Mode,
3          Abstract_State   => State,
4          Initializes      => State,
5          Initial_Condition => Is_Empty  -- Stating that Is_Empty holds
6                                         -- after initialization
7   is
8      function Is_Empty return Boolean
9        with Global => State;
10
11     function Is_Full return Boolean
12        with Global => State;
13
14     function Top return Integer
15        with Global => State,
16             Pre    => not Is_Empty;
17
18     procedure Push (X: in Integer)
19        with Global => (In_Out => State),
20             Pre    => not Is_Full,
21             Post   => Top = X;
22
23     procedure Pop (X: out Integer)
24        with Global => (In_Out => State),
25             Pre    => not Is_Empty;
26  end Stack_14;
```

Body in SPARK 2014:

```
1   package body Stack_14
2     with SPARK_Mode,
3          Refined_State => (State => (S,
```

```
4                              Pointer)) -- State refinement
5  is
6     Max_Stack_Size : constant := 1024;
7     type Pointer_Range is range 0 .. Max_Stack_Size;
8     subtype Index_Range is Pointer_Range range 1 .. Max_Stack_Size;
9     type Vector is array (Index_Range) of Integer;
10
11    -- Declaration of constituents
12    S        : Vector;
13    Pointer : Pointer_Range;
14
15    -- The subprogram contracts are refined in terms of the constituents.
16    -- Expression functions could be used where applicable
17
18    function Is_Empty  return Boolean is (Pointer = 0)
19      with Refined_Global => Pointer;
20
21    function Is_Full   return Boolean is (Pointer = Max_Stack_Size)
22      with Refined_Global => Pointer;
23
24    function Top return Integer is (S (Pointer))
25      with Refined_Global => (Pointer, S);
26
27    procedure Push(X: in Integer)
28      with Refined_Global => (In_Out => (Pointer, S))
29    is
30    begin
31       Pointer := Pointer + 1;
32       S (Pointer) := X;
33    end Push;
34
35    procedure Pop(X: out Integer)
36      with Refined_Global => (Input  => S,
37                              In_Out => Pointer)
38    is
39    begin
40       X := S (Pointer);
41       Pointer := Pointer - 1;
42    end Pop;
43 begin
44    -- Initialization - we promised to initialize the state
45    -- and that initially the stack will be empty
46    Pointer := 0;  -- Is_Empty is True.
47    S := Vector'(Index_Range => 0);
48 end Stack_14;
```

Private, abstract state, refining onto state of private child

The following example shows a parent package Power that contains an own variable (a state abstraction). This state abstraction is refined onto state abstractions of two private children Source_A and Source_B.

Specification of Parent in SPARK 2005:

```
1  -- Use of child packages to encapsulate state
2  package Power_05
3  --# own State;
4  --# initializes State;
```

```
5   is
6      procedure Read_Power(Level : out Integer);
7      --# global State;
8      --# derives Level from State;
9   end Power_05;
```

Body of Parent in SPARK 2005:

```
1   with Power_05.Source_A_05, Power_05.Source_B_05;
2
3   package body Power_05
4   --# own State is Power_05.Source_A_05.State,
5   --#               Power_05.Source_B_05.State;
6   is
7
8     procedure Read_Power(Level : out Integer)
9     --# global Source_A_05.State, Source_B_05.State;
10    --# derives
11    --#     Level
12    --#     from
13    --#           Source_A_05.State,
14    --#           Source_B_05.State;
15    is
16       Level_A : Integer;
17       Level_B : Integer;
18    begin
19       Source_A_05.Read (Level_A);
20       Source_B_05.Read (Level_B);
21       Level := Level_A + Level_B;
22    end Read_Power;
23
24  end Power_05;
```

Specifications of Private Children in SPARK 2005:

```
1   --# inherit Power_05;
2   private package Power_05.Source_A_05
3   --# own State;
4   --# initializes State;
5   is
6      procedure Read (Level : out Integer);
7      --# global State;
8      --# derives Level from State;
9   end Power_05.Source_A_05;
```

```
1   --# inherit Power_05;
2   private package Power_05.Source_B_05
3   --# own State;
4   --# initializes State;
5   is
6      procedure Read (Level : out Integer);
7      --# global State;
8      --# derives Level from State;
9   end Power_05.Source_B_05;
```

Bodies of Private Children in SPARK 2005:

```
1   package body Power_05.Source_A_05
2   --# own State is S;
3   is
4      S : Integer := 0;
5
6      procedure Read (Level : out Integer)
7      --# global in S;
8      --# derives Level from S;
9      is
10     begin
11        Level := S;
12     end Read;
13  end Power_05.Source_A_05;
```

```
1   package body Power_05.Source_B_05
2   --# own State is S;
3   is
4      S : Integer := 0;
5
6      procedure Read (Level : out Integer)
7      --# global in S;
8      --# derives Level from S;
9      is
10     begin
11        Level := S;
12     end Read;
13  end Power_05.Source_B_05;
```

Specification of Parent in SPARK 2014:

```
1   -- Use of child packages to encapsulate state
2   package Power_14
3     with SPARK_Mode,
4          Abstract_State => State,
5          Initializes    => State
6   is
7      procedure Read_Power(Level : out Integer)
8        with Global  => State,
9             Depends => (Level => State);
10  end Power_14;
```

Body of Parent in SPARK 2014:

```
1   with Power_14.Source_A_14,
2        Power_14.Source_B_14;
3
4   package body Power_14
5     with SPARK_Mode,
6          Refined_State => (State => (Power_14.Source_A_14.State,
7                                      Power_14.Source_B_14.State))
8   is
9      procedure Read_Power(Level : out Integer)
10       with Refined_Global  => (Source_A_14.State, Source_B_14.State),
11            Refined_Depends => (Level => (Source_A_14.State,
12                                          Source_B_14.State))
13       is
14        Level_A : Integer;
15        Level_B : Integer;
```

```
16      begin
17          Source_A_14.Read (Level_A);
18          Source_B_14.Read (Level_B);
19          Level := Level_A + Level_B;
20      end Read_Power;
21  end Power_14;
```

Specifications of Private Children in SPARK 2014:

```
1  private package Power_14.Source_A_14
2     with SPARK_Mode,
3          Abstract_State => (State with Part_Of =>Power_14.State),
4          Initializes    => State
5  is
6     procedure Read (Level : out Integer)
7        with Global => State,
8             Depends => (Level => State);
9  end Power_14.Source_A_14;
```

```
1  private package Power_14.Source_B_14
2     with SPARK_Mode,
3          Abstract_State => (State with Part_Of => Power_14.State),
4          Initializes    => State
5  is
6     procedure Read (Level : out Integer)
7        with Global  => State,
8             Depends => (Level => State);
9  end Power_14.Source_B_14;
```

Bodies of Private Children in SPARK 2014:

```
1  package body Power_14.Source_A_14
2     with SPARK_Mode,
3          Refined_State => (State => S)
4  is
5     S : Integer := 0;
6
7     procedure Read (Level : out Integer)
8        with Refined_Global  => (Input => S),
9             Refined_Depends => (Level => S)
10    is
11    begin
12       Level := S;
13    end Read;
14 end Power_14.Source_A_14;
```

```
1  package body Power_14.Source_B_14
2     with SPARK_Mode,
3          Refined_State => (State => S)
4  is
5     S : Integer := 0;
6
7     procedure Read (Level : out Integer)
8        with Refined_Global  => (Input => S),
9             Refined_Depends => (Level => S)
10    is
11    begin
```

```
12      Level := S;
13    end Read;
14 end Power_14.Source_B_14;
```

Private, abstract state, refining onto concrete state of embedded package

This example is based around the packages from section *Private, abstract state, refining onto concrete state of embedded package*, with the private child packages converted into embedded packages and the refinement onto concrete visible state.

Specification in SPARK 2005:

```
1  -- Use of embedded packages to encapsulate state
2  package Power_05
3  --# own State;
4  is
5     procedure Read_Power(Level : out Integer);
6     --# global State;
7     --# derives Level from State;
8  end Power_05;
```

Body in SPARK 2005:

```
1  package body Power_05
2  --# own State is Source_A.State,
3  --#                Source_B.State;
4  is
5
6     --  Embedded package spec for Source_A
7     package Source_A
8     --# own State;
9     is
10       procedure Read (Level : out Integer);
11       --# global State;
12       --# derives Level from State;
13    end Source_A;
14
15    --  Embedded package spec for Source_B.
16    package Source_B
17    --# own State;
18    is
19      procedure Read (Level : out Integer);
20      --# global State;
21      --# derives Level from State;
22    end Source_B;
23
24    --  Embedded package body for Source_A
25    package body Source_A
26    is
27      State : Integer;
28
29      procedure Read (Level : out Integer)
30      is
31      begin
32        Level := State;
33      end Read;
34    end Source_A;
```

```
35
36      -- Embedded package body for Source_B
37    package body Source_B
38    is
39       State : Integer;
40
41       procedure Read (Level : out Integer)
42       is
43       begin
44          Level := State;
45       end Read;
46
47    end Source_B;
48
49    procedure Read_Power(Level : out Integer)
50    --# global Source_A.State, Source_B.State;
51    --# derives
52    --#      Level
53    --#      from
54    --#           Source_A.State,
55    --#           Source_B.State;
56    is
57       Level_A : Integer;
58       Level_B : Integer;
59    begin
60       Source_A. Read (Level_A);
61       Source_B.Read (Level_B);
62       Level := Level_A + Level_B;
63    end Read_Power;
64
65  end Power_05;
```

Specification in SPARK 2014:

```
1   -- Use of embedded packages to encapsulate state
2   package Power_14
3     with SPARK_Mode,
4          Abstract_State => State,
5          Initializes    => State
6   is
7      procedure Read_Power(Level : out Integer)
8        with Global  => State,
9             Depends => (Level => State);
10  end Power_14;
```

Body in SPARK 2014:

```
1   package body Power_14
2     with SPARK_Mode,
3          Refined_State => (State => (Source_A.State,
4                                      Source_B.State))
5   is
6      -- Embedded package spec for Source_A
7      package Source_A
8        with Initializes => State
9      is
10        State : Integer := 0;
11
```

```
12      procedure Read (Level : out Integer)
13         with Global   => State,
14              Depends => (Level => State);
15      end Source_A;
16
17      --  Embedded package spec for Source_B.
18      package Source_B
19        with Initializes => State
20      is
21         State : Integer := 0;
22
23         procedure Read (Level : out Integer)
24            with Global   => State,
25                 Depends => (Level => State);
26      end Source_B;
27
28      --  Embedded package body for Source_A
29      package body Source_A is
30         procedure Read (Level : out Integer) is
31         begin
32            Level := State;
33         end Read;
34      end Source_A;
35
36      --  Embedded package body for Source_B
37      package body Source_B is
38         procedure Read (Level : out Integer) is
39         begin
40            Level := State;
41         end Read;
42      end Source_B;
43
44      procedure Read_Power (Level : out Integer)
45         with Refined_Global  => (Source_A.State,
46                                  Source_B.State),
47              Refined_Depends => (Level => (Source_A.State,
48                                            Source_B.State))
49      is
50         Level_A : Integer;
51         Level_B : Integer;
52      begin
53         Source_A. Read (Level_A);
54         Source_B.Read (Level_B);
55         Level := Level_A + Level_B;
56      end Read_Power;
57   end Power_14;
```

Private, abstract state, refining onto mixture of the above

This example is based around the packages from sections *Private, abstract state, refining onto state of private child* and *Private, abstract state, refining onto concrete state of embedded package*. Source_A is an embedded package, while Source_B is a private child. In order to avoid repetition, the code of this example is not being presented.

A.3.3 External Variables

Basic Input and Output Device Drivers

The following example shows a main program - Copy - that reads all available data from a given input port, stores it internally during the reading process in a stack and then outputs all the data read to an output port. The specifications of the stack packages are not presented since they are identical to previous examples.

Specification of main program in SPARK 2005:

```
1   with Input_Port_05, Output_Port_05, Stacks_05;
2   --# inherit Input_Port_05, Output_Port_05, Stacks_05;
3   --# main_program;
4   procedure Copy_05
5   --# global in     Input_Port_05.Input_State;
6   --#        out    Output_Port_05.Output_State;
7   --# derives Output_Port_05.Output_State from Input_Port_05.Input_State;
8   is
9       The_Stack   : Stacks_05.Stack;
10      Value       : Integer;
11      Done        : Boolean;
12      Final_Value : constant Integer := 999;
13  begin
14      Stacks_05.Clear(The_Stack);
15      loop
16          Input_Port_05.Read_From_Port(Value);
17          Stacks_05.Push(The_Stack, Value);
18          Done := Value = Final_Value;
19          exit when Done;
20      end loop;
21      loop
22          Stacks_05.Pop(The_Stack, Value);
23          Output_Port_05.Write_To_Port(Value);
24          exit when Stacks_05.Is_Empty(The_Stack);
25      end loop;
26  end Copy_05;
```

Specification of input port in SPARK 2005:

```
1   package Input_Port_05
2     --# own in Input_State;
3   is
4       procedure Read_From_Port(Input_Value : out Integer);
5       --# global in Input_State;
6       --# derives Input_Value from Input_State;
7
8   end Input_Port_05;
```

Body of input port in SPARK 2005:

```
1   package body Input_Port_05
2   is
3
4       Input_State : Integer;
5       for Input_State'Address use
6          System.Storage_Elements.To_Address (16#ACECAE0#);
7       pragma Volatile (Input_State);
8
9       procedure Read_From_Port(Input_Value : out Integer)
10      is
11      begin
```

```
12        Input_Value := Input_State;
13     end Read_From_Port;
14
15 end Input_Port_05;
```

Specification of output port in SPARK 2005:

```
1 package Output_Port_05
2    --# own out Output_State;
3 is
4    procedure Write_To_Port(Output_Value : in Integer);
5    --# global out Output_State;
6    --# derives Output_State from Output_Value;
7 end Output_Port_05;
```

Body of output port in SPARK 2005:

```
1  package body Output_Port_05
2  is
3
4     Output_State : Integer;
5     for Output_State'Address use
6        System.Storage_Elements.To_Address (16#ACECAF0#);
7     pragma Volatile (Output_State);
8
9     procedure Write_To_Port(Output_Value : in Integer)
10    is
11    begin
12       Output_State := Output_Value;
13    end Write_To_Port;
14
15 end Output_Port_05;
```

Specification of main program in SPARK 2014:

```
1  with Input_Port_14,
2       Output_Port_14,
3       Stacks_14;
4  --  No need to specify that Copy_14 is a main program
5
6  procedure Copy_14
7    with SPARK_Mode,
8         Global  => (Input  => Input_Port_14.Input_State,
9                     Output => Output_Port_14.Output_State),
10        Depends => (Output_Port_14.Output_State => Input_Port_14.Input_State)
11 is
12    The_Stack   : Stacks_14.Stack;
13    Value       : Integer;
14    Done        : Boolean;
15    Final_Value : constant Integer := 999;
16 begin
17    Stacks_14.Clear(The_Stack);
18    loop
19       Input_Port_14.Read_From_Port(Value);
20       Stacks_14.Push(The_Stack, Value);
21       Done := Value = Final_Value;
22       exit when Done;
23    end loop;
```

```
24   loop
25      Stacks_14.Pop(The_Stack, Value);
26      Output_Port_14.Write_To_Port(Value);
27      exit when Stacks_14.Is_Empty(The_Stack);
28   end loop;
29 end Copy_14;
```

Specification of input port in SPARK 2014:

```
1 package Input_Port_14
2   with SPARK_Mode,
3        Abstract_State => (Input_State with External => Async_Writers)
4 is
5   procedure Read_From_Port(Input_Value : out Integer)
6     with Global  => (Input => Input_State),
7          Depends => (Input_Value => Input_State);
8 end Input_Port_14;
```

Specification of output port in SPARK 2014:

```
1 package Output_Port_14
2   with SPARK_Mode,
3        Abstract_State => (Output_State with External => Async_Readers)
4 is
5   procedure Write_To_Port(Output_Value : in Integer)
6     with Global  => (Output => Output_State),
7          Depends => (Output_State => Output_Value);
8 end Output_Port_14;
```

Body of input port in SPARK 2014:

This is as per SPARK 2005, but uses aspects instead of representation clauses and pragmas.

```
1  with System.Storage_Elements;
2
3  package body Input_Port_14
4    with SPARK_Mode,
5         Refined_State => (Input_State => Input_S)
6  is
7    Input_S : Integer
8      with Volatile,
9           Async_Writers,
10          Address => System.Storage_Elements.To_Address (16#ACECAE0#);
11
12   procedure Read_From_Port(Input_Value : out Integer)
13     with Refined_Global  => (Input => Input_S),
14          Refined_Depends => (Input_Value => Input_S)
15   is
16   begin
17      Input_Value := Input_S;
18   end Read_From_Port;
19 end Input_Port_14;
```

Body of output port in SPARK 2014:

This is as per SPARK 2005, but uses aspects instead of representation clauses and pragmas.

```
1  with System.Storage_Elements;
2
```

```
 3   package body Output_Port_14
 4     with SPARK_Mode,
 5          Refined_State => (Output_State => Output_S)
 6   is
 7      Output_S : Integer
 8        with Volatile,
 9             Async_Readers,
10             Address => System.Storage_Elements.To_Address (16#ACECAF0#);
11
12      procedure Write_To_Port(Output_Value : in Integer)
13        with Refined_Global  => (Output => Output_S),
14             Refined_Depends => (Output_S => Output_Value)
15      is
16      begin
17         Output_S := Output_Value;
18      end Write_To_Port;
19   end Output_Port_14;
```

Input driver using 'Tail in a contract

This example uses the Input_Port package from section *Basic Input and Output Device Drivers* and adds a contract using the 'Tail attribute. The example also use the Always_Valid attribute in order to allow proof to succeed (otherwise, there is no guarantee in the proof context that the value read from the port is of the correct type).

SPARK 2014 does not have the attribute 'Tail but, often, an equivalent proof can be achieved using assert pragmas. Neither is there a direct equivalent of the Always_Valid attribute but the paragma Assume may be used to the same effect.

Specification in SPARK 2005:

```
 1   package Input_Port
 2     --# own in Inputs : Integer;
 3   is
 4      procedure Read_From_Port(Input_Value : out Integer);
 5      --# global in Inputs;
 6      --# derives Input_Value from Inputs;
 7      --# post (Inputs~ = 0  -> (Input_Value = Inputs'Tail (Inputs~))) and
 8      --#      (Inputs~ /= 0 -> (Input_Value = Inputs~));
 9
10   end Input_Port;
```

Body in SPARK 2005:

```
 1   package body Input_Port
 2   is
 3
 4      Inputs : Integer;
 5      for Inputs'Address use
 6        System.Storage_Elements.To_Address (16#ACECAF0#);
 7
 8      --# assert Inputs'Always_Valid;
 9      pragma Volatile (Inputs);
10
11      procedure Read_From_Port(Input_Value : out Integer)
12      is
13      begin
14         Input_Value := Inputs;
```

```
15        if Input_Value = 0 then
16            Input_Value := Inputs;
17        end if;
18     end Read_From_Port;
19
20 end Input_Port;
```

Specification in **SPARK 2014**:

```
1  package Input_Port_14
2    with SPARK_Mode,
3         Abstract_State => (Inputs with External => Async_Writers)
4  is
5     procedure Read_From_Port(Input_Value : out Integer)
6        with Global  => Inputs,
7             Depends => (Input_Value => Inputs);
8  end Input_Port_14;
```

Body in **SPARK 2014**:

```
1  with System.Storage_Elements;
2
3  package body Input_Port_14
4    with SPARK_Mode,
5         Refined_State => (Inputs => Input_Port)
6  is
7     Input_Port : Integer
8        with Volatile,
9             Async_Writers,
10            Address => System.Storage_Elements.To_Address (16#ACECAF0#);
11
12    procedure Read_From_Port(Input_Value : out Integer)
13       with Refined_Global  => Input_Port,
14            Refined_Depends => (Input_Value => Input_Port)
15    is
16       First_Read  : Integer;
17       Second_Read : Integer;
18    begin
19       Second_Read := Input_Port;    -- Ensure Second_Read is initialized
20       pragma Assume (Second_Read'Valid);
21       First_Read  := Second_Read;   -- but it is infact the First_Read.
22       if First_Read = 0 then
23          Second_Read := Input_Port; -- Now it is the Second_Read
24          pragma Assume (Second_Read'Valid);
25          Input_Value := Second_Read;
26       else
27          Input_Value := First_Read;
28       end if;
29       pragma Assert ((First_Read = 0 and then Input_Value = Second_Read)
30                      or else (Input_Value = First_Read));
31    end Read_From_Port;
32 end Input_Port_14;
```

Output driver using 'Append in a contract

This example uses the Output package from section *Basic Input and Output Device Drivers* and adds a contract using the 'Append attribute.

SPARK 2014 does not have the attribute 'Append but, often, an equivalent proof can be achieved using assert pragmas.

Specification in SPARK 2005:

```
1  package Output_Port
2    --# own out Outputs : Integer;
3  is
4    procedure Write_To_Port(Output_Value : in Integer);
5    --# global out Outputs;
6    --# derives Outputs from Output_Value;
7    --# post ((Output_Value = -1) ->
8    --#          (Outputs =
9    --#              Outputs'Append (Outputs'Append (Outputs~, 0), Output_Value)))
10   --#  and
11   --#        ((Output_Value /= -1) ->
12   --#          (Outputs =
13   --#              Outputs'Append (Outputs~, Output_Value)));
14 end Output_Port;
```

Body in SPARK 2005:

```
1  package body Output_Port
2  is
3
4    Outputs : Integer;
5    for Outputs'Address use System.Storage_Elements.To_Address (16#ACECAF10#);
6    pragma Volatile (Outputs);
7
8    procedure Write_To_Port(Output_Value : in Integer)
9    is
10   begin
11     if Output_Value = -1 then
12        Outputs := 0;
13     end if;
14
15     Outputs := Output_Value;
16   end Write_To_Port;
17
18 end Output_Port;
```

Specification in SPARK 2014:

```
1  package Output_Port_14
2    with SPARK_Mode,
3         Abstract_State => (Outputs with External => Async_Readers)
4  is
5    procedure Write_To_Port(Output_Value : in Integer)
6      with Global  => (Output => Outputs),
7           Depends => (Outputs => Output_Value);
8  end Output_Port_14;
```

Body in SPARK 2014:

```
1  with System.Storage_Elements;
2
3  package body Output_Port_14
4    with SPARK_Mode,
5         Refined_State => (Outputs => Output_Port)
6  is
```

```
 7    Output_Port : Integer
 8      with Volatile,
 9           Async_Readers,
10           Address => System.Storage_Elements.To_Address (16#ACECAF10#);
11
12    -- This is a simple subprogram that always updates the Output_Shadow with
13    -- the single value which is written to the output port.
14    procedure Write_It (Output_Value : in Integer; Output_Shadow : out Integer)
15      with Global   => (Output => Output_Port),
16           Depends  => ((Output_Port, Output_Shadow) => Output_Value),
17           Post     => Output_Shadow = Output_Value
18    is
19    begin
20       Output_Shadow := Output_Value;
21       Output_Port := Output_Shadow;
22    end Write_It;
23
24
25    procedure Write_To_Port(Output_Value : in Integer)
26      with Refined_Global  => (Output => Output_Port),
27           Refined_Depends => (Output_Port => Output_Value)
28    is
29       Out_1, Out_2 : Integer;
30    begin
31       if Output_Value = -1 then
32          Write_It (0, Out_1);
33          Write_It (Output_Value, Out_2);
34       else
35          Write_It (Output_Value, Out_1);
36          Out_2 := Out_1;   -- Avoids flow error.
37       end if;
38
39       pragma Assert (if Output_Value = -1 then
40                         Out_1 = 0 and Out_2 = Output_Value
41                      else
42                         Out_1 = Output_Value);
43    end Write_To_Port;
44 end Output_Port_14;
```

Refinement of external state - voting input switch

The following example presents an abstract view of the reading of 3 individual switches and the voting performed on the values read.

Abstract Switch specification in SPARK 2005:

```
 1  package Switch
 2  --# own in State;
 3  is
 4
 5     type Reading is (on, off, unknown);
 6
 7     function ReadValue return Reading;
 8     --# global in State;
 9
10  end Switch;
```

Component Switch specifications in SPARK 2005:

```
1   --# inherit Switch;
2   private package Switch.Val1
3   --# own in State;
4   is
5       function Read return Switch.Reading;
6       --# global in State;
7
8   end Switch.Val1;
```

```
1   --# inherit Switch;
2   private package Switch.Val2
3   --# own in State;
4   is
5       function Read return Switch.Reading;
6       --# global in State;
7
8   end Switch.Val2;
```

```
1   --# inherit Switch;
2   private package Switch.Val3
3   --# own in State;
4   is
5       function Read return Switch.Reading;
6       --# global in State;
7
8   end Switch.Val3;
```

Switch body in SPARK 2005:

```
1   with Switch.Val1;
2   with Switch.Val2;
3   with Switch.Val3;
4   package body Switch
5   --# own State is in Switch.Val1.State,
6   --#               in Switch.Val2.State,
7   --#               in Switch.Val3.State;
8   is
9
10      subtype Value is Integer range -1 .. 1;
11      subtype Score is Integer range -3 .. 3;
12      type ConvertToValueArray is array (Reading) of Value;
13      type ConvertToReadingArray is array (Score) of Reading;
14
15      ConvertToValue : constant ConvertToValueArray := ConvertToValueArray'(on => 1,
16                                                                            unknown => 0,
17                                                                            off => -1);
18      ConvertToReading : constant ConvertToReadingArray :=
19                                      ConvertToReadingArray'(-3 .. -2 => off,
20                                                             -1 .. 1 => unknown,
21                                                             2 ..3 => on);
22
23      function ReadValue return Reading
24      --# global in Val1.State;
25      --#        in Val2.State;
26      --#        in Val3.State;
27      is
```

```
28        A, B, C : Reading;
29     begin
30        A := Val1.Read;
31        B := Val2.Read;
32        C := Val3.Read;
33        return ConvertToReading (ConvertToValue (A) +
34           ConvertToValue (B) + ConvertToValue (C));
35     end ReadValue;
36
37  end Switch;
```

Abstract Switch specification in SPARK 2014:

```
1   package Switch
2     with SPARK_Mode,
3          Abstract_State => (State with External => Async_Writers)
4   is
5      type Reading is (on, off, unknown);
6
7      function ReadValue return Reading
8        with Volatile_Function,
9             Global => (Input => State);
10  end Switch;
```

Component Switch specifications in SPARK 2014:

```
1   private package Switch.Val1
2     with SPARK_Mode,
3          Abstract_State => (State with External => Async_Writers,
4                                            Part_Of   => Switch.State)
5   is
6      function Read return Switch.Reading
7        with Volatile_Function,
8             Global => (Input => State);
9   end Switch.Val1;
```

```
1   private package Switch.Val2
2     with SPARK_Mode,
3          Abstract_State => (State with External => Async_Writers,
4                                            Part_Of   => Switch.State)
5   is
6      function Read return Switch.Reading
7        with Volatile_Function,
8             Global => (Input => State);
9   end Switch.Val2;
```

```
1   private package Switch.Val3
2     with SPARK_Mode,
3          Abstract_State => (State with External => Async_Writers,
4                                            Part_Of   => Switch.State)
5   is
6      function Read return Switch.Reading
7        with Volatile_Function,
8             Global => (Input => State);
9   end Switch.Val3;
```

Switch body in SPARK 2014:

```
1   with Switch.Val1,
2        Switch.Val2,
3        Switch.Val3;
4
5   package body Switch
6      -- State is refined onto three states, each of which has properties
7      --   Volatile and Input
8     with SPARK_Mode,
9          Refined_State => (State => (Switch.Val1.State,
10                                     Switch.Val2.State,
11                                     Switch.Val3.State))
12  is
13     subtype Value is Integer range -1 .. 1;
14     subtype Score is Integer range -3 .. 3;
15     type ConvertToValueArray is array (Reading) of Value;
16     type ConvertToReadingArray is array (Score) of Reading;
17
18     ConvertToValue : constant ConvertToValueArray :=
19       ConvertToValueArray'(on => 1,
20                            unknown => 0,
21                            off => -1);
22     ConvertToReading : constant ConvertToReadingArray :=
23       ConvertToReadingArray'(-3 .. -2 => off,
24                              -1 .. 1  => unknown,
25                               2 .. 3  => on);
26
27     function ReadValue return Reading
28       with Refined_Global => (Input => (Val1.State, Val2.State, Val3.State))
29     is
30        A, B, C : Reading;
31     begin
32        A := Val1.Read;
33        B := Val2.Read;
34        C := Val3.Read;
35        return ConvertToReading (ConvertToValue (A) +
36          ConvertToValue (B) + ConvertToValue (C));
37     end ReadValue;
38  end Switch;
```

Complex I/O Device

The following example illustrates a more complex I/O device: the device is fundamentally an output device but an acknowledgement has to be read from it. In addition, a local register stores the last value written to avoid writes that would just re-send the same value. The own variable is then refined into a normal variable, an input external variable and an output external variable.

Specification in SPARK 2005:

```
1   package Device
2   --# own State;
3   --# initializes State;
4   is
5     procedure Write (X : in Integer);
6     --# global in out State;
7     --# derives State from State, X;
8   end Device;
```

Body in SPARK 2005:

```
1   package body Device
2   --# own State is        OldX,
3   --#              in      StatusPort,
4   --#                  out Register;
5   -- refinement on to mix of external and ordinary variables
6   is
7       type Status_Port_Type is mod 2**32;
8
9     OldX : Integer := 0; -- only component that needs initialization
10    StatusPort : Status_Port_Type;
11    pragma Volatile (StatusPort);
12    -- address clause would be added here
13
14    Register : Integer;
15    pragma Volatile (Register);
16    -- address clause would be added here
17
18    procedure WriteReg (X : in Integer)
19    --# global out Register;
20    --# derives Register from X;
21    is
22    begin
23      Register := X;
24    end WriteReg;
25
26    procedure ReadAck (OK : out Boolean)
27    --# global in StatusPort;
28    --# derives OK from StatusPort;
29    is
30      RawValue : Status_Port_Type;
31    begin
32      RawValue := StatusPort; -- only assignment allowed here
33      OK := RawValue = 16#FFFF_FFFF#;
34    end ReadAck;
35
36    procedure Write (X : in Integer)
37    --# global in out OldX;
38    --#            out Register;
39    --#        in     StatusPort;
40    --# derives OldX,Register from OldX, X &
41    --#         null        from StatusPort;
42    is
43      OK : Boolean;
44    begin
45      if X /= OldX then
46        OldX := X;
47        WriteReg (X);
48        loop
49          ReadAck (OK);
50          exit when OK;
51        end loop;
52      end if;
53    end Write;
54  end Device;
```

Specification in SPARK 2014:

```
1   package Device
2     with SPARK_Mode,
3          Abstract_State => (State with External => (Async_Readers,
4                                                     Async_Writers)),
5          Initializes    => State
6   is
7     procedure Write (X : in Integer)
8       with Global  => (In_Out => State),
9            Depends => (State =>+ X);
10  end Device;
```

Body in SPARK 2014:

```
1   package body Device
2     with SPARK_Mode,
3          Refined_State => (State => (OldX,
4                                      StatusPort,
5                                      Register))
6     -- refinement on to mix of external and ordinary variables
7   is
8     type Status_Port_Type is mod 2**32;
9
10    OldX : Integer := 0; -- only component that needs initialization
11
12    StatusPort : Status_Port_Type
13      with Volatile,
14           Async_Writers;
15    -- address clause would be added here
16
17    Register : Integer
18      with Volatile,
19           Async_Readers;
20    -- address clause would be added here
21
22    procedure WriteReg (X : in Integer)
23      with Global  => (Output => Register),
24           Depends => (Register => X)
25    is
26    begin
27       Register := X;
28    end WriteReg;
29
30    procedure ReadAck (OK : out Boolean)
31      with Global  => (Input => StatusPort),
32           Depends => (OK => StatusPort)
33    is
34       RawValue : Status_Port_Type;
35    begin
36       RawValue := StatusPort; -- only assignment allowed here
37       OK := RawValue = 16#FFFF_FFFF#;
38    end ReadAck;
39
40    procedure Write (X : in Integer)
41      with Refined_Global  => (Input  => StatusPort,
42                               Output => Register,
43                               In_Out => OldX),
44           Refined_Depends => ((OldX,
45                                Register) => (OldX,
```

```
46                                                               X),
47                                     null => StatusPort)
48       is
49          OK : Boolean;
50       begin
51          if X /= OldX then
52             OldX := X;
53             WriteReg (X);
54             loop
55                ReadAck (OK);
56                exit when OK;
57             end loop;
58          end if;
59       end Write;
60    end Device;
```

Increasing values in input stream

The following example illustrates an input port from which values are read. According to its postcondition, procedure Increases checks whether the first values read from the sequence are in ascending order. This example shows that postconditions can refer to multiple individual elements of the input stream.

In SPARK 2014 we can use assert pragmas in the subprogram instead of specifying the action in the postcondition, as was done in *Input driver using 'Tail in a contract*. Another alternative, as shown in this example, is to use a formal parameter of a private type to keep a trace of the values read.

Specification in SPARK 2005:

```
1    package Inc
2    --# own in Sensor : Integer;
3    is
4       procedure Increases (Result : out Boolean;
5                            Valid  : out Boolean);
6       --# global in Sensor;
7       --# post Valid -> (Result <-> Sensor'Tail (Sensor~) > Sensor~);
8
9    end Inc;
```

Body in SPARK 2005:

```
1    with System.Storage_Elements;
2    package body Inc
3    -- Cannot refine own variable Sensor as it has been given a concrete type.
4    is
5       Sensor : Integer;
6       for Sensor'Address use System.Storage_Elements.To_Address (16#DEADBEE0#);
7       pragma Volatile (Sensor);
8
9       procedure Read (V     : out Integer;
10                      Valid : out Boolean)
11      --# global in Sensor;
12      --# post (Valid -> V = Sensor~) and
13      --#      (Sensor = Sensor'Tail (Sensor~));
14      is
15         Tmp : Integer;
16      begin
17         Tmp := Sensor;
```

```
18        if Tmp'Valid then
19            V := Tmp;
20            Valid := True;
21            --# check Sensor = Sensor'Tail (Sensor~);
22        else
23            V := 0;
24            Valid := False;
25        end if;
26    end Read;
27
28    procedure Increases (Result : out Boolean;
29                         Valid  : out Boolean)
30    is
31        A, B : Integer;
32    begin
33        Result := False;
34        Read (A, Valid);
35        if Valid then
36            Read (B, Valid);
37            if Valid then
38                Result := B > A;
39            end if;
40        end if;
41    end Increases;
42
43 end Inc;
```

Specification in SPARK 2014:

```
1  package Inc
2    with SPARK_Mode,
3         Abstract_State => (Sensor with External => Async_Writers)
4  is
5    -- Declare a private type which will keep a trace of the
6    -- values read.
7    type Increasing_Indicator is private;
8
9    -- Access (ghost) functions for the private type only intended for
10   -- use in pre and post conditions or other assertion expressions
11   function First (Indicator : Increasing_Indicator) return Integer
12     with Ghost;
13
14   function Second (Indicator : Increasing_Indicator) return Integer
15     with Ghost;
16
17   -- Used to check that the value returned by procedure Increases
18   -- is valid (Invalid values have not been read from the Sensor).
19   function Is_Valid (Indicator : Increasing_Indicator) return Boolean;
20
21   -- Use this function to determine whether the result of the procedure
22   -- Increases indicates an increasing value.
23   -- It can only be called if Is_Valid (Indicator)
24   function Is_Increasing (Indicator : Increasing_Indicator) return Boolean
25     with Pre => Is_Valid (Indicator);
26
27   procedure Increases (Result : out Increasing_Indicator)
28     with Global => Sensor,
29          Post   => (if Is_Valid (Result) then Is_Increasing (Result)=
```

```
30                        (Second (Result) > First (Result)));
31
32  private
33     type Increasing_Indicator is record
34        Valid : Boolean;
35        First, Second : Integer;
36     end record;
37  end Inc;
```

Body in SPARK 2014:

```
1   with System.Storage_Elements;
2
3   package body Inc
4     with SPARK_Mode,
5          Refined_State => (Sensor => S)
6   is
7      pragma Warnings (Off);
8      S : Integer
9        with Volatile,
10            Async_Writers,
11            Address => System.Storage_Elements.To_Address (16#DEADBEE0#);
12     pragma Warnings (On);
13
14     function First (Indicator : Increasing_Indicator) return Integer is
15       (Indicator.First);
16
17     function Second (Indicator : Increasing_Indicator) return Integer is
18       (Indicator.Second);
19
20     function Is_Valid (Indicator : Increasing_Indicator) return Boolean is
21       (Indicator.Valid);
22
23     function Is_Increasing (Indicator : Increasing_Indicator) return Boolean is
24       (Indicator.Second > Indicator.First);
25
26     pragma Warnings (Off);
27     procedure Read (V     : out Integer;
28                     Valid : out Boolean)
29       with Global => S,
30            Post   => (if Valid then V'Valid)
31     is
32        Tmp : Integer;
33     begin
34        pragma Warnings (On);
35        Tmp := S;
36        pragma Warnings (Off);
37        if Tmp'Valid then
38        pragma Warnings (On);
39           V := Tmp;
40           Valid := True;
41        else
42           V := 0;
43           Valid := False;
44        end if;
45     end Read;
46
47     procedure Increases (Result : out Increasing_Indicator)
```

```
48        with Refined_Global => S
49     is
50     begin
51        Read (Result.First, Result.Valid);
52        if Result.Valid then
53           Read (Result.Second, Result.Valid);
54        else
55           Result.Second := 0;
56        end if;
57     end Increases;
58  end Inc;
```

A.3.4 Package Inheritance

SPARK 2014 does not have the SPARK 2005 concept of package inheritance. It has the same package visibility rules as Ada 2012.

Contracts with remote state

The following example illustrates indirect access to the state of one package by another via an intermediary. Raw_Data stores some data, which has preprocessing performed on it by Processing and on which Calculate performs some further processing (although the corresponding bodies are not given, Read_Calculated_Value in Calculate calls through to Read_Processed_Data in Processing, which calls through to Read in Raw_Data).

Specifications in SPARK 2005:

```
1   package Raw_Data
2   --# own State;
3   --# Initializes State;
4   is
5
6      function Data_Is_Valid return Boolean;
7      --# global State;
8
9      function Get_Value return Integer;
10     --# global State;
11
12     procedure Read_Next;
13     --# global in out State;
14     --# derives State from State;
15
16
17  end Raw_Data;
```

```
1   with Raw_Data;
2   --# inherit Raw_Data;
3   package Processing
4   --# own State;
5   --# Initializes State;
6   is
7
8      procedure Get_Processed_Data (Value : out Integer);
9      --# global in      Raw_Data.State;
10     --#        in out State;
11     --# derives Value, State  from State, Raw_Data.State;
```

```
12      --# pre Raw_Data.Data_Is_Valid (Raw_Data.State);
13
14   end Processing;
```

```
1    with Processing;
2    --# inherit Processing, Raw_Data;
3    package Calculate
4    is
5
6       procedure Read_Calculated_Value (Value : out Integer);
7       --# global in out Processing.State;
8       --#           in     Raw_Data.State;
9       --# derives Value, Processing.State from Processing.State, Raw_Data.State;
10      --# pre Raw_Data.Data_Is_Valid (Raw_Data.State);
11
12   end Calculate;
```

Specifications in **SPARK 2014**:

```
1    package Raw_Data
2      with SPARK_Mode,
3           Abstract_State => (State with External => Async_Writers),
4           Initializes    => State
5    is
6       function Data_Is_Valid return Boolean
7         with Volatile_Function,
8              Global => State;
9
10      function Get_Value return Integer
11        with Volatile_Function,
12             Global => State;
13
14      procedure Read_Next
15        with Global  => (In_Out => State),
16             Depends => (State => State);
17   end Raw_Data;
```

```
1    with Raw_Data;
2
3    package Processing
4      with SPARK_Mode,
5           Abstract_State => State
6    is
7       procedure Get_Processed_Data (Value : out Integer)
8         with Global  => (Input  => Raw_Data.State,
9                          In_Out => State),
10            Depends => ((Value,
11                         State) => (State,
12                                    Raw_Data.State)),
13            Pre     => Raw_Data.Data_Is_Valid;
14   end Processing;
```

```
1    with Processing,
2         Raw_Data;
3
4    package Calculate
5      with SPARK_Mode
```

```
6   is
7      procedure Read_Calculated_Value (Value : out Integer)
8        with Global  => (In_Out => Processing.State,
9                         Input  => Raw_Data.State),
10            Depends => ((Value,
11                         Processing.State) => (Processing.State,
12                                               Raw_Data.State)),
13            Pre     => Raw_Data.Data_Is_Valid;
14  end Calculate;
```

Package nested inside package

See section *Private, abstract state, refining onto concrete state of embedded package*.

Package nested inside subprogram

This example is a modified version of that given in section *Refinement of external state - voting input switch*. It illustrates the use of a package nested within a subprogram.

Abstract Switch specification in SPARK 2005:

```
1   package Switch
2   --# own in State;
3   is
4
5      type Reading is (on, off, unknown);
6
7      function ReadValue return Reading;
8      --# global in State;
9
10  end Switch;
```

Component Switch specifications in SPARK 2005:

As in *Refinement of external state - voting input switch*

Switch body in SPARK 2005:

```
1   with Switch.Val1;
2   with Switch.Val2;
3   with Switch.Val3;
4   package body Switch
5   --# own State is in Switch.Val1.State,
6   --#              in Switch.Val2.State,
7   --#              in Switch.Val3.State;
8   is
9
10     subtype Value is Integer range -1 .. 1;
11     subtype Score is Integer range -3 .. 3;
12
13
14     function ReadValue return Reading
15     --# global in Val1.State;
16     --#        in Val2.State;
17     --#        in Val3.State;
18     is
```

```ada
      A, B, C : Reading;

      --  Embedded package to provide the capability to synthesize three inputs
      --  into one.
      --# inherit Switch;
      package Conversion
      is

          function Convert_To_Reading
             (Val_A : Switch.Reading;
              Val_B : Switch.Reading;
              Val_C : Switch.Reading) return Switch.Reading;

      end Conversion;

      package body Conversion
      is

          type ConvertToValueArray is array (Switch.Reading) of Switch.Value;
          type ConvertToReadingArray is array (Switch.Score) of Switch.Reading;
          ConvertToValue : constant ConvertToValueArray := ConvertToValueArray'(Switch.
  on => 1,
                                                              Switch.
  unknown => 0,
                                                              Switch.off =>
  -1);

          ConvertToReading : constant ConvertToReadingArray :=
                                  ConvertToReadingArray'(-3 .. -2 => Switch.off,
                                                 -1 .. 1 => Switch.
  unknown,
                                                 2 ..3   => Switch.on);

          function Convert_To_Reading
             (Val_A : Switch.Reading;
              Val_B : Switch.Reading;
              Val_C : Switch.Reading) return Switch.Reading
          is
          begin

              return ConvertToReading (ConvertToValue (Val_A) +
                      ConvertToValue (Val_B) + ConvertToValue (Val_C));
          end Convert_To_Reading;

      end Conversion;

   begin
       A := Val1.Read;
       B := Val2.Read;
       C := Val3.Read;
       return Conversion.Convert_To_Reading
                  (Val_A => A,
                   Val_B => B,
                   Val_C => C);
   end ReadValue;

end Switch;
```

Abstract Switch specification in SPARK 2014:

```
1  package Switch
2    with SPARK_Mode,
3         Abstract_State => (State with External => Async_Writers)
4  is
5     type Reading is (on, off, unknown);
6
7     function ReadValue return Reading
8       with Volatile_Function,
9            Global => (Input => State);
10 end Switch;
```

Component Switch specification in SPARK 2014:

As in *Refinement of external state - voting input switch*

Switch body in SPARK 2014:

```
1  with Switch.Val1,
2       Switch.Val2,
3       Switch.Val3;
4
5  package body Switch
6    --  State is refined onto three states, each of which has properties
7    --  Volatile and Input.
8    with SPARK_Mode,
9         Refined_State => (State => (Switch.Val1.State,
10                                    Switch.Val2.State,
11                                    Switch.Val3.State))
12 is
13    subtype Value is Integer range -1 .. 1;
14    subtype Score is Integer range -3 .. 3;
15
16    function ReadValue return Reading
17      with Refined_Global => (Input => (Val1.State, Val2.State, Val3.State))
18    is
19       A, B, C : Reading;
20
21       --  Embedded package to provide the capability to synthesize three inputs
22       --  into one.
23       package Conversion is
24          function Convert_To_Reading
25            (Val_A : Switch.Reading;
26             Val_B : Switch.Reading;
27             Val_C : Switch.Reading) return Switch.Reading;
28       end Conversion;
29
30       package body Conversion is
31          type ConvertToValueArray is array (Switch.Reading) of Switch.Value;
32          type ConvertToReadingArray is array (Switch.Score) of Switch.Reading;
33          ConvertToValue : constant ConvertToValueArray :=
34            ConvertToValueArray'(Switch.on => 1,
35                                 Switch.unknown => 0,
36                                 Switch.off => -1);
37
38          ConvertToReading : constant ConvertToReadingArray :=
39            ConvertToReadingArray'(-3 .. -2 => Switch.off,
40                                   -1 .. 1  => Switch.unknown,
```

```
41                                    2 .. 3  => Switch.on);
42
43           function Convert_To_Reading
44              (Val_A : Switch.Reading;
45               Val_B : Switch.Reading;
46               Val_C : Switch.Reading) return Switch.Reading is
47           (ConvertToReading (ConvertToValue (Val_A) +
48                              ConvertToValue (Val_B) +
49                              ConvertToValue (Val_C)));
50        end Conversion;
51     begin  -- begin statement of ReadValue function
52        A := Val1.Read;
53        B := Val2.Read;
54        C := Val3.Read;
55        return Conversion.Convert_To_Reading
56                 (Val_A => A,
57                  Val_B => B,
58                  Val_C => C);
59     end ReadValue;
60  end Switch;
```

Circular dependence and elaboration order

SPARK 2005 avoided issues of circular dependence and elaboration order dependencies through a combination of the inherit annotation and the restrictions that initialization expressions are constant, user defined subprograms cannot be called in the sequence of statements of a package body and a package can only initialize variables declared in its delarative part.

SPARK 2014 does not have the inherit annotation and only enforces the restriction that a package can only initialize an object declared in its declarative region. Hence, in SPARK 2014 two package bodies that depend on each other's specification may be legal, as is calling a user defined suprogram.

Instead of the elaboration restrictions of SPARK 2005 a set of rules is applied in SPARK 2014 which determines when elaboration order control pragmas such as Elaborate_Body or Elaborate_All are required. These rules ensure the absence of elaboration order dependencies.

Examples of the features of SPARK 2014 elaboration order rules are given below. In the example described below the partial elaboration order would be either of P_14 or Q_14 specifications first followed by P_14 body because of the Elaborate_All on the specification of R_14 specification and the body of Q_14, then the elaboration of Q_14 body or the specification of R_14 and the body of R_14 after the elaboration of Q_14. Elaboration order dependencies are avoided by the (required) use of elaboration control pragmas.

Package Specifications in SPARK 2014:

```
1   package P_14
2     with SPARK_Mode,
3          Abstract_State => P_State,
4          Initializes    => (P_State, Global_Var),
5          Elaborate_Body
6   is
7      Global_Var : Integer;
8
9      procedure Init (S : out Integer);
10  end P_14;
```

```
1   package Q_14
2     with SPARK_Mode,
```

```
 3          Abstract_State => Q_State,
 4          Initializes    => Q_State
 5   is
 6      type T is new Integer;
 7
 8      procedure Init (S : out T);
 9   end Q_14;
```

```
 1   with P_14;
 2   pragma Elaborate_All (P_14);  -- Required because P_14.Global_Var
 3                                 -- Is mentioned as input in the Initializes aspect
 4   package R_14
 5     with SPARK_Mode,
 6          Abstract_State => State,
 7          Initializes    => (State => P_14.Global_Var)
 8   is
 9      procedure Op ( X : in Positive)
10        with Global => (In_Out => State);
11   end R_14;
```

Package Bodies in SPARK 2014

```
 1   with Q_14;
 2
 3   package body P_14
 4     with SPARK_Mode,
 5          Refined_State => (P_State => P_S)
 6   is
 7      P_S : Q_14.T;   -- The use of type Q.T does not require
 8                      -- the body of Q to be elaborated.
 9
10      procedure Init (S : out Integer) is
11      begin
12         S := 5;
13      end Init;
14   begin
15      -- Cannot call Q_14.Init here beacuse
16      -- this would require an Elaborate_All for Q_14
17      -- and would be detected as a circularity
18      Init (Global_Var);
19      P_S := Q_14.T (Global_Var);
20   end P_14;
```

```
 1   with P_14;
 2   pragma Elaborate_All (P_14);  -- Required because the elaboration of the
 3                                 -- body of Q_14 (indirectly) calls P_14.Init
 4   package body Q_14
 5     with SPARK_Mode,
 6          Refined_State => (Q_State => Q_S)
 7   is
 8      Q_S : T;
 9
10      procedure Init (S : out T) is
11         V : Integer;
12      begin
13         P_14.Init (V);
14         if V > 0 and then  V <= Integer'Last - 5 then
```

```
15          S := T (V + 5);
16      else
17          S := 5;
18      end if;
19   end Init;
20 begin
21   Init (Q_S);
22 end Q_14;
```

```
1  with Q_14;
2  pragma Elaborate_All (Q_14); -- Required because Q_14.Init is called
3                               -- in the elaboration of the body of R_14
4  use type Q_14.T;
5
6  package body R_14
7    with SPARK_Mode,
8         Refined_State => (State => R_S)
9  is
10    R_S : Q_14.T;
11    procedure Op ( X : in Positive)
12      with Refined_Global => (In_Out => R_S)
13    is
14    begin
15      if R_S <= Q_14.T'Last - Q_14.T (X) then
16          R_S := R_S + Q_14.T (X);
17      else
18          R_S := 0;
19      end if;
20    end Op;
21 begin
22    Q_14.Init (R_S);
23    if P_14.Global_Var > 0
24      and then R_S <= Q_14.T'Last - Q_14.T (P_14.Global_Var)
25    then
26        R_S := R_S + Q_14.T (P_14.Global_Var);
27    else
28        R_S := Q_14.T (P_14.Global_Var);
29    end if;
30 end R_14;
```

A.4 Bodies and Proof

A.4.1 Assert, Assume, Check contracts

Assert (in loop) contract

The following example demonstrates how the SPARK 2005 *assert* annotation is used inside a loop as a loop invariant. It cuts the loop and on each iteration of the loop the list of existing hypotheses for the path is cleared. A verification condition is generated to prove that the assert expression is True, and the expression is the basis of the new hypotheses.

SPARK 2014 has a specific pragma for defining a loop invariant, *pragma Loop_Invariant* which is more sophisticated than the SPARK 2005 assert annotation and often requires less conditions in the invariant expression than in SPARK 2005. As in SPARK 2005 a default loop invariant will be used if one is not provided which, often, may be sufficient to prove absence of run-time exceptions. Like all SPARK 2014 assertion expressions the loop invariant is executable.

Note in the example below the SPARK 2014 version proves absence of run-time exceptions without an explicit loop invariant being provided.

Specification in SPARK 2005:

```
1  package Assert_Loop_05
2  is
3     subtype Index is Integer range 1 .. 10;
4     type A_Type is Array (Index) of Integer;
5
6     function Value_present (A: A_Type; X : Integer) return Boolean;
7     --# return for some M in Index => (A (M) = X);
8  end Assert_Loop_05;
```

Body in SPARK 2005:

```
1  package body Assert_Loop_05
2  is
3     function Value_Present (A: A_Type; X : Integer) return Boolean
4     is
5        I : Index := Index'First;
6     begin
7        while A (I) /= X and I < Index'Last loop
8           --# assert I < Index'Last and
9           --#         (for all M in Index range Index'First .. I => (A (M) /= X));
10          I := I + 1;
11       end loop;
12       return A (I) = X;
13    end Value_Present;
14 end Assert_Loop_05;
```

Specification in SPARK 2014:

```
1  package Assert_Loop_14
2    with SPARK_Mode
3  is
4     subtype Index is Integer range 1 .. 10;
5     type A_Type is Array (Index) of Integer;
6
7     function Value_present (A : A_Type; X : Integer) return Boolean
8       with Post => Value_present'Result = (for some M in Index => A (M) = X);
9  end Assert_Loop_14;
```

Body in SPARK 2014:

```
1  package body Assert_Loop_14
2    with SPARK_Mode
3  is
4     function Value_Present (A : A_Type; X : Integer) return Boolean is
5        I : Index := Index'First;
6     begin
7        while A (I) /= X and I < Index'Last loop
8           pragma Loop_Invariant
9             (I < Index'Last
10             and (for all M in Index'First .. I => A (M) /= X));
11          I := I + 1;
12       end loop;
13
14       return A (I) = X;
```

```
15      end Value_Present;
16  end Assert_Loop_14;
```

Assert (no loop) contract

While not in a loop, the SPARK 2005 *assert* annotation maps to *pragma Assert_And_Cut* in SPARK 2014. Both the assert annotation and pragma assert clear the list of hypotheses on the path, generate a verification condition to prove the assertion expression and use the assertion expression as the basis of the new hypotheses.

Assume contract

The following example illustrates use of an Assume annotation. The assumed expression does not generate a verification condition and is not proved (although it is executed in SPARK 2014 if assertion expressions are not ignored at run-time).

In this example, the Assume annotation is effectively being used to implement the SPARK 2005 Always_Valid attribute.

Specification for Assume annotation in SPARK 2005:

```
1  package Input_Port
2    --# own in Inputs;
3  is
4     procedure Read_From_Port(Input_Value : out Integer);
5     --# global in Inputs;
6     --# derives Input_Value from Inputs;
7
8  end Input_Port;
```

Body for Assume annotation in SPARK 2005:

```
1   with System.Storage_Elements;
2   package body Input_Port
3   is
4
5      Inputs : Integer;
6      for Inputs'Address use System.Storage_Elements.To_Address (16#CAFE0#);
7      pragma Volatile (Inputs);
8
9      procedure Read_From_Port(Input_Value : out Integer)
10     is
11     begin
12        --# assume Inputs in Integer;
13        Input_Value := Inputs;
14     end Read_From_Port;
15
16  end Input_Port;
```

Specification for Assume annotation in SPARK 2014:

```
1  package Input_Port
2    with SPARK_Mode,
3         Abstract_State => (State_Inputs with External => Async_Writers)
4  is
5     procedure Read_From_Port(Input_Value : out Integer)
```

```
6       with Global   => (Input => State_Inputs),
7            Depends  => (Input_Value => State_Inputs);
8    end Input_Port;
```

Body for Assume annotation in SPARK 2014:

```
1    with System.Storage_Elements;
2
3    package body Input_Port
4      with SPARK_Mode,
5           Refined_State => (State_Inputs => Inputs)
6    is
7       Inputs : Integer
8         with Volatile,
9              Async_Writers,
10             Address => System.Storage_Elements.To_Address (16#CAFE0#);
11
12      procedure Read_From_Port(Input_Value : out Integer)
13        with Refined_Global   => (Input => Inputs),
14             Refined_Depends  => (Input_Value => Inputs)
15      is
16      begin
17         Input_Value := Inputs;
18         pragma Assume(Input_Value in Integer);
19      end Read_From_Port;
20   end Input_Port;
```

Check contract

The SPARK 2005 *check* annotation is replaced by *pragma assert* in SPARK 2014. This annotation generates a verification condition to prove the checked expression and adds the expression as a new hypothesis to the list of existing hypotheses.

Specification for Check annotation in SPARK 2005:

```
1    package Check_05
2    is
3       subtype Small is Integer range 1 .. 10;
4       subtype Big   is Integer range 1 .. 21;
5
6       procedure Compare(A, B : in Small; C : in out Big);
7    end Check_05;
```

Body for Check annotation in SPARK 2005:

```
1    package body Check_05
2    is
3       procedure Compare(A, B : in Small; C : in out Big)
4       is
5       begin
6          if (A + B >= C) then
7             C := A;
8             C := C + B;
9             C := C + 1;
10         end if;
11         --# check A + B < C;
```

```
12     end Compare;
13  end Check_05;
```

Specification for Check annotation in SPARK 2014:

```
1   package Check_14
2     with SPARK_Mode
3   is
4       subtype Small is Integer range 1 .. 10;
5       subtype Big   is Integer range 1 .. 21;
6
7       procedure Compare (A, B : in Small; C : in out Big);
8   end Check_14;
```

Body for Check annotation in SPARK 2014:

```
1   package body Check_14
2     with SPARK_Mode
3   is
4       procedure Compare(A, B : in Small; C : in out Big) is
5       begin
6          if A + B >= C then
7             C := A;
8             C := C + B;
9             C := C + 1;
10         end if;
11         pragma Assert (A + B < C);
12      end Compare;
13  end Check_14;
```

A.4.2 Assert used to control path explosion

This capability is in general not needed with the SPARK 2014 toolset where path explosion is handled automatically. In the rare cases where this is needed you can use *pragma Assert_And_Cut*.

A.5 Other Contracts and Annotations

A.5.1 Always_Valid assertion

See section *Input driver using 'Tail in a contract* for use of an assertion involving the Always_Valid attribute.

A.5.2 Rule declaration annotation

See section *Proof types and proof functions*.

A.5.3 Proof types and proof functions

The following example gives pre- and postconditions on operations that act upon the concrete representation of an abstract own variable. This means that proof functions and proof types are needed to state those pre- and postconditions. In addition, it gives an example of the use of a rule declaration annotation - in the body of procedure Initialize - to introduce a rule related to the components of a constant record value.

SPARK 2014 does not have a direct equivalent of proof types and proof functions. State abstractions cannot have a type and all functions in SPARK 2014 are Ada functions. Functions may be defined to be ghost functions which means that they can only be called within an assertion expression such as a pre or postcondition. Assertion expressions may be executed or ignored at run-time and if they are ignored Ghost functions behave much like SPARK 2005 proof functions.

Rule declaration annotations for structured constants are not required in SPARK 2014.

The SPARK 2005 version of the example given below will require user defined proof rules to discharge the proofs because refined definitions of some of the proof functions cannot be provided as they would have different formal parameters. The SPARK 2014 version does not suffer from this problem as functions called within assertion expressions may have global items.

Specification in SPARK 2005:

```
 1  package Stack
 2  --# own State : Abstract_Stack;
 3  is
 4     --  It is not possible to specify that the stack will be
 5     --  initialized to empty except by having an initialization
 6     --  subprogram called during program execution (as opposed to
 7     --  package elaboration).
 8
 9     --  Proof functions to indicate whether or not the Stack is empty
10     --  and whether or not it is full.
11     --# type Abstract_Stack is abstract;
12
13     --# function Max_Stack_Size return Natural;
14
15     --  Proof function to give the number of elements on the stack.
16     --# function Count(Input : Abstract_Stack) return Natural;
17
18     --  Proof function returns the Nth entry on the stack.
19     --  Stack_Entry (Count (State)) is the top of stack
20     --# function Stack_Entry (N : Natural; S : Abstract_Stack) return Integer;
21     --# pre N in 1 .. Count (S);
22     --  A refined version of this function cannot be written because
23     --  the abstract view has a formal parameter of type Abstract_Stack
24     --  whereas the refined view would not have this parameter but use
25     --  a global. A user defined proof rule would be required to define
26     --  this function. Alternatively, it could be written as an Ada
27     --  function where the the global and formal parameter views would
28     --  be available. However, the function would then be callable and
29     --  generate implementation code.
30
31     --# function Is_Empty(Input : Abstract_Stack) return Boolean;
32     --# return Count (Input) = 0;
33
34     --# function Is_Full(Input : Abstract_Stack) return Boolean;
35     --# return Count (Input) = Max_Stack_Size;
36
37     --  The precondition requires the stack is not full when a value, X,
38     --  is pushed onto it.
39     --  The postcondition indicates that the count of the stack will be
40     --  incremented after a push and therefore the stack will be non-empty.
41     --  The item X is now the top of the stack.
42     procedure Push(X : in Integer);
43     --# global in out State;
44     --# pre  not Is_Full(State);
```

```
45    --# post Count (State) = Count (State~) + 1 and
46    --#       Count (State) <= Max_Stack_Size and
47    --#       Stack_Entry (Count (State), State) = X;
48
49    --  The precondition requires the stack is not empty when we
50    --  pull a value from it.
51    --  The postcondition indicates the stack count is decremented.
52    procedure Pop (X : out Integer);
53    --# global in out State;
54    --# pre not Is_Empty (State);
55    --# post Count (State) = Count (State~) - 1;
56
57    --  Procedure that swaps the first two elements in a stack.
58    procedure Swap2;
59    --# global in out State;
60    --# pre  Count(State) >= 2;
61    --# post Count(State) =  Count(State~) and
62    --#       Stack_Entry (Count (State), State) =
63    --#           Stack_Entry (Count (State) - 1, State~) and
64    --#       Stack_Entry (Count (State) - 1, State) =
65    --#           Stack_Entry (Count (State), State~);
66
67    --  Initializes the Stack.
68    procedure Initialize;
69    --# global out State;
70    --# post Is_Empty (State);
71 end Stack;
```

Body in SPARK 2005:

```
1  package body Stack
2  --# own State is My_Stack;
3  is
4     Stack_Size : constant := 100;
5     type    Pointer_Range is range 0 .. Stack_Size;
6     subtype Index_Range  is Pointer_Range range 1..Stack_Size;
7     type    Vector       is array(Index_Range) of Integer;
8
9     type Stack_Type is record
10       S : Vector;
11       Pointer : Pointer_Range;
12    end record;
13
14    Initial_Stack : constant Stack_Type :=
15       Stack_Type'(S        => Vector'(others => 0),
16                   Pointer => 0);
17
18    My_Stack : Stack_Type;
19
20    procedure Push(X : in Integer)
21    --# global in out My_Stack;
22    --# pre My_Stack.Pointer < Stack_Size;
23    is
24    begin
25       My_Stack.Pointer := My_Stack.Pointer + 1;
26       My_Stack.S(My_Stack.Pointer) := X;
27    end Push;
28
```

```
29   procedure Pop (X : out Integer)
30   --# global in out My_Stack;
31   --# pre My_Stack.Pointer >= 1;
32   is
33   begin
34      X := My_Stack.S (My_Stack.Pointer);
35      My_Stack.Pointer := My_Stack.Pointer - 1;
36   end Pop;
37
38   procedure Swap2
39   --# global in out My_Stack;
40   --# post My_Stack.Pointer = My_Stack~.Pointer;
41   is
42      Temp : Integer;
43   begin
44      Temp := My_Stack.S (1);
45      My_Stack.S (1) := My_Stack.S (2);
46      My_Stack.S (2) := Temp;
47   end Swap2;
48
49   procedure Initialize
50   --# global out My_Stack;
51   --# post My_Stack.Pointer = 0;
52   is
53      --# for Initial_Stack declare Rule;
54   begin
55      My_Stack := Initial_Stack;
56   end Initialize;
57 end Stack;
```

Specification in SPARK 2014

```
1  package Stack
2    with SPARK_Mode,
3         Abstract_State   => State,
4         Initializes      => State,
5         Initial_Condition => Is_Empty
6  is
7     --   In SPARK 2014 we can specify an initial condition for the
8     --   elaboration of a package and so initialization may be done
9     --   during the elaboration of the package Stack, rendering the need
10    --   for an initialization procedure unnecessary.
11
12    --   Abstract states do not have types in SPARK 2014 they can only
13    --   be directly referenced in Global and Depends aspects.
14
15    --   Proof functions are actual functions but they may have the
16    --   convention Ghost meaning that they can only be called from
17    --   assertion expressions, e.g., pre and postconditions
18    function Max_Stack_Size return Natural
19      with Ghost;
20
21    --   Returns the number of elements on the stack
22    function Count return Natural
23      with Global      => (Input => State),
24           Ghost;
25
26    --   Returns the Nth entry on the stack. Stack_Entry (Count) is the
```

```
27     -- top of stack
28     function Stack_Entry (N : Natural) return Integer
29       with Global      => (Input => State),
30            Pre         => N in 1 .. Count,
31            Ghost;
32     -- A body (refined) version of this function can (must) be
33     -- provided in the body of the package.
34
35     function Is_Empty return Boolean is (Count = 0)
36       with Global      => State,
37            Ghost;
38
39     function Is_Full return Boolean is (Count = Max_Stack_Size)
40       with Global      => State,
41            Ghost;
42
43     -- The precondition requires the stack is not full when a value,
44     -- X, is pushed onto it. Functions with global items (Is_Full
45     -- with global State in this case) can be called in an assertion
46     -- expression such as the precondition here.  The postcondition
47     -- indicates that the count of the stack will be incremented after
48     -- a push and therefore the stack will be non-empty.  The item X
49     -- is now the top of the stack.
50     procedure Push (X : in Integer)
51       with Global => (In_Out => State),
52            Pre    => not Is_Full,
53            Post   => Count = Count'Old + 1 and
54                      Count <= Max_Stack_Size and
55                      Stack_Entry (Count) = X;
56
57     -- The precondition requires the stack is not empty when we pull a
58     -- value from it. The postcondition indicates the stack count is
59     -- decremented.
60     procedure Pop (X : out Integer)
61       with Global => (In_Out => State),
62            Pre    => not Is_Empty,
63            Post   => Count = Count'Old - 1;
64
65     -- Procedure that swaps the top two elements in a stack.
66     procedure Swap2
67       with Global => (In_Out => State),
68            Pre    => Count >= 2,
69            Post   => Count = Count'Old and
70                      Stack_Entry (Count) = Stack_Entry (Count - 1)'Old and
71                      Stack_Entry (Count - 1) = Stack_Entry (Count)'Old;
72 end Stack;
```

Body in SPARK 2014:

```
1 package body Stack
2   with SPARK_Mode,
3        Refined_State => (State => My_Stack)
4 is
5    Stack_Size : constant := 100;
6    type    Pointer_Range is range 0 .. Stack_Size;
7    subtype Index_Range   is Pointer_Range range 1 .. Stack_Size;
8    type    Vector        is array(Index_Range) of Integer;
9
```

```
10    type Stack_Type is record
11       S : Vector;
12       Pointer : Pointer_Range;
13    end record;
14
15    Initial_Stack : constant Stack_Type :=
16       Stack_Type'(S        => Vector'(others => 0),
17                   Pointer => 0);
18    My_Stack : Stack_Type;
19
20    function Max_Stack_Size return Natural is (Stack_Size);
21
22    function Count return Natural is (Natural (My_Stack.Pointer))
23       with Refined_Global => My_Stack;
24
25    function Stack_Entry (N : Natural) return Integer is
26       (My_Stack.S (Index_Range (N)))
27       with Refined_Global => My_Stack;
28
29
30    procedure Push(X : in Integer)
31       with Refined_Global => (In_Out => My_Stack)
32    is
33    begin
34       My_Stack.Pointer := My_Stack.Pointer + 1;
35       My_Stack.S(My_Stack.Pointer) := X;
36    end Push;
37
38    procedure Pop (X : out Integer)
39       with Refined_Global => (In_Out => My_Stack)
40    is
41    begin
42       X := My_Stack.S (My_Stack.Pointer);
43       My_Stack.Pointer := My_Stack.Pointer - 1;
44    end Pop;
45
46    procedure Swap2
47       with Refined_Global => (In_Out => My_Stack)
48    is
49       Temp : Integer;
50    begin
51       Temp := My_Stack.S (My_Stack.Pointer);
52       My_Stack.S (My_Stack.Pointer) := My_Stack.S (My_Stack.Pointer - 1);
53       My_Stack.S (My_Stack.Pointer - 1) := Temp;
54    end Swap2;
55 begin
56    My_Stack := Initial_Stack;
57 end Stack;
```

A.5.4 Using an External Prover

One may wish to use an external prover such as Isabelle, with rules defining a ghost function written in the prover input language. This can be done in SPARK 2014 by denoting the ghost function as an Import in lieu of providing a body for it. Of course such ghost functions cannot be executed.

Specification in SPARK 2014 using an external prover:

```ada
package Stack_External_Prover
  with SPARK_Mode,
       Abstract_State   => State,
       Initializes      => State,
       Initial_Condition => Is_Empty
is
  -- A Ghost function may be an Import which means that no body is
  -- given in the SPARK 2014 code and the proof has to be discharged
  -- by an external prover. Of course, such functions are not
  -- executable.
  function Max_Stack_Size return Natural
    with Global => null,
         Ghost,
         Import;

  -- Returns the number of elements on the stack
  function Count return Natural
    with Global => (Input => State),
         Ghost,
         Import;

  -- Returns the Nth entry on the stack. Stack_Entry (Count) is the
  -- top of stack
  function Stack_Entry (N : Natural) return Integer
    with Global => (Input => State),
         Ghost,
         Import;

  function Is_Empty return Boolean
    with Global => State,
         Ghost,
         Import;

  function Is_Full return Boolean
    with Global => State,
         Ghost,
         Import;

  procedure Push (X : in Integer)
    with Global => (In_Out => State),
         Pre    => not Is_Full,
         Post   => Count = Count'Old + 1 and Count <= Max_Stack_Size and
                   Stack_Entry (Count) = X;

  procedure Pop (X : out Integer)
    with Global => (In_Out => State),
         Pre    => not Is_Empty,
         Post   => Count = Count'Old - 1;

  procedure Swap2
    with Global => (In_Out => State),
         Pre    => Count >= 2,
         Post   => Count = Count'Old and
                   Stack_Entry (Count) = Stack_Entry (Count - 1)'Old and
                   Stack_Entry (Count - 1) = Stack_Entry (Count)'Old;
end Stack_External_Prover;
```

A.5.5 Quoting an Own Variable in a Contract

Sometimes it is necessary to reference an own variable (a state abstraction) in a contract. In SPARK 2005 this was achieved by declaring the own variable with a type, either concrete or abstract. As seen in *Proof types and proof functions*. Once the own variable has a type it can be used in a SPARK 2005 proof context.

A state abstraction in SPARK 2014 does not have a type. Instead, an Ada type to represent the abstract state is declared. A function which has the state abstraction as a global item is then declared which returns an object of the type. This function may have the same name as the state abstraction (the name is overloaded). References which appear to be the abstract state in an assertion expression are in fact calls to the overloaded function.

An example of this technique is given in the following example which is a version of the stack example given in *Proof types and proof functions* but with the post conditions extended to express the functional properties of the stack.

The extension requires the quoting of the own variable/state abstraction in the postcondition in order to state that the contents of the stack other than the top entries are not changed.

Specification in SPARK 2005:

```
1   package Stack_Functional_Spec
2   --# own State : Abstract_Stack;
3   is
4      --   It is not possible to specify that the stack will be
5      --   initialized to empty except by having an initialization
6      --   subprogram called during program execution (as opposed to
7      --   package elaboration).
8
9      --   Proof functions to indicate whether or not the Stack is empty
10     --   and whether or not it is full.
11     --# type Abstract_Stack is abstract;
12
13     --# function Max_Stack_Size return Natural;
14
15     --   Proof function to give the number of elements on the stack.
16     --# function Count(Input : Abstract_Stack) return Natural;
17
18     --   Proof function returns the Nth entry on the stack.
19     --   Stack_Entry (Count (State)) is the top of stack
20     --# function Stack_Entry (S : Abstract_Stack; N : Natural) return Integer;
21     --# pre N in 1 .. Count (S);
22     --   A refined version of this function cannot be written because
23     --   the abstract view has a formal parameter of type Abstract_Stack
24     --   whereas the refined view would not have this parameter but use
25     --   a global. A user defined proof rule would be required to
26     --   define this function. Alternatively, it could be written as an
27     --   Ada function where the the global and formal parameter views
28     --   would be available. However, the function would then be
29     --   callable and generate implementation code.
30
31     --# function Is_Empty(Input : Abstract_Stack) return Boolean;
32     --# return Count (Input) = 0;
33
34     --# function Is_Full(Input : Abstract_Stack) return Boolean;
35     --# return Count (Input) = Max_Stack_Size;
36
37     --   The precondition requires the stack is not full when a value, X,
38     --   is pushed onto it.
39     --   Functions with global items (Is_Full with global State in this case)
40     --   can be called in an assertion expression such as the precondition here.
```

```
41      --   The postcondition indicates that the count of the stack will be
42      --   incremented after a push and therefore the stack will be non-empty.
43      --   The item X is now the top of the stack and the contents of the rest of
44      --   the stack are unchanged.
45      procedure Push(X : in Integer);
46      --# global in out State;
47      --# pre   not Is_Full(State);
48      --# post Count (State) = Count (State~) + 1 and
49      --#        Count (State) <= Max_Stack_Size and
50      --#        Stack_Entry (State, Count (State)) = X and
51      --#        (for all I in Natural range 1 .. Count (State~) =>
52      --#             (Stack_Entry (State, I) = Stack_Entry (State~, I)));
53
54      --   The precondition requires the stack is not empty when we
55      --   pull a value from it.
56      --   The postcondition indicates that the X = the old top of stack,
57      --   the stack count is decremented, and the contents of the stack excluding
58      --   the old top of stack are unchanged.
59      procedure Pop (X : out Integer);
60      --# global in out State;
61      --# pre not Is_Empty (State);
62      --# post Count (State) = Count (State~) - 1 and
63      --#        X = Stack_Entry (State~, Count (State~)) and
64      --#        (for all I in Natural range 1 .. Count (State) =>
65      --#             (Stack_Entry (State, I) = Stack_Entry (State~, I)));
66
67      --   The precondition requires that the stack has at least 2 entries
68      --   (Count >= 2).
69      --   The postcondition states that the top two elements of the stack are
70      --   transposed but the remainder of the stack is unchanged.
71      procedure Swap2;
72      --# global in out State;
73      --# pre   Count(State) >= 2;
74      --# post Count(State) =  Count(State~) and
75      --#        Stack_Entry (State, Count (State)) =
76      --#            Stack_Entry (State~, Count (State) - 1) and
77      --#        Stack_Entry (State, Count (State) - 1) =
78      --#            Stack_Entry (State~, Count (State)) and
79      --#        (for all I in Natural range 1 .. Count (State) =>
80      --#             (Stack_Entry (State, I) = Stack_Entry (State~, I)));
81
82      --   Initializes the Stack.
83      procedure Initialize;
84      --# global out State;
85      --# post Is_Empty (State);
86  end Stack_Functional_Spec;
```

Body in SPARK 2005:

```
1  package body Stack_Functional_Spec
2  --# own State is My_Stack;
3  is
4     Stack_Size : constant := 100;
5     type    Pointer_Range is range 0 .. Stack_Size;
6     subtype Index_Range   is Pointer_Range range 1..Stack_Size;
7     type    Vector        is array(Index_Range) of Integer;
8
9     type Stack_Type is
```

```
10        record
11            S : Vector;
12            Pointer : Pointer_Range;
13        end record;
14
15    Initial_Stack : constant Stack_Type :=
16        Stack_Type'(S        => Vector'(others => 0),
17                    Pointer => 0);
18
19    My_Stack : Stack_Type;
20
21    procedure Push(X : in Integer)
22    --# global in out My_Stack;
23    --# pre My_Stack.Pointer < Stack_Size;
24    is
25    begin
26        My_Stack.Pointer := My_Stack.Pointer + 1;
27        My_Stack.S(My_Stack.Pointer) := X;
28    end Push;
29
30    procedure Pop (X : out Integer)
31    --# global in out My_Stack;
32    --# pre My_Stack.Pointer >= 1;
33    is
34    begin
35        X := My_Stack.S (My_Stack.Pointer);
36        My_Stack.Pointer := My_Stack.Pointer - 1;
37    end Pop;
38
39    procedure Swap2
40    --# global in out My_Stack;
41    --# post My_Stack.Pointer = My_Stack~.Pointer;
42    is
43        Temp : Integer;
44    begin
45        Temp := My_Stack.S (1);
46        My_Stack.S (1) := My_Stack.S (2);
47        My_Stack.S (2) := Temp;
48    end Swap2;
49
50    procedure Initialize
51    --# global out My_Stack;
52    --# post My_Stack.Pointer = 0;
53    is
54        --# for Initial_Stack declare Rule;
55    begin
56        My_Stack := Initial_Stack;
57    end Initialize;
58
59 end Stack_Functional_Spec;
```

Specification in SPARK 2014

```
1 pragma Unevaluated_Use_Of_Old(Allow);
2 package Stack_Functional_Spec
3   with SPARK_Mode,
4        Abstract_State    => State,
5        Initializes       => State,
```

```ada
6           Initial_Condition => Is_Empty
7  is
8     --  Abstract states do not have types in SPARK 2014 but to provide
9     --  functional specifications it is sometimes necessary to refer to
10    --  the abstract state in an assertion expression such as a post
11    --  condition. To do this in SPARK 2014 an Ada type declaration is
12    --  required to represent the type of the abstract state, then a
13    --  function applied to the abstract state (as a global) can be
14    --  written which returns an object of the declared type.
15    type Stack_Type is private;
16
17    --  The Abstract_State name may be overloaded by the function which
18    --  represents it in assertion expressions.
19    function State return Stack_Type
20      with Global => State;
21
22    function Max_Stack_Size return Natural
23      with Ghost;
24
25    --  Returns the number of elements on the stack
26    --  A function may have a formal parameter (or return a value)
27    --  of the abstract state.
28    function Count (S : Stack_Type) return Natural
29      with Ghost;
30
31    --  Returns the Nth entry on the stack.
32    --  Stack_Entry (S, Count (S)) is the top of stack
33    function Stack_Entry (S : Stack_Type; N : Natural) return Integer
34      with Pre       => N in 1 .. Count (S),
35           Ghost;
36
37    --  The ghost function Count can be called in the function
38    --  expression because Is_Empty is also a ghost function.
39    function Is_Empty return Boolean is (Count (State) = 0)
40      with Global     => State,
41           Ghost;
42
43    function Is_Full return Boolean is (Count(State) = Max_Stack_Size)
44      with Global     => State,
45           Ghost;
46
47    --  The precondition requires the stack is not full when a value, X,
48    --  is pushed onto it.
49    --  Functions with global items (Is_Full with global State in this case)
50    --  can be called in an assertion expression such as the precondition here.
51    --  The postcondition indicates that the count of the stack will be
52    --  incremented after a push and therefore the stack will be non-empty.
53    --  The item X is now the top of the stack and the contents of the rest of
54    --  the stack are unchanged.
55    procedure Push (X : in Integer)
56      with Global => (In_Out => State),
57           Pre    => not Is_Full,
58           Post   => Count (State) = Count (State'Old) + 1 and
59                     Count (State) <= Max_Stack_Size and
60                     Stack_Entry (State, Count (State)) = X and
61                     (for all I in 1 .. Count (State'Old) =>
62                          Stack_Entry (State, I) = Stack_Entry (State'Old, I));
63
```

```
64      --   The precondition requires the stack is not empty when we
65      --   pull a value from it.
66      --   The postcondition indicates that the X = the old top of stack,
67      --   the stack count is decremented, and the contents of the stack excluding
68      --   the old top of stack are unchanged.
69      procedure Pop (X : out Integer)
70        with Global => (In_Out => State),
71             Pre    => not Is_Empty,
72             Post   => Count (State) = Count (State'Old) - 1 and
73                       X = Stack_Entry (State'Old, Count (State'Old)) and
74                       (for all I in 1 .. Count (State) =>
75                           Stack_Entry (State, I) = Stack_Entry (State'Old, I));
76
77      --   The precondition requires that the stack has at least 2 entries
78      --   (Count >= 2).
79      --   The postcondition states that the top two elements of the stack are
80      --   transposed but the remainder of the stack is unchanged.
81      procedure Swap2
82        with Global => (In_Out => State),
83             Pre    => Count (State) >= 2,
84             Post   => Count (State) = Count (State'Old) and
85                       Stack_Entry (State, Count (State)) =
86                           Stack_Entry (State'Old, Count (State) - 1) and
87                       Stack_Entry (State, Count (State) - 1) =
88                           Stack_Entry (State'Old, Count (State)) and
89                       (for all I in 1 .. Count (State) - 2 =>
90                           Stack_Entry (State, I) = Stack_Entry (State'Old, I));
91
92   private
93      -- The full type declarion used to represent the abstract state.
94      Stack_Size : constant := 100;
95      type     Pointer_Range is range 0 .. Stack_Size;
96      subtype  Index_Range   is Pointer_Range range 1 .. Stack_Size;
97      type     Vector        is array(Index_Range) of Integer;
98
99      type Stack_Type is record
100        S : Vector;
101        Pointer : Pointer_Range;
102     end record;
103  end Stack_Functional_Spec;
```

Body in **SPARK 2014**:

```
1   package body Stack_Functional_Spec
2     with SPARK_Mode,
3          Refined_State => (State => My_Stack)
4   is
5      Initial_Stack : constant Stack_Type :=
6        Stack_Type'(S       => Vector'(others => 0),
7                    Pointer => 0);
8
9      --  In this example the type used to represent the state
10     --  abstraction and the actual type used in the implementation are
11     --  the same, but they need not be. For instance S and Pointer
12     --  could have been declared as distinct objects rather than
13     --  composed into a record. Where the type representing the
14     --  abstract state and the implementation of that state are
15     --  different the function representing the abstract state has to
```

```
16      --  convert implementation representation into the abstract
17      --  representation. For instance, if S and Pointer were distinct
18      --  objects the function State would have to return (S => S,
19      --  Pointer => Pointer).
20    My_Stack : Stack_Type;
21
22      --  No convertion necessary as the abstract and implementation type
23      --  is the same.
24    function State return Stack_Type is (My_Stack)
25      with Refined_Global => My_Stack;
26
27    function Max_Stack_Size return Natural is (Stack_Size);
28
29    function Count (S : Stack_Type) return Natural is (Natural (S.Pointer));
30
31    function Stack_Entry (S : Stack_Type; N : Natural) return Integer is
32      (S.S (Index_Range (N)));
33
34    procedure Push(X : in Integer)
35      with Refined_Global => (In_Out => My_Stack)
36    is
37    begin
38      My_Stack.Pointer := My_Stack.Pointer + 1;
39      My_Stack.S(My_Stack.Pointer) := X;
40    end Push;
41
42    procedure Pop (X : out Integer)
43      with Refined_Global => (In_Out => My_Stack)
44    is
45    begin
46      X := My_Stack.S (My_Stack.Pointer);
47      My_Stack.Pointer := My_Stack.Pointer - 1;
48    end Pop;
49
50    procedure Swap2
51      with Refined_Global => (In_Out => My_Stack)
52    is
53      Temp : Integer;
54    begin
55      Temp := My_Stack.S (My_Stack.Pointer);
56      My_Stack.S (My_Stack.Pointer) := My_Stack.S (My_Stack.Pointer - 1);
57      My_Stack.S (My_Stack.Pointer - 1) := Temp;
58    end Swap2;
59 begin
60    My_Stack := Initial_Stack;
61 end Stack_Functional_Spec;
```

A.5.6 Main_Program annotation

This annotation isn't needed. Currently any parameterless procedure declared at library-level is considered as a potential main program and analyzed as such.

A.6 Update Expressions

SPARK 2005 has update expressions for updating records and arrays. They can only be used in SPARK 2005 proof contexts.

The equivalent in SPARK 2014 is the '*Update* attribute. This can be used in any Ada expression.

Specification in SPARK 2005:

```
package Update_Examples
is
   type Rec is record
      X, Y : Integer;
   end record;

   type Index is range 1 ..3;

   type Arr is array (Index) of Integer;

   type Arr_2D is array (Index, Index) of Integer;

   type Nested_Rec is record
      A : Integer;
      B : Rec;
      C : Arr;
      D : Arr_2D;
   end record;

   type Nested_Arr is array (Index) of Nested_Rec;

   -- Simple record update
   procedure P1 (R : in out Rec);
   --# post R = R~ [X => 1];

   -- Simple 1D array update
   procedure P2 (A : in out Arr);
   --# post A = A~ [1 => 2];

   -- 2D array update
   procedure P3 (A2D : in out Arr_2D);
   --# post A2D = A2D~ [1, 1 => 1;
   --#                  2, 2 => 2;
   --#                  3, 3 => 3];

   -- Nested record update
   procedure P4 (NR : in out Nested_Rec);
   --# post NR = NR~ [A => 1;
   --#                B => NR~.B [X => 1];
   --#                C => NR~.C [1 => 5]];

   -- Nested array update
   procedure P5 (NA : in out Nested_Arr);
   --# post NA = NA~ [1 => NA~ (1) [A => 1;
   --#                              D => NA~ (1).D [2, 2 => 0]];
   --#                2 => NA~ (2) [B => NA~ (2).B [X => 2]];
   --#                3 => NA~ (3) [C => NA~ (3).C [1 => 5]]];
end Update_Examples;
```

Specification in SPARK 2014

```
1   package Update_Examples
2     with SPARK_Mode
3   is
4      type Rec is record
5         X, Y : Integer;
6      end record;
7
8      type Arr is array (1 .. 3) of Integer;
9
10     type Arr_2D is array (1 .. 3, 1 .. 3) of Integer;
11
12     type Nested_Rec is record
13        A : Integer;
14        B : Rec;
15        C : Arr;
16        D : Arr_2D;
17     end record;
18
19     type Nested_Arr is array (1 .. 3) of Nested_Rec;
20
21     -- Simple record update
22     procedure P1 (R : in out Rec)
23       with Post => R = R'Old'Update (X => 1);
24     -- this is equivalent to:
25     --    R = (X => 1,
26     --         Y => R'Old.Y)
27
28     -- Simple 1D array update
29     procedure P2 (A : in out Arr)
30       with Post => A = A'Old'Update (1 => 2);
31     -- this is equivalent to:
32     --    A = (1 => 2,
33     --         2 => A'Old (2),
34     --         3 => A'Old (3));
35
36     -- 2D array update
37     procedure P3 (A2D : in out Arr_2D)
38       with Post => A2D = A2D'Old'Update ((1, 1) => 1,
39                                           (2, 2) => 2,
40                                           (3, 3) => 3);
41     -- this is equivalent to:
42     --    A2D = (1 => (1 => 1,
43     --                 2 => A2D'Old (1, 2),
44     --                 3 => A2D'Old (1, 3)),
45     --           2 => (2 => 2,
46     --                 1 => A2D'Old (2, 1),
47     --                 3 => A2D'Old (2, 3)),
48     --           3 => (3 => 3,
49     --                 1 => A2D'Old (3, 1),
50     --                 2 => A2D'Old (3, 2)));
51
52     -- Nested record update
53     procedure P4 (NR : in out Nested_Rec)
54       with Post => NR = NR'Old'Update (A => 1,
55                                         B => NR'Old.B'Update (X => 1),
56                                         C => NR'Old.C'Update (1 => 5));
57     -- this is equivalent to:
```

```
58    --      NR = (A => 1,
59    --            B.X => 1,
60    --            B.Y => NR'Old.B.Y,
61    --            C (1) => 5,
62    --            C (2) => NR'Old.C (2),
63    --            C (3) => NR'Old.C (3),
64    --            D => NR'Old.D)
65
66    -- Nested array update
67    procedure P5 (NA : in out Nested_Arr)
68      with Post =>
69        NA = NA'Old'Update (1 => NA'Old (1)'Update
70                                   (A => 1,
71                                    D => NA'Old (1).D'Update ((2, 2) => 0)),
72                            2 => NA'Old (2)'Update
73                                   (B => NA'Old (2).B'Update (X => 2)),
74                            3 => NA'Old (3)'Update
75                                   (C => NA'Old (3).C'Update (1 => 5)));
76    -- this is equivalent to:
77    --      NA = (1 => (A => 1,
78    --                  B => NA'Old (1).B,
79    --                  C => NA'Old (1).C,
80    --                  D => NA'Old (1).D),
81    --            2 => (B.X => 2,
82    --                  B.Y => NA'Old (2).B.Y,
83    --                  A => NA'Old (2).A,
84    --                  C => NA'Old (2).C,
85    --                  D => NA'Old (2).D),
86    --            3 => (C => (1 => 5,
87    --                        2 => NA'Old (3).C (2),
88    --                        3 => NA'Old (3).C (3)),
89    --                  A => NA'Old (3).A,
90    --                  B => NA'Old (3).B,
91    --                  D => NA'Old (3).D));
92
93    end Update_Examples;
```

A.7 Value of Variable on Entry to a Loop

In SPARK 2005 the entry value of a for loop variable variable, X, can be referenced using the notation X%. This notation is required frequently when the variable is referenced in a proof context within the loop. Often it is needed to state that the value of X is not changed within the loop by stating X = X%. This notation is restricted to a variable which defines the lower or upper range of a for loop.

SPARK 2014 has a more general scheme whereby the loop entry value of any variable can be denoted within any sort of loop using the 'Loop_Entry attribute. However, its main use is not for showing that the value of a for loop variable has not changed as the SPARK 2014 tools are able to determine this automatically. Rather it is used instead of ~ in loops because the attribute 'Old is only permitted in postconditions (including Contract_Cases).

Specification in SPARK 2005:

```
1    package Loop_Entry
2    is
3
4      subtype ElementType is Natural range 0..1000;
5      subtype IndexType is Positive range 1..100;
```

```
6    type ArrayType is array (IndexType) of ElementType;

7

8    procedure Clear (A: in out ArrayType; L,U: in IndexType);
9    --# derives A from A, L, U;
10   --# post (for all N in IndexType range L..U => (A(N) = 0)) and
11   --#      (for all N in IndexType => ((N<L or N>U) -> A(N) = A~(N)));

12

13 end Loop_Entry;
```

Body in SPARK 2005:

```
1  package body Loop_Entry
2  is
3
4    procedure Clear (A: in out ArrayType; L,U: in IndexType)
5    is
6    begin
7      for I in IndexType range L..U loop
8        A(I) := 0;
9        --# assert (for all N in IndexType range L..I => (A(N) = 0)) and
10       --#        (for all N in IndexType => ((N<L or N>I) -> A(N) = A~(N))) and
11       --#        U = U% and L <= I;
12       -- Note U = U% is required to show that the vaule of U does not change
13       -- within the loop.
14     end loop;
15   end Clear;
16
17 end Loop_Entry;
```

Specification in SPARK 2014:

```
1  pragma SPARK_Mode (On);
2  package Loop_Entry
3  is
4
5    subtype ElementType is Natural range 0..1000;
6    subtype IndexType is Positive range 1..100;
7    type ArrayType is array (IndexType) of ElementType;
8
9    procedure Clear (A: in out ArrayType; L,U: in IndexType)
10     with Depends => (A => (A, L, U)),
11          Post    => (for all N in L..U => A(N) = 0) and
12                     (for all N in IndexType =>
13                          (if N<L or N>U then A(N) = A'Old(N)));
14
15 end Loop_Entry;
```

Body in SPARK 2014:

```
1  pragma SPARK_Mode (On);
2  package body Loop_Entry
3  is
4
5    procedure Clear (A: in out ArrayType; L,U: in IndexType)
6    is
7    begin
8      for I in IndexType range L..U loop
9        A(I) := 0;
```

```ada
10          pragma Loop_Invariant ((for all N in L..I => (A(N) = 0)) and
11             (for all N in IndexType =>
12                (if N < L or N > I then A(N) = A'Loop_Entry(N))));
13       -- Note it is not necessary to show that the vaule of U does not change
14       -- within the loop.
15       -- However 'Loop_Entry must be used rather than 'Old.
16    end loop;
17  end Clear;
18
19 end Loop_Entry;
```

GNU FREE DOCUMENTATION LICENSE

Version 1.3, 3 November 2008

Copyright (C) 2000, 2001, 2002, 2007, 2008 Free Software Foundation, Inc.

B.1 PREAMBLE

The purpose of this License is to make a manual, textbook, or other functional and useful document 'free' in the sense of freedom: to assure everyone the effective freedom to copy and redistribute it, with or without modifying it, either commercially or noncommercially. Secondarily, this License preserves for the author and publisher a way to get credit for their work, while not being considered responsible for modifications made by others.

This License is a kind of 'copyleft', which means that derivative works of the document must themselves be free in the same sense. It complements the GNU General Public License, which is a copyleft license designed for free software.

We have designed this License in order to use it for manuals for free software, because free software needs free documentation: a free program should come with manuals providing the same freedoms that the software does. But this License is not limited to software manuals; it can be used for any textual work, regardless of subject matter or whether it is published as a printed book. We recommend this License principally for works whose purpose is instruction or reference.

B.2 APPLICABILITY AND DEFINITIONS

This License applies to any manual or other work, in any medium, that contains a notice placed by the copyright holder saying it can be distributed under the terms of this License. Such a notice grants a world-wide, royalty-free license, unlimited in duration, to use that work under the conditions stated herein. The 'Document', below, refers to any such manual or work. Any member of the public is a licensee, and is addressed as 'you'. You accept the license if you copy, modify or distribute the work in a way requiring permission under copyright law.

A 'Modified Version' of the Document means any work containing the Document or a portion of it, either copied verbatim, or with modifications and/or translated into another language.

A 'Secondary Section' is a named appendix or a front-matter section of the Document that deals exclusively with the relationship of the publishers or authors of the Document to the Document's overall subject (or to related matters) and contains nothing that could fall directly within that overall subject. (Thus, if the Document is in part a textbook of mathematics, a Secondary Section may not explain any mathematics.) The relationship could be a matter of historical connection with the subject or with related matters, or of legal, commercial, philosophical, ethical or political position regarding them.

The 'Invariant Sections' are certain Secondary Sections whose titles are designated, as being those of Invariant Sections, in the notice that says that the Document is released under this License. If a section does not fit the above definition of Secondary then it is not allowed to be designated as Invariant. The Document may contain zero Invariant Sections. If the Document does not identify any Invariant Sections then there are none.

The 'Cover Texts' are certain short passages of text that are listed, as Front-Cover Texts or Back-Cover Texts, in the notice that says that the Document is released under this License. A Front-Cover Text may be at most 5 words, and a Back-Cover Text may be at most 25 words.

A 'Transparent' copy of the Document means a machine-readable copy, represented in a format whose specification is available to the general public, that is suitable for revising the document straightforwardly with generic text editors or (for images composed of pixels) generic paint programs or (for drawings) some widely available drawing editor, and that is suitable for input to text formatters or for automatic translation to a variety of formats suitable for input to text formatters. A copy made in an otherwise Transparent file format whose markup, or absence of markup, has been arranged to thwart or discourage subsequent modification by readers is not Transparent. An image format is not Transparent if used for any substantial amount of text. A copy that is not 'Transparent' is called 'Opaque'.

Examples of suitable formats for Transparent copies include plain ASCII without markup, Texinfo input format, LaTeX input format, SGML or XML using a publicly available DTD, and standard-conforming simple HTML, PostScript or PDF designed for human modification. Examples of transparent image formats include PNG, XCF and JPG. Opaque formats include proprietary formats that can be read and edited only by proprietary word processors, SGML or XML for which the DTD and/or processing tools are not generally available, and the machine-generated HTML, PostScript or PDF produced by some word processors for output purposes only.

The 'Title Page' means, for a printed book, the title page itself, plus such following pages as are needed to hold, legibly, the material this License requires to appear in the title page. For works in formats which do not have any title page as such, 'Title Page' means the text near the most prominent appearance of the work's title, preceding the beginning of the body of the text.

The 'publisher' means any person or entity that distributes copies of the Document to the public.

A section 'Entitled XYZ' means a named subunit of the Document whose title either is precisely XYZ or contains XYZ in parentheses following text that translates XYZ in another language. (Here XYZ stands for a specific section name mentioned below, such as 'Acknowledgements', 'Dedications', 'Endorsements', or 'History'.) To 'Preserve the Title' of such a section when you modify the Document means that it remains a section 'Entitled XYZ' according to this definition.

The Document may include Warranty Disclaimers next to the notice which states that this License applies to the Document. These Warranty Disclaimers are considered to be included by reference in this License, but only as regards disclaiming warranties: any other implication that these Warranty Disclaimers may have is void and has no effect on the meaning of this License.

B.3 VERBATIM COPYING

You may copy and distribute the Document in any medium, either commercially or noncommercially, provided that this License, the copyright notices, and the license notice saying this License applies to the Document are reproduced in all copies, and that you add no other conditions whatsoever to those of this License. You may not use technical measures to obstruct or control the reading or further copying of the copies you make or distribute. However, you may accept compensation in exchange for copies. If you distribute a large enough number of copies you must also follow the conditions in section 3.

You may also lend copies, under the same conditions stated above, and you may publicly display copies.

B.4 COPYING IN QUANTITY

If you publish printed copies (or copies in media that commonly have printed covers) of the Document, numbering more than 100, and the Document's license notice requires Cover Texts, you must enclose the copies in covers that carry, clearly and legibly, all these Cover Texts: Front-Cover Texts on the front cover, and Back-Cover Texts on the back cover. Both covers must also clearly and legibly identify you as the publisher of these copies. The front cover must present the full title with all words of the title equally prominent and visible. You may add other material on the covers in addition. Copying with changes limited to the covers, as long as they preserve the title of the Document and satisfy these conditions, can be treated as verbatim copying in other respects.

If the required texts for either cover are too voluminous to fit legibly, you should put the first ones listed (as many as fit reasonably) on the actual cover, and continue the rest onto adjacent pages.

If you publish or distribute Opaque copies of the Document numbering more than 100, you must either include a machine-readable Transparent copy along with each Opaque copy, or state in or with each Opaque copy a computer-network location from which the general network-using public has access to download using public-standard network protocols a complete Transparent copy of the Document, free of added material. If you use the latter option, you must take reasonably prudent steps, when you begin distribution of Opaque copies in quantity, to ensure that this Transparent copy will remain thus accessible at the stated location until at least one year after the last time you distribute an Opaque copy (directly or through your agents or retailers) of that edition to the public.

It is requested, but not required, that you contact the authors of the Document well before redistributing any large number of copies, to give them a chance to provide you with an updated version of the Document.

B.5 MODIFICATIONS

You may copy and distribute a Modified Version of the Document under the conditions of sections 2 and 3 above, provided that you release the Modified Version under precisely this License, with the Modified Version filling the role of the Document, thus licensing distribution and modification of the Modified Version to whoever possesses a copy of it. In addition, you must do these things in the Modified Version:

- Use in the Title Page (and on the covers, if any) a title distinct from that of the Document, and from those of previous versions (which should, if there were any, be listed in the History section of the Document). You may use the same title as a previous version if the original publisher of that version gives permission.

- List on the Title Page, as authors, one or more persons or entities responsible for authorship of the modifications in the Modified Version, together with at least five of the principal authors of the Document (all of its principal authors, if it has fewer than five), unless they release you from this requirement.

- State on the Title page the name of the publisher of the Modified Version, as the publisher.

- Preserve all the copyright notices of the Document.

- Add an appropriate copyright notice for your modifications adjacent to the other copyright notices.

- Include, immediately after the copyright notices, a license notice giving the public permission to use the Modified Version under the terms of this License, in the form shown in the Addendum below.

- Preserve in that license notice the full lists of Invariant Sections and required Cover Texts given in the Document's license notice.

- Include an unaltered copy of this License.

- Preserve the section Entitled 'History', Preserve its Title, and add to it an item stating at least the title, year, new authors, and publisher of the Modified Version as given on the Title Page. If there is no section Entitled 'History' in the Document, create one stating the title, year, authors, and publisher of the Document as given on its Title Page, then add an item describing the Modified Version as stated in the previous sentence.

- Preserve the network location, if any, given in the Document for public access to a Transparent copy of the Document, and likewise the network locations given in the Document for previous versions it was based on. These may be placed in the 'History' section. You may omit a network location for a work that was published at least four years before the Document itself, or if the original publisher of the version it refers to gives permission.

- For any section Entitled 'Acknowledgements' or 'Dedications', Preserve the Title of the section, and preserve in the section all the substance and tone of each of the contributor acknowledgements and/or dedications given therein.

- Preserve all the Invariant Sections of the Document, unaltered in their text and in their titles. Section numbers or the equivalent are not considered part of the section titles.

- Delete any section Entitled 'Endorsements'. Such a section may not be included in the Modified Version.

- Do not retitle any existing section to be Entitled 'Endorsements' or to conflict in title with any Invariant Section.

- Preserve any Warranty Disclaimers.

If the Modified Version includes new front-matter sections or appendices that qualify as Secondary Sections and contain no material copied from the Document, you may at your option designate some or all of these sections as invariant. To do this, add their titles to the list of Invariant Sections in the Modified Version's license notice. These titles must be distinct from any other section titles.

You may add a section Entitled 'Endorsements', provided it contains nothing but endorsements of your Modified Version by various parties – for example, statements of peer review or that the text has been approved by an organization as the authoritative definition of a standard.

You may add a passage of up to five words as a Front-Cover Text, and a passage of up to 25 words as a Back-Cover Text, to the end of the list of Cover Texts in the Modified Version. Only one passage of Front-Cover Text and one of Back-Cover Text may be added by (or through arrangements made by) any one entity. If the Document already includes a cover text for the same cover, previously added by you or by arrangement made by the same entity you are acting on behalf of, you may not add another; but you may replace the old one, on explicit permission from the previous publisher that added the old one.

The author(s) and publisher(s) of the Document do not by this License give permission to use their names for publicity for or to assert or imply endorsement of any Modified Version.

B.6 COMBINING DOCUMENTS

You may combine the Document with other documents released under this License, under the terms defined in section 4 above for modified versions, provided that you include in the combination all of the Invariant Sections of all of the original documents, unmodified, and list them all as Invariant Sections of your combined work in its license notice, and that you preserve all their Warranty Disclaimers.

The combined work need only contain one copy of this License, and multiple identical Invariant Sections may be replaced with a single copy. If there are multiple Invariant Sections with the same name but different contents, make the title of each such section unique by adding at the end of it, in parentheses, the name of the original author or publisher of that section if known, or else a unique number. Make the same adjustment to the section titles in the list of Invariant Sections in the license notice of the combined work.

In the combination, you must combine any sections Entitled 'History' in the various original documents, forming one section Entitled 'History'; likewise combine any sections Entitled 'Acknowledgements', and any sections Entitled 'Dedications'. You must delete all sections Entitled 'Endorsements'.

B.7 COLLECTIONS OF DOCUMENTS

You may make a collection consisting of the Document and other documents released under this License, and replace the individual copies of this License in the various documents with a single copy that is included in the collection, provided that you follow the rules of this License for verbatim copying of each of the documents in all other respects.

You may extract a single document from such a collection, and distribute it individually under this License, provided you insert a copy of this License into the extracted document, and follow this License in all other respects regarding verbatim copying of that document.

B.8 AGGREGATION WITH INDEPENDENT WORKS

A compilation of the Document or its derivatives with other separate and independent documents or works, in or on a volume of a storage or distribution medium, is called an 'aggregate' if the copyright resulting from the compilation is not used to limit the legal rights of the compilation's users beyond what the individual works permit. When the Document is included in an aggregate, this License does not apply to the other works in the aggregate which are not themselves derivative works of the Document.

If the Cover Text requirement of section 3 is applicable to these copies of the Document, then if the Document is less than one half of the entire aggregate, the Document's Cover Texts may be placed on covers that bracket the Document within the aggregate, or the electronic equivalent of covers if the Document is in electronic form. Otherwise they must appear on printed covers that bracket the whole aggregate.

B.9 TRANSLATION

Translation is considered a kind of modification, so you may distribute translations of the Document under the terms of section 4. Replacing Invariant Sections with translations requires special permission from their copyright holders, but you may include translations of some or all Invariant Sections in addition to the original versions of these Invariant Sections. You may include a translation of this License, and all the license notices in the Document, and any Warranty Disclaimers, provided that you also include the original English version of this License and the original versions of those notices and disclaimers. In case of a disagreement between the translation and the original version of this License or a notice or disclaimer, the original version will prevail.

If a section in the Document is Entitled 'Acknowledgements', 'Dedications', or 'History', the requirement (section 4) to Preserve its Title (section 1) will typically require changing the actual title.

B.10 TERMINATION

You may not copy, modify, sublicense, or distribute the Document except as expressly provided under this License. Any attempt otherwise to copy, modify, sublicense, or distribute it is void, and will automatically terminate your rights under this License.

However, if you cease all violation of this License, then your license from a particular copyright holder is reinstated (a) provisionally, unless and until the copyright holder explicitly and finally terminates your license, and (b) permanently, if the copyright holder fails to notify you of the violation by some reasonable means prior to 60 days after the cessation.

Moreover, your license from a particular copyright holder is reinstated permanently if the copyright holder notifies you of the violation by some reasonable means, this is the first time you have received notice of violation of this License (for any work) from that copyright holder, and you cure the violation prior to 30 days after your receipt of the notice.

Termination of your rights under this section does not terminate the licenses of parties who have received copies or rights from you under this License. If your rights have been terminated and not permanently reinstated, receipt of a copy of some or all of the same material does not give you any rights to use it.

B.11 FUTURE REVISIONS OF THIS LICENSE

The Free Software Foundation may publish new, revised versions of the GNU Free Documentation License from time to time. Such new versions will be similar in spirit to the present version, but may differ in detail to address new problems or concerns. See http://www.gnu.org/copyleft/.

Each version of the License is given a distinguishing version number. If the Document specifies that a particular numbered version of this License 'or any later version' applies to it, you have the option of following the terms and conditions either of that specified version or of any later version that has been published (not as a draft) by the Free Software Foundation. If the Document does not specify a version number of this License, you may choose any version ever published (not as a draft) by the Free Software Foundation. If the Document specifies that a proxy can decide which future versions of this License can be used, that proxy's public statement of acceptance of a version permanently authorizes you to choose that version for the Document.

B.12 RELICENSING

'Massive Multiauthor Collaboration Site' (or 'MMC Site') means any World Wide Web server that publishes copyrightable works and also provides prominent facilities for anybody to edit those works. A public wiki that anybody can edit is an example of such a server. A 'Massive Multiauthor Collaboration' (or 'MMC') contained in the site means any set of copyrightable works thus published on the MMC site.

'CC-BY-SA' means the Creative Commons Attribution-Share Alike 3.0 license published by Creative Commons Corporation, a not-for-profit corporation with a principal place of business in San Francisco, California, as well as future copyleft versions of that license published by that same organization.

'Incorporate' means to publish or republish a Document, in whole or in part, as part of another Document.

An MMC is 'eligible for relicensing' if it is licensed under this License, and if all works that were first published under this License somewhere other than this MMC, and subsequently incorporated in whole or in part into the MMC, (1) had no cover texts or invariant sections, and (2) were thus incorporated prior to November 1, 2008.

The operator of an MMC Site may republish an MMC contained in the site under CC-BY-SA on the same site at any time before August 1, 2009, provided the MMC is eligible for relicensing.

B.13 ADDENDUM: How to use this License for your documents

To use this License in a document you have written, include a copy of the License in the document and put the following copyright and license notices just after the title page:

```
Copyright (C)  YEAR  YOUR NAME.
Permission is granted to copy, distribute and/or modify this document
under the terms of the GNU Free Documentation License, Version 1.3
or any later version published by the Free Software Foundation;
with no Invariant Sections, no Front-Cover Texts, and no Back-Cover Texts.
A copy of the license is included in the section entitled 'GNU
Free Documentation License'.
```

If you have Invariant Sections, Front-Cover Texts and Back-Cover Texts, replace the 'with ... Texts.' line with this:

```
with the Invariant Sections being LIST THEIR TITLES, with the
Front-Cover Texts being LIST, and with the Back-Cover Texts being LIST.
```

If you have Invariant Sections without Cover Texts, or some other combination of the three, merge those two alternatives to suit the situation.

If your document contains nontrivial examples of program code, we recommend releasing these examples in parallel under your choice of free software license, such as the GNU General Public License, to permit their use in free software.

www.ingramcontent.com/pod-product-compliance
Lightning Source LLC
Chambersburg PA
CBHW060537060326
40690CB00017B/3525